Meaning

Meaning in Action

Outline of an Integral Theory of Culture

Rein Raud

polity

The right of Rein Raud to be identified as Author of this Work has been asserted in accordance with the UK Copyright, Designs and Patents Act 1988.

First published in 2016 by Polity Press

Polity Press
65 Bridge Street
Cambridge CB2 1UR, UK

Polity Press
350 Main Street
Malden, MA 02148, USA

ISBN-13: 978-1-5095-1124-2
ISBN-13: 978-1-5095-1125-9 (pb)

A catalogue record for this book is available from the British Library.

Library of Congress Cataloging-in-Publication Data

Names: Raud, Rein, author.
Title: Meaning in action : outline of an integral theory of culture / Rein Raud.
Description: Cambridge, UK ; Malden, MA : Polity Press, [2016] | Includes bibliographical references and index.
Identifiers: LCCN 2016000161| ISBN 9781509511242 (hardback : alk. paper) | ISBN 9781509511259 (pbk. : alk. paper)
Subjects: LCSH: Culture--Semiotic models. | Language and culture. | Culture--Philosophy.
Classification: LCC GN357 .R38 2016 | DDC 306.01--dc23
LC record available at https://lccn.loc.gov/2016000161

Typeset in 10.5 on 12 pt Sabon by
Servis Filmsetting Ltd, Stockport, Cheshire
Printed and bound in the UK by CPI Group Ltd, Croydon, CR0 4YY

For further information on Polity, visit our website:
politybooks.com

Civilization consists in giving an inappropriate name to something and then dreaming what results from that. And in fact the false name and the true dream do create a new reality. The object really does become other, because we have made it so. We manufacture realities. We use the raw material we always used but the form lent it by art effectively prevents it from remaining the same.

Fernando Pessoa, *The Book of Disquiet* (2002:53)

CONTENTS

ACKNOWLEDGEMENTS

The first ideas for this book were formulated during the summer of 1989, when I had just become a graduate student. So it has been quite a long journey, during which many initially promising ideas have turned out to be dead ends and hundreds of pages have not made it to the final version. Over all these years, I have been lucky to have the support of too many people to list them all here, but some deserve special mention: Tarmo Jüristo, Mihhail Lotman, Ülar Ploom and Marek Tamm for their thorough comments on previous versions of the book; Zygmunt Bauman for his support and wisdom; as well as Hannes Palang for constant encouragement. I would also like to thank my friends and colleagues in Cambridge, particularly Richard Bowring, Peter Kornicki and Mark Morris, for their hospitality and help. Some of the research for this book was financed by grants ETF7218, SF0130129s08, IUT3-2 and TK18U01 from various Estonian funding authorities. Last, but not least, my heartfelt gratitude goes to Leigh Mueller, whose sensitive editing has greatly contributed to the readability of my text, as well as to John Thompson, without whom the book would not have become possible.

This book is dedicated to my family – Rosita, Juhan and Laura Liina. Thank you for having faith in me.

INTRODUCTION

This book is primarily motivated by the current situation in the study of culture(s), which has become rather narrow in its interests. Even though books with titles promising new theoretical advances in the field continue to appear, in fact these almost invariably turn out to be case studies with little ambition for generalization, or discussions of other authors who have had such ambition in the past. No real breakthroughs have been made for decades. It has almost become improper to theorize about culture in broader terms. Under the conditions of increased specialization, the bigger picture is getting hazier and hazier. At the same time, the concept of culture, defined sloppily or not at all, is occupying an increasingly central place in social and political debate. Globalization, culture shocks, multiculturality and 'civilization conflicts' are being discussed by the general public almost daily – but with the help of a conceptual apparatus from about fifty years ago, which has been simplified to the extreme. In the process, the word 'culture' itself has come to refer to 'the exact opposite of what it was originally intended to mean' (Trouillot 2003:104), lending itself to bolstering conservative, reductionist and determinist agendas.

This is not to say there has been no positive development at all. The long overdue dialogue with natural sciences, genetics and neuroscience in particular – something called for already in the classic discussion of Kroeber and Kluckhohn on the definitions of culture (1952) – has gradually gained momentum. But all of it is happening entirely on the partner's terms. Cultural theorists do not seem to have anything to contribute and helplessly watch how their subject is being explained away in hard science terms (Blackmore 1999; Laland 2011; Lynch 1996), both for an academic audience and in more popular form.

1

Undoubtedly, quite a lot about human behaviour can be described in biological terms and should be put into a larger context, but this does not mean that cultural phenomena can be fully clarified in these terms only. In a differing context, the focus of the field is shifting away from cultural phenomena in the direction of the social and the economical. For example, the influential 'strong program' of Jeffrey Alexander and Philip Smith (2001), its recognition of the autonomous nature of cultural processes notwithstanding, is primarily aimed at the explanation of cultural phenomena as a part of the social whole. The 'cultural science' of John Hartley (2008) is programmatically opened up towards economics, while distancing itself from the study of particular phenomena for their semantic content. Most certainly the social and economic background is extremely important for understanding particular phenomena as well as the processes that generate and influence them, but taking such factors into account should not lead us back into economic or any other kind of determinism.

Another characteristic of current research on cultural matters is the trend to restrict its subject matter to fairly recent phenomena. Under the influence of the Birmingham school, most of what is now called 'cultural studies', or sometimes even 'culture and media studies', is engaged with practices of current popular culture, lifestyles and consumer products. This is not to say that our immediate cultural surroundings should not be analysed and criticized – just to point out that 'culture' still might refer to more than certain practices of the post-industrial West.

In yet another department, anthropologists operate with a wholly different concept of culture, derived from, but not restricted to, the modes of being human of the cultural Other. Here, too, long conceptual wars have been fought over the idea of culture as such (see, e.g., Fox and King 2002). Recent anthropological research has done a fine job in extrapolating its approaches to the human condition as such, and not just societies operating on different premises from our own. And yet, for most anthropologists 'culture' means primarily lived practice, actions rather than ideas or texts, which only come to the fore as elements shaping collective experience. As a result, the views on culture current in anthropological writing, tuned as they are to the solving of particular research questions, also remain limited in the range of phenomena they address.

Unquestionably, all these approaches are both legitimate and productive. However, culture cannot and should not be reduced to biological and socio-economic mechanisms only. All their insights notwithstanding, biocentric and sociocentric theories are unable

2

to explain the enormous variativity of human cultural experience. Nor should 'culture' be reduced to popular media or ethnographic descriptions. In order to understand culture, we need a broader view that would integrate all these approaches and complement them with the specific methods of textual theory, cultural history and other disciplines that have traditionally engaged in the study of our intellectual heritage and its present forms.

Indeed, the need for such a theory is being articulated by many. An increasing (even if subdued) chorus of voices critical of the current trends suggests that the separation of cultural analysis from the actual study of texts and the exclusive concentration on the present may already have taken the pendulum of cultural theory to the end of its current trajectory. To cite but a few examples from scholars working in various fields: Sheldon Pollock points out a widespread 'shallow presentism of scholarship and even antipathy to the past as such' (2009:935), while Robert Eaglestone doubts even the capacity of the discipline to handle the present: 'we fail to respond to the contemporary nature of our field, the "now"-ness of it' because 'we do not even have a clear idea of what the problems are. It is not that there is a consensus: there is not even a dissensus. We do not even know what the "basic concepts" are that need to undergo a radical revision' (2013:1093). Rita Felski, in turn, points out a hidden elitist agenda behind the rhetoric of subversion, 'a covert bid for moral superiority and cutting edge radicalism in the highly charged fray of academic politics. The vanguardism of cultural studies takes a distinctive form; it lies not in vaunting the authority of intellectuals vis-à-vis the people but in trumping its own superiority as a field vis-à-vis the conventional disciplines' (2003:502). Perhaps we should say more: in spite of its original opposition to the oppressive hierarchies of its day, 'cultural studies' have by now become the new orthodoxy, a conservative and stale field within which nothing really new has appeared for decades. Even one of the founding fathers of the discipline, Stuart Hall, has been reported as saying, towards the end of his life, that he 'really cannot read another cultural-studies analysis of Madonna or The Sopranos' (Bérubé 2009). This, of course, is not to deny the important contribution that this discipline has historically made to the study of cultures by broadening the extent of the field to include the 'uncanonical', or the phenomena not endorsed by the elites, as well as by alerting researchers to always pay attention to the power relations and the specifics of production behind the cultural process. And yet, after the theoretical 'explosion' of the 1970s and 1980s, we have been slowly drifting onto a rather uninspiring trail, where well-tested ideas are recycled and applied to whatever cases the author happens to be studying. 'Cultural studies', in their present form, have exhausted their potential, and the study of cultures – which is not the same thing – needs to be reinvigorated. This is not a conservative call back to the progressivist, hierarchical and totalizing views of culture from the nineteenth century, but an invitation to move on, towards an integral and holistic, but not determinist or reductive view of the human effort to make sense of our living environment.

For what it is worth, this book presents an attempt to construct such an integral theory that would bring textual analysis back into the discussion of cultural phenomena while at the same time not isolating them from their broader context of social practice or biological ground. Its second objective is to construct a rigorous but nonetheless flexible conceptual apparatus that can be used to address all cultural phenomena, present or past, that are meaningful for us, as well as being able to open up the results of the text-oriented and the practice-oriented investigations of cultural phenomena to each other. I believe the latter is essential – for a holistic understanding of culture, it is insufficient to view its phenomena only from one, however well-formed, single perspective.

Thus, the book sets itself the ambitious goal of bringing together several separate and influential traditions of speaking about its topic: the cultural semiotics of Umberto Eco (1976, 1979, 1984, 2000) and Yuri Lotman (1970, 1992, 1993, 2010a, 2010b), the cultural sociologies of Pierre Bourdieu (1977, 1988, 1991, 1993, 2007) and Zygmunt Bauman (1987, 1992, 1999, 2007a, 2007b), as well as a number of meaning-oriented anthropological approaches (D'Andrade 1995; de Certeau 1993; Geertz 1993; Strauss and Quinn 1997) that recognize the autonomy of individual cultural systems. I also admit a considerable debt to the cultural pragmatics of Jeffrey Alexander and his school (2006, 2011a, 2011b, 2013), the school of cultural psychology (Boyer and Wertsch 2009; Simão and Valsiner 2007; Valsiner and Rosa 2007; Valsiner and van der Veer 2000) and most certainly to Michel Foucault (2002a, 2002b), whose thought first led me to theorize about culture as a discursive system in practice, even if he is not evoked by name too often.

However, even though it stands on the shoulders of giants, just as any academic project necessarily does, this book is not primarily a response to or reflection on previous work, but a systematic and theoretical endeavour, distilled from the multitude of my own micro-level methodological solutions to problems I have encountered during years of research on cultural phenomena, Western and Asian, past and present. I am convinced that a theory should be evaluated on the basis not of its structural qualities (for example, elegance or complexity), but of its explanatory power. I believe that the analysis of an object of research is successful if and only if it is able to generate a broader and more adequate view of that object. I also think that, even though the objects of research in the humanities are necessarily vague, their terminology should not be, just as natural scientists observing fog employ no less strict language than those classifying rocks. The notorious difficulties that plague the conceptualization of cultural phenomena should not be considered a valid reason to give up the effort. Obviously, I do not believe that any judgement on the realities of social and cultural processes could be passed from a value-free, ideologically neutral viewpoint. But, following Karl Mannheim (1985:78–80), I hold that a position that is able to consider its own inevitable ideological bias is to be preferred to one that cannot.

This is why I have tried to keep the theory as simple as possible (admittedly not always succeeding), yet without compromises in the content. I have coined as few new concepts and redefined as few current ones as possible. Some of both has still proved to be necessary, even if fine-tuning and adjusting to the context does not count. In a word, I have tried to keep the theoretical construction reasonably compact and clear without simplifying its objects. The theory also does not seek to divorce itself from the hands-on analysis of particular cultural phenomena, contemporary and historical, familiar and structurally different.

AN OUTLINE OF THE THEORY
AND THE BOOK

Any theory of culture has to start with the definition of its object. In chapter 1, I argue for an approach to culture that is able to account for all phenomena related to the production, dissemination, transmission and interpretation of meaning. If culture constitutes the sum total of our efforts to make sense of our world, from the most individual and personal level to the most universal, then meaning should indeed be the common denominator for all phenomena we consider cultural. But meaning is not something abstract; it is itself produced in and by individual minds when they confront their reality.

Throughout the book, I stress the binary nature of cultural phenomena. On the one hand, there are more or less stable and shareable fixtures of meaning from images and narratives to laws, dress codes and domesticated spaces such as cities. A cultural subject comes into being in dialogue with such entities – texts – and inevitably participates in their production as well. On the other hand, culture manifests itself in all kinds of activities, from real rituals to ritualistic behaviour, from displaying curiosities to auditions for reality shows, from witch-trials to defences of dissertations. All activities grounded in meaning, or cultural practices, also construct their participants while being constructed by them in the process: you become a 'player' by 'playing'. I will proceed from the description of the signifying act – the elementary cultural event – to the nature of the mechanisms that combine and organize singular moments of signification into larger meaningful wholes, 'texts' and 'textualities', and from there to the cultural practices that relate the signifying wholes to the behaviour of people towards each other as well as all levels of their environment.

Chapter 2 will outline the theory of meaning used in this book. Just as cultural activity iterates between textuality and practice, the human subject also conceptualizes the world in two different ways that result in two different kinds of concepts – through direct experience, when the empirical flux is structured into a manageable reality, and with the help of acquired tools: by learning, for instance, that an unknown city is situated in a certain country of which the person has no experience. Concepts learned this way are, in Saussurean terms, more closely related to the signifier while the ones deduced from lived experience are inherent in the signified. It can be said that the moment of becoming meaningful, or the act of signification, takes place when these two concepts converge. This does not happen solely through an internal realization, but rather as a response to a *claim*. When an adult is speaking with a child and points to a furry barking animal, saying 'This is a dog!', she makes the claim that the signifier [dog], which the child may already know from a bedtime story, is associated with the animal they are observing. Of course, it is possible to use signs – for example, for abstract concepts – that hark back only to other signs that form their definitions, the only reality to which they refer. But all these derive, in the last resort, from similarly accepted claims, just as physically non-existent fictional characters are imagined through an analogy with real people. It is also possible *not* to accept claims others are making by saying, for example, 'this is what being a real man is all about', when the experiential concept does not fit the one acquired through learning. Moments like this highlight the difference between the two kinds of concepts, unnoticed in uncritical situations. And, from within, it is also possible to construct private-language signifiers with which one can refer to personally relevant reality slices. Nonetheless, reality on the whole becomes culturally meaningful to the perceiver through acts of signification that claim the identity of intralinguistic, learned concepts and experiential concepts, and it is these *claims*, not actually existing relations of meaning, that become reified in signs. And this is precisely what constitutes their irreducible arbitrariness. In a claim, the relation between the intralinguistic concept, definable through linguistically expressed characteristics, and the experiential concept, derived from our observation of reality, is necessarily arbitrary.

But stand-alone signs or their random combinations do not constitute cultural phenomena. Various sets of rules that govern cultural expression make it possible for us to express ourselves – to engage in practices and produce texts – and for others to interpret our utterances. These 'grammars' are modulated by the mentalities, the structures of knowledge, the worldviews of their historical context, which, deep down, have a similarly cultural origin. Although most of our cultural environment is handed down to us in a ready-made form, the elements that constitute it have all been produced by the same dynamic processes that are taking place in our minds when they encounter something unknown.

It should also be noted that cultural phenomena do not automatically enter circulation. At this next level, there is a mechanism at work similar to that within the elementary act of signification. Any new cultural expression (text or pattern of practice) that seeks to be acknowledged by the community makes a *bid*, a promise to be meaningful to its recipients in certain ways. Thousands of clothes designers produce new models each year and each of them makes a bid to be the expression of the new trends in fashion. Thousands of new poets make their debut and each of them makes the bid to be the voice of the new generation. Especially in the present times, when the equipment for producing a sample CD, a portfolio of photographs or a video is accessible to a much larger proportion of aspiring creative personalities than ever before, the number of bids greatly outweighs the number of those texts that are accepted by cultural institutions. At the same time, more democratic as well as more cheaply available new channels of communication, such as the internet, have also made alternative dissemination possible. Nevertheless, even after a text has initially entered circulation, it remains only a bid until it is endorsed by a critical mass of its intended recipients – tens of thousands of dedicated fans if the bid is to be a pop idol, or perhaps a dozen academics if it is a bid for the reinterpretation of the seventeenth-century Ethiopian philosopher Zera Yacob. If a bid is accepted, it will gain access to proper channels of circulation, which, in turn, determine the rules for its reception. Each cultural text comes with an implicit operation manual. A romantic comedy shown at an arthouse cinema may be poorly welcomed, even if the majority of the audience likes to see a romantic comedy now and then, but in another setting.

At this point it will be useful to start describing the mechanisms of the cultural system with the help of not one, but two separate models, a text-centred and a practice-centred one, sketched here in the barest outline. It is possible to look at a culture as primarily the sum total of all products of meaning production, or texts in the widest sense of the word – written and oral, verbal and visual, aural, corporal, spatial. But it is also possible to describe the cultural system as a totality of different, sometimes mingling, mostly collective but occasionally private, practices in which its carriers engage, producing and consuming texts in the process, sometimes simply as negligible by-products. For a holistic view, it is important not to privilege one of these perspectives over the other, though (or actually because) they operate with incompatible sets of concepts.

Chapter 3 will be dedicated to the text-centred model of culture. I will first distinguish between two categories of texts that differ in status and function. First, there are the texts that every carrier of the culture could be expected to know – at least to some extent or by hearsay – and the extent of her knowledge is a measure of her level of education. The Gospel, *Hamlet*, elementary table manners, *Mona Lisa*, the beginning of Beethoven's Fifth Symphony, basic traffic rules and the Eiffel Tower are examples of such texts in contemporary Western culture. I will call these nodes of meanings *base-texts*. No cultural system is totally homogeneous, and one way to identify its different layers is by the differences in their sets of base-texts. The heavy metal cultural community counts 'War Pigs' and *Smoke on the Water* among them, while *Giselle* and *The Nutcracker* belong to the base-texts of ballet enthusiasts, but the Eiffel Tower, traffic rules and *Mona Lisa* are shared by both. Obviously, the borders of these communities are not closed and a person with somewhat more catholic tastes can actually appreciate ballet and heavy metal alike. This also demonstrates that the category of base-texts has no fixed boundaries – immediately next to those actually shared by the over- whelming majority of the carriers of a culture are texts that are still only making the bid to be accepted on this level, emerging from a sub- culture and claiming their spot on the central stage. Similarly, there are texts, such as the catechism or novels by Mikhail Sholokhov, the Nobelist classic author of socialist realism, that have previously been base-texts in their respective cultures, but are no longer.

At the opposite end of the status scale are *result-texts*, bids that have just been accepted and entered circulation, as well as those that have done so some time ago but are still being considered recent arrivals by their recipients. Some of them may eventually acquire a more solid position, become the base-texts of a subculture, and finally perhaps even of the whole cultural system, while others will have a brief span of active life and will soon fade out of circulation. There are various mechanisms in action that may prolong or shorten the life span of a text, and some of them are completely accidental. For example, it is possible that an actress who will later become a major star has played the heroine in a film based on a mediocre novel, which will induce her fans-to-be to rediscover the book they would otherwise hardly have bothered to read. In any case, the status trajectory of a text, its trail through the operational memory (see below) of the cultural system, may take different turns and, accordingly, the group of result-texts is even more mixed in terms of status than that of base-texts.

Apart from their life span, there are also other differences between the layers of base- and result-texts. The most important of them is the role of the former in generating the latter. Base-texts keep appearing in new cultural expressions as intertextual material – narrative templates, imitated style registers, wandering motifs, parodied elements and simply quotes that will be recognized by the majority of their intended recipients. This also upholds their status. New generations of recipients may never have actually read *Romeo and Juliet*, but they continue to be aware of the story because of its many reincarnations in contemporary culture. Some other classical love stories, such as that of Tristan and Isolde, for example, have gone almost completely out of circulation. Result-texts do not have such generative potential, and if an author has assumed that a recent text can be confidently alluded to with a broader audience in mind, this means her acceptance of the text's bid for base-text status, which also contributes to the rise of that text towards this goal.

A model of textuality also needs a description of the space where base-texts are processed and result-texts produced. I call it the *operational memory* of culture, using the term without a very consistent analogy with either neurophysiological processes or computer technology, but more resemblant of the latter. This operational memory contains the normative theories of the period, or the assumed proper ways of symbolization and interpretation. It is also the space for struggle between ideological, moral, aesthetical and other kinds of standards, as well as many other modes of cultural thinking, verbal, visual, corporal – in short, everything that can influence textual production and interpretation. These modes are not necessarily in correlation with the two layers of texts, and there are tensions within this layer itself. For instance, it is possible that the modes of cultural thinking change, but a critical amount of the base-texts stay intact, as in the time of the Reformation, which made a bid for a new regime for reading the Bible and more or less successfully challenged the status of many of the result-texts produced by the Catholic Church. Or, conversely, base-texts may change in a historical rupture, but the modes of cultural thinking remain largely the same, as in the switch from communism to nationalism in Russia and some other parts of Eastern Europe during and after the decline of the USSR. In due time, a significant change in one of these two will also affect the other, but the impact on the result-texts is almost always immediate.

Culture as textuality is also dependent on cultural institutions, which play a seminal role in the production and dissemination of result-texts as well as the maintenance of base-texts along with their canonized interpretations. Some of these are real places and people (galleries, publishing houses, newspaper columns, cafés); others, just instances of the social imaginary (the average TV viewer, the powers-that-be). In the text-centred model of the cultural system, these institutions are important for the ways in which they highlight some aspects of the texts in the operational memory and downplay others, encourage and support the bids for status of particular texts and stop the advancement of those that do not conform to their standards, and can distort the semantic content of the texts they handle, both the ones they favour and the ones they dislike. Cultural institutions may be in alignment with certain dominant modes of cultural thinking, but they may also be at odds with them, challenging the mainstream taste or the preferences of the powers-that-be.

The text-centred model of the cultural system thus consists of two groups of texts, base and result, which are separated by a layer of operational memory and cultural institutions. The two groups of texts communicate with each other through this layer, and the components of this layer also influence each other. During stable periods, all the constituent parts of the system are in contact with each other (a certain degree of necessary subcultural fragmentation aside), but in times of cultural turmoil, which are frequently also the turning points that produce more texts with base-text potential than other periods in history, there can be strong tensions between the elements of the system. By identifying the key features of each of the constituent elements and their relation to each other, we have a picture of the background system within which both old and new texts circulate, are (re)interpreted, interact while competing for status and, collectively, make up the stuff of which the larger part of the cultural consciousness of the people in this particular timespace consists. An understanding of this system is necessary in order to turn close readings into truly 'thick' descriptions and to put technical studies of textual form and style into perspective.

But the terms of textuality are, as stated above, not the only coordinates for mapping a cultural system. A different picture arises when it is conceived as a flux that merges together a large number of heterogeneous practices, whose tangible products command attention only as junctions guiding the movement of meanings in action. Some of these practices support each other, some contradict one another, some are unrelated, but all of them are shaped by their common context, which they themselves actively shape in turn. A text-centred

11

model must therefore necessarily be complemented by a practice-oriented one that foregrounds the activities of cultural subjects, and not the stable clusters of meaning these practices produce. A tentative description of such a model will be undertaken in chapter 4. Even a cursory cross-cultural inquiry reveals, however, that the structures of practices vary to a considerable extent across genres, historically and geographically. Indeed, it seems difficult to compare auguries based on birds' entrails to weather forecasts on cable TV networks. On the other hand, we might find it useful to observe that there is a certain similarity between the cultural logic that requires of all adult men that they write a poem to prove their suitability for public office (as was the case during many centuries in China) and another that presupposes that marriageable women can play chess (as was traditionally the case in Georgia) which distinguishes them from logics that reserve these and other analogous cultural activities for professionals.

To enable such comparisons, I have identified eight aspects that each cultural practice necessarily has. First of all, we can identify a *function* for each cultural practice – a certain task or a set of tasks that it performs in the socio-cultural environment (entertainment, education, transmission of values, recording of historical events, or even the suspension of other socio-cultural activities, as is claimed for 'pure art', etc.). This is not necessarily identical to the *goal* of the practice, or the task that it has set for itself and proclaims to be its true purpose. Moreover, the function of the practice may change – for instance, when a once-entertaining text becomes a historical source – but its goal cannot; the text may also proclaim 'false' goals or conceal its true ones, which should then be deduced from its reception.

Each cultural practice necessarily has a certain type of *carrier* – people who are actively engaged in it as producers or consumers. The carrier of a practice can be expected to have a certain kind of education and social standing, they can belong to an age group or gender, or have some specific personal characteristics. The group of carriers can be homogeneous, or not very. It could be closed to anybody but the initiated, or open to all. There might be differences between the active performers and passive recipients of the practice, or it could be that everybody involved should be both. The carrier type may be in correlation with the *status* of the practice. It is always likely that practices of the aristocrats would be considered aristocratic. But they might be reserved for them and only them, or be available for imitation by everybody else. The decadent habits of the nobility, such as orgiastic debauchery or impious investigations of heathen religions, can also be abhorred by the common people on moral grounds. The

12

practices of carriers of similar standing may also have a hierarchy –
some of them could be serious pursuits; others, pastimes for leisure.
It could be that practices of originally low status, such as the singing
of folksongs, could be elevated to a high status by a sudden gust of
fashion. It could even be that the richest and most powerful would
construct for themselves an artificial world in which to imitate the
allegedly pure and primitive life or the socially deprived, as has happened in various forms of pastoralism. The status of a practice does
not immediately follow from who its carriers are, and vice versa.

Next, it is necessary for each cultural practice to have a range
of *materials* it regularly uses. A cultural language, or a mixture of
several languages, or only a small part of the vocabulary and stylistic
registers, but also material objects and technologies, such as cos-
tumes, artefacts, paints, typewriters, wines, ritual objects, computer
software or the full moon, can all be necessary for practising certain
cultural phenomena. Artefacts used in a practice perhaps have to be
manufactured only according to established rules and by licensed
masters. Musical instruments may have long histories of prestigious
owners and be traced back to makers of high reputation. The authen-
ticity of a painting may be confirmed or disputed by chemical analysis
of the paints used.

Regulations on what can and should be used in a cultural practice
are complemented by sets of *rules* about how the materials are to
be exploited. Approximately the same set of percussion instruments
can be used for pop, rock, heavy metal or jazz music, and even if we
consider these separate languages (because all of them are difficult to
use outside the subpractices they define), then the variety of styles and
forms within each of them is still considerable and has been changing
over time. The same is obvious for any other cultural practice. The
rules of the practice are sometimes adequately described by the normative theory of its timespace, but at some other times they are not,
which usually means that the normative theory is being challenged by
actual practice. It is permissible to use swear-words in contemporary
poetry, but it is precisely that permission that marks the poetry as
contemporary – the absence of certain restrictions is itself also a rule.
The rules are thus closely related to the materials and, through them,
to their immediate context, but also to other rules in other similar
practices that use similar materials in their expression.

The final pair of characteristics is formed by the *means of circulation* and the *means of preservation and transmission* of the practice.
On the one hand, it is important to know how the practice reaches
its immediate audience. There is a difference between public readings,

13

manuscripts, books and files – each of them implies a specific mode of organizing time, materials and distribution; some are more costly than others, and some are more easily controlled than others. Circulation is usually managed and monitored by specific institutions that can impose their regulations on the process; they can be elitist or democratic, selling for profit or interested in the diffusion of their message, centralized or heterogeneous; they can have the monopoly over a particular practice, compete with each other on an equal basis or set up alternative systems that a dictatorship cannot hold in check even though it censors official publications. In a different world, there are websites for downloading pirated files, persecuted by distribution companies and copyright agencies that try to restrict their circulation to commercial channels.

Each cultural practice also seeks to sustain itself and ensure its continuity by teaching itself to new possible performers and educating new recipients to appreciate it. Practices with a sufficient degree of self-consciousness frequently try to preserve even those of their historical forms, genres and subpractices that are falling out of circulation, but may be kept alive in some other form. Ballroom dancing, once a widespread social skill, has been transformed into a form of sport, while folk dance has become a social activity, and medieval dance a form of entertainment performed by professionals. As the function of these practices has changed, so have their means of transmission. Societies, schools, fraternities, clubs, universities, lodges, libraries, archives, museums, wandering teachers and many other kinds of cultural institutions preserve and transmit specific skills and kinds of cultural knowledge, instrumental and theoretical. Some of these are simultaneously engaged in organizing the circulation of the practice; others are specialized in transmission. And what is being preserved and taught there may one day, when the suitable moment arrives, make a new bid for being restored to general circulation, albeit usually in a new form.

In the last chapters, I will present two case studies, applying the concepts proposed here to two cultural moments, one historical – the 'new sweet style' poetry in Italy in the thirteenth century – and one more recent – the transformation of the art scene in Eastern Europe after the fall of the Iron Curtain. As I hope will be seen from these brief studies, the description of a cultural phenomenon – be it a stylistic trend in TV series, or the work of a school of medieval Persian manuscript illuminators, or American adaptations of Japanese food – can gain a lot in explanatory power by employing simultaneously the two sets of concepts proposed here. If so, this could perhaps also lead to more dialogue between the disciplines engaged in the study of culture(s), something sorely needed in the present times, when humanities programmes in universities worldwide constantly have to struggle for survival.

— 1 —

LOOKING FOR CULTURE,
LOOKING AT THINGS

'Culture' is a notoriously ambiguous concept with hundreds of definitions, and its very use has been criticized by a number of researchers (Abu-Lughod 1991; Fox 1985; Kuper 1999, and many others) because of its allegedly totalizing nature. Indeed, in the late nineteenth and early twentieth centuries, it was often hastily assumed that cultural systems are in complete correlation with communities, and people's life-worlds are inescapably shaped by them (Frobenius 1921; Tylor 1871). If that were true, then all the carriers of a given culture would somehow intrinsically have to share the same values and norms, even if they contradicted them with their actions. This is obviously false. However, the concept of culture still continues to be plagued by the ontologizing character of language. The prototype of the referent of any noun is imagined to be a particular thing, self-identical throughout, continuous in time and fully contained within its borders. But culture is not such a thing, and to conceive it as such is misleading. As Marilyn Strathern puts it, speaking about the analogous concept of society:

> To think of society as a thing is to think of it as a discrete entity. The theoretical task then becomes one of elucidating 'the relationship' between it and other entities. This is a mathematic, if you will, that sees the world as inherently divided up into units. The significant corollary of this view is that relationships appear as extrinsic to such units: they appear as secondary ways of connecting things up. (1996:61)

In fact, such relationships are actually what these 'things' consist of.

Thus, sentences such as 'the sky is blue', built on the same structural pattern as 'the rose is red', imply a similar existence for things such as 'the sky' and 'the rose' and that they have properties in the same way, which is not true – there is no such object as 'the sky'. Nonetheless, the difference in ontological status does not mean things of the non-rose category do not exist at all. For example, they can enter chains of causal relations. 'The flight was cancelled because of the weather' describes a real situation: 'the flight' (itself a non-rose) did not take place because of a number of conditions, such as poor visibility, probable turbulence, heavy rainfall, etc., which collectively make up another non-rose called 'the weather'. Analogically, it would make things clearer if we think of entities such as 'culture' as unstable sets of heterogeneous elements, processes, environments, webs of relations similar to the weather, rather than, for example, the statutes of a legal entity. The same is indeed true for 'societies'. 'Cultures' share a certain amount of encompassing characteristics, although this does not mean that the results of their study can describe their individual carriers with precision. In such investigations, as in many soft sciences in general, the object of research does not necessarily exist independently of the research, but comes into being, in a Heisenbergian way, only in and through the language with which it is spoken about. Thus, in the paradigmatic case, it is not a discrete object or category of objects, but rather a group of similar, though not necessarily connected, things, relations, activities, or of all these linked together, either on a more or less permanent basis or just for a brief moment. Nevertheless, such phenomena – called 'hybrids' by Bruno Latour (1993:10–11, 41–3) – are no less real than concrete, physical things, because they, too, have the capacity to shape the life-world of human beings as conscious social agents moving around in it. To de-ontologize culture – to remove it from the group of self-identical and non-fuzzy things – thus does not mean to dismiss it. On the contrary, this is the prerequisite of seeing it clearly. A more flexible approach makes it possible to think about culture not as a strictly tangible object, but as a loose network of heterogeneous, at times contradictory, phenomena that is nevertheless essential for each single person in her efforts to make sense of her world, as well as for integrating such persons into groups capable of communication and collaboration. And this is the approach I am going to adopt. Nearly all phenomena under scrutiny in this book are 'non-roses' – not tangible, not self-identical, not graspable as wholes – but nonetheless constantly affect what we are and what we do.

Social/cultural

For the purposes of this book, 'culture' embraces all those and only those phenomena that involve a certain degree of expression and are open to interpretation, or different interpretations – in other words, that are definable by their meaning. This is a distinction made already back in the 1970s by scholars such as Clifford Geertz (1993:144–5) and Michel de Certeau (1993:121–2), for whom 'social' referred to the relationships and 'cultural' to the meanings that link subjects with each other. The distinction still remains highly useful, although the borders between social sciences and the humanities are today even more blurred than then. Obviously, relationships depend on meanings and meanings only function in relationships.[1] The overlap is not quite complete, however. Analogous or structurally similar relationships of power can take place in different cultures, having been encoded in completely different ways and therefore having different meanings for their participants. Conversely, people may well be involved in ritualistic or bureaucratic relationships which they fail – or at least have to make considerable effort – to understand. These are cases where the cultural and social aspects of one particular situation are not in accordance with each other, and it is in such spots that the tension between them becomes visible. Jeffrey Alexander has neatly captured this dialectic in his discussion of Geertz: 'social facts as events, institutions, and collective actions are like art in the sense that they do their work as art does – via the imagination', he writes, but reminds us immediately that it is a mistake to reduce the effect of such phenomena to their artistic significance (2011a:61). And neither should cultural phenomena be read solely as aestheticized social meanings. I quite agree with Alexander when he writes that 'in order to understand power, we must give relative autonomy to culture' (2011b:107) – a statement I take to mean simultaneously that

[1] Roger Friedland and John Mohr have questioned the necessity for this distinction in their discussion of William Sewell's (1999) theories of structure and cultural practice, rejecting, in particular, Sewell's claims for a relative autonomy of the semiotic: 'Neither interests, powers, nor resources can be specified independently of the meanings which organize specific institutional fields. Materiality is a way of producing meaning; meaning is a way of producing materiality. Materiality and meaning are not exterior to each other, as the conceptual divide between social and cultural systems, or resource and structure, or the term "embedded", all variously imply' (2004:9). But when they then observe that, in sociological writing, 'cultural meanings, both categorical and expressive, are usually subservient to a social logic and do not participate in its making' (2004:11), it becomes obvious that the reduction of the difference has tacitly served to justify the primacy of the social over the semiotic, between which they continue to distinguish.

the mechanisms of culture can and should be analysed for their own, autonomous principles of operation. Social relations and mechanisms of power are just one aspect of the basic ways of being human in the world, as are the repertoires of making sense of oneself as well as reality, and navigating that reality on all its levels. 'Culture', in the sense in which the word is used in this book, is a collective designation for all phenomena, stable and momentary, that take place in order to facilitate this task. In short, I take the social and the cultural to be two heterogeneous, but strongly overlapping, spheres of human activity, both of them dependent on the other, and of equal standing.

Moreover, cultural phenomena are characteristically able to survive their original context and the power-games that have shaped them. A language (as a system of meanings) does not completely cease to be a language when it dies out. The texts surviving in it continue to mean after their initial practical relevance is long forgotten. The same is even more true of rituals that continue to perform social functions after their meaningful content is lost or has ceased to be relevant to their participants. Old rituals may even acquire cardinally new symbolic content when their cultural environment changes, and thus, in a sense, become new rituals. This is how Christmas and Easter have evolved into Christian religious holidays from pagan calendric feasts and, in the contemporary world, developed into commercial events that also influence the behaviour of consumers in countries where Christianity is not very widespread. These are examples of the internal distance cultural languages may take from the social reality they are describing.

Following Lotman (2010a:144), I am going to use the term 'cultural languages' in a broad sense, as a category that enables us to group together specific uses of natural languages, artificial symbolic codes (such as traffic signs or dress codes) and a large variety of other means of self-expression, such as artistic practices. However, this will be done with Zygmunt Bauman's warning in mind:

> the logic of culture is the logic of the self-regulating system rather than the logic of the code or of the generative grammar of language . . . we are justified in extrapolating (to the non-linguistic spheres of culture) only the most general features of language; exactly those features, which characterize the linguistic interaction in its capacity as a case of a more inclusive class of self-regulating systems. (1999:77)

Thus, the generic use of the word 'language' does not imply that there is a deep unity between all the signifying systems of a culture that is patterned on natural language and allows its users to 'read' dance in a way that is somehow fundamentally the same as the way

19

they read newspapers. A cultural language is never a straightforward code, as traffic lights are, but a much more complicated affair within which several signifying systems of different types normally operate at the same time. This is, in fact, also true of a natural language to a certain extent. To be sure, a natural language is describable in terms of vocabulary and grammatical structure, but in any event where it is actually used there are several other signifying systems simultaneously in operation, without which it does not really work. Socially endorsed codes such as rules of etiquette or significant registers of style, 'body language' and repertoires of rhetoric are always there. Any practical use of language is also informed by other significatory devices pertaining to aspects of the speech situation, whether it be a long-distance telephone call, an abdication speech of a monarch, or a simulation of an abdication speech by a monarch, performed by an actor in a theatre play. In real-life situations, expression is produced at the same time on different levels, which support each other when the underlying impulse is itself more or less unambiguous, but may also contradict each other, creating tensions and confusion. This is what always makes the use of 'natural' languages in practice already cultural, and the same applies to all cultural languages – much more strongly, most of the time.

Cultural phenomena are produced as results of self-expression, conscious or unconscious, purposeful or random. All human beings constantly produce cultural phenomena, even if very short-lived ones, such as conversations with neighbours or order on our desks. From the position of the recipient, however, a 'cultural phenomenon' is any delimited slice of the culturally mediated reality that she tries to interpret. Ancient Romans examined the livers of sacrificed animals for purposes of divination, thus converting them to cultural phenomena. Most of the time, however, people define and construct for themselves only such 'texts' as actually help them to get a better grasp of things. This constructedness is characteristic of all texts and practices, regardless of how distinctly visible it is to the naked eye. A text, as is well known, is not simply the material surface of the cultural product, but contains trails of signification chains, allusions, influences and so forth, which connect it to other texts of different kinds. It is also accompanied by explicitly indicated or implicitly assumed ways of access that make it possible for its recipients to partake of it. By actualizing other layers of its significance and making use of some particular ways of access, recipients construct the text as it is 'for them', and produce interpretations that are actually representations. Such modes of reception may also differ among groups and individuals as well as change over time. The same applies to practices. Together, texts and

20

practices form the bulk of cultural phenomena and, as we saw earlier, each phenomenon normally contains some of both.

A cultural text or practice can never occur alone and in isolation, but is necessarily linked to others through what will here be called 'cultural systems'. This term has a history in the older anthropological tradition and its critics (see Bauman 1999:xx–xxix), but will be used here in the sense Geertz gives to it, when he defines culture as 'an historically transmitted pattern of meanings embodied in symbols, a system of inherited conceptions expressed in symbolic forms by means of which men communicate, perpetuate, and develop their knowledge about and attitudes toward life' (1993:89). In a particular timespace, cultural phenomena may be related to each other either directly (one film parodies another), indirectly (avant-garde art and experimental poetry share the same critical attitude towards the establishment) or obliquely (the physically same CD player may be used to play the music of the parents and the children). What will here be called 'cultural systems' consist of everything that is involved in such relations, within the completely hypothetical outer limits to which they reach. Cultural systems do not have universal structural patterns, because they arise in particular environments wherein certain groups of people live, and they build on the knowledge and understanding these people have. Even if they might be reasonably graspable in their institutional power-centres, they become ambiguous and vague and tend to fade away at the edges. There, they either fall apart or fork into countless specialized or subcultural streams less accessible to the statistically average inhabitant of the cultural space, and yet remain capable of unnegligible input to some salient 'central' cultural practice or another. Needless to say, the statistically average inhabitant of a cultural environment is herself a complete abstraction, because the cultural identities of each particular person are necessarily constructed at the converging point of heterogeneous streams. Everybody is an exception to general rules in some respect. Nobody is ever in full control of their cultural resources, and nobody can survive with the help of one specific, homogeneous and unambiguous set of cultural resources alone. There is no 'pure' culture – and never has been. No community of people has ever invented and designed absolutely everything they use in order to interact meaningfully with each other and their environment, materially and mentally. Every language contains loan-words and bears traces of syntactic influence from other languages, and similarly the invention of a useful tool or the discovery of the intoxicating properties of a plant hardly ever remain the intellectual monopoly of those who first came by them.

Efficient gods win new worshippers, and cardinal beliefs about the structure of the universe spread likewise. 'Cultural purity', wherever and whenever proclaimed as a value, has not necessarily been very beneficial for the well-being of a community, although it can be an effective means of control and domination. This is why descriptive myths of original cultural purity are willingly taken up by politicians of a certain sort in order to use them to bolster their own agendas. Despite the simplifying traditionalist (or tradition-bashing) claims to the contrary, a completely homogeneous, isolated and unchanging cultural system with no memory of its past is simply not possible.

Of course, it also has to be noted that the relations between different cultural systems, although inevitable and necessary for their maintenance, are rarely just, equal and innocent interactions. It is typical of a culture to assume initially that its own view of the world is the basically 'correct' one – otherwise it has simply failed in its primary task to explain the world to its carriers. This is why a cultural system also normally sees no problem in trying to spread itself, imposing itself even by force on others, if need be. There is a certain dose of imperialist ambition in the core of every culture, but only some have actually historically had a chance to act on it. Much has been written on how colonial empires have raped and disfigured all the cultural systems they came into contact with, creating a mythology of their own superiority and culturalizing mission in the process.[2] The cultural mix resulting from such interaction is clearly of a different kind from the *mélange* that emerges in a cultural system that adopts and adapts foreign elements suited to it and on its own terms. There is, of course, a degree of affinity to be found between brutal imperialist domination and the more covert cultural imperialism based on techniques akin to Baudrillard's 'seduction' (1990). Ways of imposing one's systemic characteristics on other cultures with the help of powerful methods of persuasion and advanced technologies of text dissemination may also result in the erosion and eventual disappearance of these cultures. However, there remains a crucial difference. In the colonial context, the mix is composed of elements that are in systemic disagreement: they obstruct and do not complement each other, as is well illustrated in the discussion of the 'subaltern' condition (see Spivak 1988). In comparison, a 'seduced' culture willingly adjusts itself internally in order to accommodate the imposed elements, even if it has no pressing need for them.

[2] Moreover, Jonathan Friedman has shown how the allegedly primitive societies in Africa, Melanesia and other places have actually emerged as a result of contact with European trade that has eroded the native social structures and rendered their social and cultural institutions powerless (1994:9–12).

Cultural communities

There is a long tradition in culture-related debates of criticizing the term 'community', mostly with the arguments summarized in the first section of this chapter. In traditional usage, 'communities' have indeed claimed a rather high degree of coherence that is clearly not justified. Nevertheless, the converse position – single individuals against a heterogeneous and variable cultural background – also has its problems. If cultural phenomena are approached with a Wittgensteinian view of meanings derived from use – meanings 'taking place' and not just 'being there' – this already presupposes an intersubjective environment where that happens. The relation between the processes of meaning production and the collective of people for whom they are happening thus needs to be clarified in more detail. Therefore, I suggest we also redefine 'community' for the present purposes, and see it as any group capable of sharing meanings, from temporary, ad hoc associations to more solidly established social institutions, on the sole basis of sharing cultural languages. As Lotman insists, cultural communities are always such that individuals as their parts do not cease to be distinct wholes in them (1992:45).

A cultural system normally allocates different sets of languages to various groups of carriers, to be used for different purposes and in different situations, so that nobody is in complete active command of the entire repertoire. The same indeed happens to natural languages, which circulate in numerous dialects, as well as jargonistic and other subcultural variations that may be mutually almost unintelligible. And neither do cultural and textual communities constitute strongly cohesive groups of like-minded people who all share the same values, cultural habits and attitudes.[3] What they do share, however, is texts and practices. Texts can be shared by a teacher in a class (who reveres them) and students (who are bored by them), practices can be shared by prison wardens and inmates, both sides having their own ideas about them. However, both of them can make more authoritative statements about prison life than someone who has never experienced it. Of course, it goes without saying that wardens and inmates

---

[3] The term 'textual communities' was initially coined by Brian Stock to describe virtual groups of medieval religious dissenters who 'may not have shared profound doctrinal similarities or common social origins, but ... demonstrated a parallel use of texts, both to structure the internal behaviour of the groups' members and to provide solidarity against the outside world' (1987:90). In my usage, the term is broader and includes also the sharing of texts with much more limited life-defining potential.

23

belong to different and mutually opposed 'communities of meaning' in Booth's sense of 'communities of (some type of) sameness defined from within by the presence of a morally/politically relevant past' (2006:52). The same kind of diversity can be found in most cultural communities, perhaps with the exception of some closed religious sects or quasi-religious groups, where it is suppressed. It is, in principle, possible to speak about single-text and single-practice communities – or nano-communities, to use a term aptly coined by Jonathan Zittrain (2008:143) – such as groups of people united only by the fact that they collect stamps or went to Woodstock. Nonetheless, it makes more sense to imagine larger communities, with a longer list of shared texts or practices, or both, and perhaps also some attitudes towards them (Fish 1980; Rosenwein 2006). A conscious feeling of belonging to the same group may connect them, or parts of them, but is not strictly necessary. In other words, cultural communities don't need to be coherent, spatially contiguous, or internally homogeneous in any other respect. This is not only a characteristic of the present times, as opposed to more cohesive, pre-(post-)modern *Gemeinschafts*. Consider, for example, the various networks of monasteries in medieval Europe, from Ireland and Norway to Spain and Italy. These were certainly cultural communities connected by flows of information traffic, but still divided between monastic orders, as well as diversified by local cultural input and internal struggles for domination. The traders and craftsmen living in member-cities of the Hanseatic League provide another example, quite comparable to the professional networks of the present-day European Union. As discussed earlier, meanings need a social space to circulate, simply in order to be there.

A cultural system can thus also be characterized as a configuration of cultural communities and subcultures, partially overlapping, partially hierarchically organized, sometimes coexisting, sometimes challenging each other. As Jeffrey Alexander has shown, a certain distance of some groups from the core is endemic to any social system and not merely the result of contingent tensions or conflicts (2006:411), and the same applies to the organization of the cultural space. The word 'subculture' is here used in a broader sense than usual. In academic literature, the term 'subculture' normally refers to the cultural identity of marked minority groups, which themselves stress their difference from the mainstream and challenge the dominant norms. In the present context, however, the word is used for any cultural community that shares a consistently structured subset of cultural languages, texts and practices and is at least minimally self-conscious – that is, allows its carriers to identify themselves as belonging to the group. There is a subculture of hikers, just as there is one of bikers. It is therefore possible, for example, to speak about professional subcultures, not only in the sense of their being defined by their capability to use professional jargons, but also in the sense that anatomically more explicit jokes may be tolerated in the company of doctors than of lawyers. Each carrier of a culture normally belongs to a fairly large number of such subcultural groups, but some of them make stronger claims on her identity than others. It is possible to define oneself for oneself completely through any practice – to be a Sunday fisherman to the bone – but it is difficult (though perhaps not altogether impossible) to be a Sunday skinhead. Non-practising Christians are met frequently, non-practising vegetarians hard to imagine. Sometimes, the identity claims are so strong that an individual is compelled to accept them in order to have access to membership of the group; sometimes they are weak and it is up to the individual to decide how much of this group she wants to have in her life.

One way to imagine the circulation space of meanings is thus as a complex and interconnected hierarchy of cultural communities. The lowest level of this pyramid is occupied by imaginary nano-communities that share a single text or practice, gradually rising to higher levels with more and more structured overlap of shared cultural material, but always with room for non-shared meanings. The highest and most abstract level of the hierarchy would be a global culture, the heuristic 'parent-culture' of all others.[4] There is no such thing, because there are no texts and practices that are shared by absolutely all self-conscious human beings. But gradually the situation is approaching where at least some representatives of every cultural community on earth have access to a set of global channels, which carry considerable prestige and disseminate information in cultural languages that presuppose a certain core competence. Cultural erosion has already made many local traditions less meaningful to their carriers than the global popular culture, which has little or nothing to say about their own situation. Historically, this situation is rather unique, because until the twentieth century the highest level of such hierarchies has always been regional.

Except for the lowest and the highest, every level of the cultural hierarchy can be seen both as a parent-culture to a set of subcultures and as a subculture to the next level. Which level the observer places

---

[4] By this, I do not mean the cultural system that has spread all over the world as a result of globalization processes, but the abstract level at which intercultural communication could be achieved on globally shared issues – even if, in practice, the former shapes the possibility conditions of the latter (see Hopper 2007:100ff.)

herself on is always a matter of choice and purpose. A cultural critic can legitimately study something called 'French culture' which actually consists of an array of Francophone and non-Francophone cultural communities on French soil, as well as French-rooted communities elsewhere, with all their internal tensions resulting not only from class, race, gender or social position, but also from the more tangible variation of shared texts and practices, as well as their responses to them. But, just as legitimately, an anthropologist can also study the nano-community of people that daily takes the same bus and sees the same advertisements en route, developing similar desires and/or similar bursts of resentment at the same moment.

To make matters even more complicated, it has to be noted that the borders of subcultures need not respect the borders of their parent-cultures. Fans of Harry Potter may inhabit many countries and they may partake of the adventures of their hero in a multitude of languages – all being members of the same community based on a shared text. Territorial and linguistic coherence, traditionally the arguments by which national cultures have been claimed to be a natural level of abstraction to their carriers, are no longer all-important. History has certainly demonstrated that it is not difficult to produce powerful shared and agenda-oriented self-consciousness among the members of one nation and to link the result to virtually any aspect of social interaction. Even without entering into the debate on nationalisms, it should also be clear that a situation in which one set of cultural languages based on one natural language is completely shared by a homogeneous community that populates a clearly demarcated territory has never historically occurred. Therefore, accordingly, the role of 'nation' as a privileged cultural level, parent to subcultures that are fully contained by it and governed by its codes, is not really natural. When we consider the structure of the cultural world of an individual, it is not a smoothly organized hierarchy of concentric circles, but a space of overlaps and internal contradictions. In that space, cultural groups emerge as conceptualizations, either by themselves or by outsiders. And each of these groups shares some cultural languages also with people who are not a part of it.

All in all, it is incorrect to say that an individual is completely defined or moulded into predictability by the cultural system with all its groups, subgroups and communities, but neither is it true that each individual can freely take on the entire system. Culture is indeed 'an organisation of diversity' (Hannerz 1992:14), even in two opposite senses. It organizes the diversity of its carriers into a system where they can make sense of their surroundings and interact with each other, but it also organizes the ways in which the diversity of every-body else's self-expression is available to each one of them.

The cultural subject

It is now time to look at the opposite, the most particular position in the cultural process – that of the concrete individual, the cultural subject. The Western metaphysical tradition has come a long way since the Cartesian postulation of the single and undivided 'I' that looks at the process of reality from the outside, as it were – a purely mental whole uninhibited by its corporeal dimensions. But already the Kantian site of pure reason, though still a coherent whole, was internally structured, containing various *a priori* conditions of empirical knowledge. With Freud and Nietzsche, the unity broke down completely. The current understanding of the cultural subject, shaped by Lacan and Foucault, sees it primarily as the site of struggle between externally conditioned factors, conflicting influences of various kinds and origins. It is also obvious that a cultural subject is not restricted to her physical body, but includes much more, starting with appropriate clothing and ending up, as Andy Clark has suggested (1997:213–14), with the libraries, information networks and other possible resources at her disposal. After all, talking about the 'cultural' subject already implies her privileged relationship with a particular cultural environment.

But even the view of the subject as an independent entity, a continuous instance of consciousness that interacts with the world, learning from it and making assessments of it, has been challenged on many fronts by various brands of theory. On the one hand, some social and cultural constructivists (Hampson 1988; Hampson and Colman 1995) have argued that the cultural subject is not a sovereign entity, only superficially shaped by its environment, but actually comes into being purely as the result of a construction process in a particular cultural setting. On the other hand, the school of 'neurophilosophy' (Churchland 2007; Churchland and Churchland 1998; Dennett 1992) is further reducing the role of a person to that of a biological machine that only processes data fed to it from the outside, through physiological channels, and builds them into her conceptual structures with the help of cognitive software, quite often considered to be largely hard-wired to the human brain. Under such circumstances, it seems hardly appropriate to speak of the subject at all, or at least not in more substantial forms than as a purely heuristic designation of the cultural extensions of an identifiable individual physical person. This view also calls into question the critique levelled at totalizing views of culture: if personality is nothing but an almost neutral site of convergence for external influences, why do we then object to the attitudes of older theory that consider culture the primary conditioning force that bends individuals to its particular moulds?

These authors definitely make several valid points, but important issues remain to be resolved in the places where their claims differ. First of all, we must consider the way in which cultural phenomena take place in the world of 'things'. The neurophilosophers and other proponents of the cognitive turn, in their programmatic effort to bring the disciplines of cultural analysis as close to natural sciences as possible, are nearing the position of strong physicalism – which holds that everything that happens in the world *is best described* in physical terms – as opposed to a moderate or weak physicalism claiming that everything that happens in the world *can also be described* in physical terms, and, accordingly, that there can be contexts in which some other form of description is more informative. For example, a message informing two sisters about the death of their uncle can reach one via a telegram and the other via a phone call, which are parts of two distinctly different causation chains in the strong physicalist view, while the weak version allows us to think of an identical message transmitted in two forms. This latter view, called 'multiple realisability' (Putnam 1988) is actually nothing other than a principle of conceptual organization that allows us to speak of non-physical phenomena as identifiable entities, regardless of their ontological status, which is only reasonable if this helps us to increase the explanatory power of our discourse. But multiple realizability does not actually vindicate physicalism. This is because, in order to declare two phenomena with nothing material in common to be multiply realized variants of one underlying 'thing', we need a structural principle that itself cannot be reduced to physical laws but reminds us of a Platonic idea instead. If the same message can be transmitted through two different channels that have nothing in common physically, this simply proves that meaning cannot be exhaustively described in physical terms. But meanings exist insofar as they can be the causes of change in the world.

The second big issue is the question of whether the outside world has a logical structure. Strangely enough, it is the strong physicalists who tend to answer this question in the affirmative, thus subscribing to a rather naive 'strong' view, which privileges the static over the dynamic and entails at least a certain degree of essentialism in our thinking of things in the world – a position that should be incompatible with modern physics. The opposite 'weak' view holds that

28

logical structures emerge in the minds of the perceivers when they try to make sense of the world and construct categories with which to classify different slices of their experience. This view also allows any perceiver the use of whatever terms she sees fit to invent, but again without asserting for them a solid ontological status.

It is easy to see how a combination of the two strong views would commit their holder to seeing culturally constructed variativity of world-models as largely irrelevant and, where in conflict with her own views, irrational, while the weak views allow her to credit the cultural Other with an internal logic and to acknowledge the role of the cultural environment in the formation of the cognizing subject. Moreover, this latter position makes it possible to leave open the ontological status of the subject as such. The question of whether it is a psychic grain of sand around which its cultural experiences crystallize or merely a bundle of more or less stably coexisting and mutually reinforcing patterns of acquired interpretational and expressive procedures inscribed on an idiosyncratic biological waxboard can be answered by everybody according to her inclinations.[5] In neither case is the subject a sovereign instance of meaning-construction, nor a wholly passive quasi-individual forged by the supreme powers of biological and social determination, and this is all that matters for the moment. In Yuri Lotman's words, 'the core of personality can be treated as an individual set of socially significant codes', which 'changes in the process of an act of [auto]communication' (1992:78).[6] As Orlando Patterson has put it, 'agents and structural processes mutually reinforce and constitute each other in ongoing, relatively stable reproduction patterns' (2004:83). But, in Patterson's view, these patterns are more important than what they are the patterns of. Nonetheless, we can just as well speak of the subject as the organizing

---

[5] Some findings of experimental psychology are important in this context. Kelley and colleagues have shown that distinct neural regions are activated when a person answers questions about herself, as opposed to the same type of questions about someone else, or different types of questions (2002). What their data seem to indicate, however, is that though the medial prefrontal cortex is essential for self-related mental activity to occur, the latter is only possible when several regions of the brain operate in conjunction – i.e. the self is not to be localized in one particular region, but emerges as the relation between the patterns of activity of several regions.

[6] Thus, when Giorgio Agamben, having written that 'insofar as it is identifiable only through its pure reference to the event of actual speech, "I" necessarily has a *temporal* and *negative* structure', goes on to say that 'the displacement of reflection from the "I" to the third person and the Absolute (*Es, Es selbst*) corresponds to the attempt to absolve the subject of its necessary relation to the event of speech' (1999:121), he is describing not how the 'I' is set free, but how it is captured and imprisoned in a preconceived mould of subjectivity, or liberated only in the sense that one can liberate a fish from water.

29

principle of the mind of an individual carrier of a particular culture, in constant interaction with its environment and its own life-experience, with a 'native capacity to imaginatively construct situations in dialectical ways' (Jenkins 2008:183), participating actively in the construction of its life-world and adjusting itself to change if unable to carry on its activity as usual. As Marilyn Strathern writes, 'Where the individual is thus produced "in opposition to" society, the move conceals social formations and power relations' while 'Social relations are intrinsic to human existence, not extrinsic' and 'one cannot therefore conceive of persons as individual entities' (1996:66), self-sufficient and continuous Cartesian egos that are able to enter the field of interaction with others and the world on their own pre-formulated terms.

It should be immediately obvious that this activity of the subject – continuously constructing and reconstructing its life-world – is not a systematic and orderly project (in spite of what a subject itself might want to believe), but more aptly characterized by what Claude Lévi-Strauss has called 'bricolage' (Lévi-Strauss 1962:26). This assembling of bits and pieces of heterogeneous origin, value and function does not take place according to overarching structural principles, but certainly also not at random. The main, if not only, criterion for acceptance into the system by the assembler is whether a particular item somehow finds for itself a place in the pre-existing assembly (which, for us self-contradictory humans, does not necessarily imply strict compatibility with everything else that is there).[7] But the cultural subject is not a sovereignly choosing *bricoleur*, because quite often an item, or even a great many of them, may be thrust into the life-world of a person and installed there by force. Nonetheless, whatever its origin and history, each installed item becomes a part of the subject's life-world and thereby a resource for future practice.

Summary

This chapter has simultaneously dealt with how 'culture' is understood in this book and what prerequisites are needed for a theory that can

[7] Earlier experimental psychology has challenged the notion of biologically solid selfhood by showing that the reactions of test subjects were similar to questions related to themselves and to questions related to their intimate others (Bower and Gilligan 1979), or involved social desirability (Ferguson, Rule and Carlson 1983). However, a broader understanding of cultural subjectivity that emerges through the relations of the self in the narrower sense, and its meaning-endowed environment, enables us to avoid the contradiction: after all, something is socially desirable only if the self has learned to desire it as well.

adequately deal with it. For present purposes, the terms 'culture' and 'cultural' will broadly refer to all actions, processes, artefacts and other kinds of objects and practices that are perceived to be meaningful: involved in the assignation, communication or interpretation of meaning. 'Meaning' is here understood in two senses, either as referring to something else or something bigger than itself (signifying) or as being 'meaningful', i.e. relevant to the memories, experiences, beliefs and fantasies of the human beings engaged with it. Such meanings are encapsulated in repeatable strings, or texts, and articulated in spontaneous or regulated actions (cultural practices) that are associated with specific institutions and incorporated into the whole of a cultural system. This term refers to the loosely integrated totality of practices, institutions and mechanisms of production, distribution, consumption and preservation of meaning, as well as the explicit and implicit rules that govern all the relevant processes. A cultural system is shared to a significant degree by a critical mass of people. These people, the carriers of that culture, form communities that share cultural languages but do not totally define the individual identities of its members. The cultural system is thus only relatively organized, and embraces the tensions and internal contradictions of the social world in which it appears, perpetuating and subverting its norms of behaviour, relations of power or solidarity, as well as providing loopholes for escape from its everyday routines to imaginary realities.

A theory that can take on a cultural system, or just adequately and holistically describe a certain slice of it, cannot commit itself to one single disciplinary mindframe. It also has to abandon universalist claims for its findings, because any theory is dated and looks at things from within a certain context. It is therefore also impossible to discern objectively existing, 'real' underlying blueprints and structures of cultural phenomena or to reduce them to universal laws or atomic constituents. What is noise from one perspective might be relevant for another. Accordingly, the gazes with which cultural phenomena are seen are themselves also cultural, and have to be analysed as well. All of this is not to say that we have to stare helplessly at the ever-ineffable Others. Our evaluations of what they have to say are not valueless if they are not universally valid truths, as long as they make sense for us and help us to build bridges towards ways of being human we do not fully understand, as well as to have a clearer grasp of our own.

— 2 —

MEANING AND SIGNIFICATION

In this chapter, I am going to elaborate a theory of signification that will deal both with the genesis of meaning in cultural phenomena and with their capacity to mediate meaning in socio-cultural space. I will show that meaning as such can be construed as containing a certain tension, as a meeting point of two elements of different order. This tension remains unresolved whenever meanings operate in action.

If we try to generalize from the classic meaning theories of Frege (1960), Saussure (1966) and Peirce (1931) as well as Ogden and Richards (1923), we see that they collectively contain the following elements: first, there is something in the objective reality (object, referent), of which the mind has an idea (sense, concept), which becomes a part (the signified) of a functional whole (the sign). The latter also contains a material 'vehicle' (the signifier, representamen) for carrying that meaning in a certain context (the ground) shared with others. What remains unclear is how the idea that emerges in an individual mind also becomes the idea encapsulated in the shareable meaning. I would like to argue that this is the result of a wilful, even if normally unconscious, act that makes meaning happen. Signifying is not achieved just by learning and using signs that are already there. Meaning does not appear naturally; it is always produced, and it also carries the traces of its production within it when it starts to circulate in the cultural process.

I will now try to show that the production of elementary units of meaning takes place in a single crucial moment, the signifying act, in which the individual experience of the cultural subject and the shared, pre-existing signifying systems are brought together. This act is the basic constituent of any event that involves the use of a cultural language and takes place whenever and wherever cultural phenomena

32

occur, instantaneously and, in most cases, repeatedly. The signifying act is the elementary instance of connection between the outer form (signifier, representamen) and the inner content (signified, concept) of a sign, or an array of signs. I hope to show that, regardless of its scale – of whether it is the recognition of a friend in a group photograph, or the realization that Gulliver's journey to Lilliput is not simply a good story but a critique of mankind's stupidity – the architecture of the signifying act remains the same. Although signifying acts rarely occur alone and tend to form immediate chains of signification, it is more informative to view one in isolation as the moment of forging a connection between the individual mind and the shared ideas that make communication possible.[1]

The problem of reference

In order to see how a sign works, let us take a simple example, the letter H. This letter – like any other – does not have any meaning as long as it is 'just' itself, a set of lines in a certain relation to each other. Waves might toss a few logs on the shore so that they form this configuration. H becomes a letter only if we say so – a letter corresponding to the sound [h] in the Latin alphabet, or [e:] in the Greek alphabet, or [n] in the Cyrillic alphabet. If we look at it from a different angle, it could also become エ, the Japanese katakana sign for [e]. The letter remains a sign only as long as it is taken to belong to one of these signifying systems, or some other, and just to one at a time. The letter itself contains nothing that would link it with these systems. But since the primary task of a letter is to be a sign, it becomes what it is at the very moment it is seen as one, and not sooner. In the words of Umberto Eco, 'smoke *becomes* [my italics] a sign of fire not in the moment in which it is perceived but when we decide that it *stands for* [italics in the original] something else' (2000:125).

The same argument can also be extended to other, and much more vague signifying systems than alphabets are. Nothing carries meaning intrinsically: it always appears as a result of a certain

---

[1] It may well be that the general view about the shared character of meanings is too optimistic. Sperber and Wilson have demonstrated (1998) that it is not necessary that both parties of an act of communication actually share the meanings of the words they use in order for successful communication to ensue, and the same holds for all kinds of meaning circulation. In fact, Lotman maintains that 'the functionality of a highly complex sign system does not at all presuppose full comprehension, but a state of tension between comprehension and non-comprehension' (1992:99).

internal movement on the part of the perceiver. And yet meanings are functional only if shared. So what is the ground on which this sharing takes place?

In the classic version of his semiotic theory, Umberto Eco has strongly argued the case for discarding the referent as a slice of objective reality from the theory of meaning altogether (1976:58–68). In this view, 'an expression does not, in principle, designate any object, but on the contrary *conveys a cultural content*' (1976:61, italics in the original). Referents are therefore only accessible through senses and defined by them, not vice versa. The meaning of each word is thus a cultural unit, 'defined semiotically as a semantic unit inserted into a system' (1976:67) and part of 'a "cultural" world which is neither actual nor possible in the ontological sense. Its existence is linked to a cultural order, which is the way in which a society thinks, speaks and, while speaking, explains the "purport" of its thought through other thoughts' (1976:61). Thus, the referent of the word [dog] 'will certainly not be the dog x standing by me when I am pronouncing the word. For anyone who holds to the doctrine of the referent, the referent, in such a case, will be all existing dogs (and also all past and future dogs). But "all existing dogs" is not an object which can be perceived with the senses. It is a set, a class, a logical entity' (1976:66). The position is, in fact, reiterated in Eco's later theory as well: 'The problem is that man always talks in general while things are singular. Language names by blurring the irrepressible proof of the existing individual' (2000:23). The problem certainly has to be addressed, but it is not solved by assigning too strong a status to the signifier.[2] Already Bertrand Russell has pointed out that it only seems to us that

> we can utter the same word 'dog' on two occasions, but in fact we utter two examples of the same species. There is thus no difference of logical status between dog and the word 'dog': each is general, and exists only in instances. . . . But there is an almost irresistible tendency, whenever we are not on our guard, to think of the word as one thing, and to argue that, while there are many dogs, the one word 'dog' is applicable to them all'. (1940:24)

---

[2] In a lengthy footnote to *Kant and the Platypus* (2000:401–2), Eco attributes the shift in his theory to a hyperemphasis on the socio-cultural in his earlier thought, a polemical stance against Lacanian poststructuralism, in which he indulged without stating clearly enough that, for him, intelligence and signification were indeed a single process that he has now described. For the present purposes, however, his new theory has run too many risks, a number of which he admits (2000:36, 125, 397) – in particular, it tacitly assumes the transparency of language and is not sufficiently sensitive to the cultural variation of subjectivity and conceptual worldmaking.

P. F. Strawson has used the same argument to clarify the problem of sentential reference (1950): it is not possible to analyse in the same way sentence types (such as 'the present king of France is bald'), which have semantic meaning, but do not refer in principle, and their singular 'token' uses, which may or may not correspond to actual states of affairs. It is thus perfectly possible for anyone to utter the word [dog] so that it refers to Chappy and not to all the dogs of the world. By this act, the utterer of the word establishes a correlation between a tail-wagging slice of reality and an element of the cultural signifying system at her disposal.

This is indeed what happens in signifying practice. Consider 'dog' in context – for example, in the sentence 'Beware of the dog'. We can walk down a village street and observe signs with this sentence on the gate of every house, and though the sentence is identical, in each case it has a different, yet very concrete, reference, which is emphasized by the use of the definite article and does not speak of all the possible dogs of the past, the present and the future. Moreover, the sentence implies certain qualities of the dog – it has to be fierce, intimidating or otherwise dangerous. This would hold even in cases where the sign actually deceives us – for instance, when there is no dog, but an elderly person living alone has nevertheless put up the sign just like everybody else in order to discourage intruders. The signs on the gates may also be all produced by the same factory and look the same. For the passer-by, who heeds the warning and does not knock on any of the gates, their meaning is also identical in lived practice, especially if none of the animals shows itself – the dog remains abstract, although even the passer-by knows that a separate individual dog is the reference of the sentence in each individual case. A correspondence is established between a number of particular situations in the world and a repeatable chain of words. Let it be noted that the sentence 'beware of the dog' is itself a culturally set phrase. The same meaning could also be communicated by a reformulated version ('Be careful! There is a dog in the garden!'), or with a supplement (a portrait of a Rottweiler with the sentence 'Chappy does not like strangers'). These versions would nonetheless have a different cultural meaning, telling us in addition that 'we want a personal touch felt in every single aspect of our activities', while the stock phrase, in a situation where it is not the only permissible one, can be read as 'our domain of self-realisation is elsewhere than stupid personalisation of trivial affairs'. It is also important that each single use of the sentence – even if it only takes place in the perceiver's mind – is different even when the frame of reference is the same. When I visit for the first time a house with such a sign, I might feel slightly nervous, though the hosts assure me that Chappy only bites strangers, which I am not; coming for the second time I may have forgotten the dog's existence, but am unpleasantly reminded of it by the sign; next time, I am already comfortable with the dog, and the sign gradually loses its informative meaningfulness for me, becomes a mere element of the décor – until it is once again restored to its meaningful status, when I notice that the dog is not there any longer: its absence has altered the status of the sign, caused a discrepancy.

In his description of singular sense-producing units, Yuri Lotman has noted that 'first, an intellectual act is the result of the development of asymmetric and irreversible processes, necessarily related to a structural asymmetry, and secondly, it involves a complex moment of contingency' (1993:373). One site where this asymmetry works most forcefully is the contact point of the diachronical (memory and acquired cultural resources) and the synchronical (direct experience). Indeed, new meanings can appear in individual consciousnesses precisely because these two never blend seamlessly, and cultural languages are able to do what they do precisely because intersubjective, permanent and self-identical concepts and conceptual structures do not really exist. This view is not necessarily at odds with the postulation of 'cultural units', or culturally shared and constructed concepts: it only denies these concepts an objective and independent ontological status that is quite often inadvertently assigned to them. A certain asymmetry persists between abstract concept-types (describable in terms of defining properties, which are in turn divisible into sense-carrying units, and so on) and individually entertained concepts, which have irregular and different connotations, associations and memory triggers attached to them in each individual mind. We are accustomed to building up the descriptions of how we confront the reality of the world from 'simple objects' or 'simple concepts' or 'simple sensations' that are then combined into 'complex' ones, although in effect it is exactly the opposite that takes place: we dissect our complex sensations and concepts into simple building blocks, though any of these 'simple' things can only exist in the circumstances of the philosophical laboratory and are not to be met in reality.[3] In actual practice, concepts manifest themselves in the human mind

---

[3] Maurice Bloch has convincingly shown how the construction of 'simple' cultural concepts is completely arbitrary (2005:91–2). Paul Churchland has also demonstrated that such a hierarchical view is, moreover, at odds with developmental facts: children start to distinguish 'complex' concepts earlier than 'simple' ones, because these are easier to extract from reality (2007:147–8).

only in, so to speak, 'conceptual situations' or 'concept acts', which are more analogous to sentences and speech acts than to stand-alone words. Any communication that takes place between minds is structured by the means of communication used, and this determines the dialectic of linguistic systems and linguistic usage: system-level entities are abstracted from interpersonal, not impersonal, acts of communication. If one tries to define, on the level of the system, individual units in terms of opposition to other units (as linguists traditionally do), these units can only be used – actualized – through correspondence with the personalized 'systems' of individually mean-ingful concepts entertained by individual minds, and these individual systems are continually shaped and changed by interpersonal com-munication on culturally established platforms.

In this particular sense, we can speak about the concepts of a culture, not only linguistically contingent signs for expressing them. This view should not be confused with a strong version of linguistic relativism, since it does not claim that the very perception of the actual world is wholly predetermined by linguistic usage, only that the already-perceived world is structured differently in different languages. The latter is indeed a well-established fact. Already Louis Hjelmslev has famously compared the usage of words meaning 'tree'/'wood' in French ('arbre', 'bois', 'forêt'), German ('Baum', 'Holz', 'Wald'), Italian ('albero', 'legno', 'bosco', 'foresta') and Danish ('træ', 'skov') and shown that their signifieds do not coincide – there is no single concept that would sufficiently determine one signifier in each of these languages (1959:104). The same incommensurability appears even more forcefully in other cultural languages, since these are yet more dependent on arbitrarily formed signifieds.

But the recognized influence of a signifying system on the arrange-ment of the conceptual world poses a problem. On the one hand, the signifying system always maps for itself the territory on which it can signify, since its signs are defined by and reducible to other signs, thus fading away from the perceiver's grasp. Or, in post-structuralist terms, no element of language, no sign, is able to signify without an endless trail of references to other elements, and thus a sign always contains within itself 'traces of traces' of other signs (Derrida 1982:26). On the other hand, however, even if this is how meanings can exist 'out there' in the system of language, this knowledge is of little practical use to anyone who tries to make sense of her immediate experience in the world. In spite of what theoretical physics and chemistry have uncovered about the fundamental nature of things as combinations of particles in constant movement, common sense bestows a certain ontological independence upon the things it encounters in the world. Similarly, the cultural subject also assigns a fair amount of conceptual independence to the designations it uses for them. Moreover, the grammar of these designations determines how experientially relevant things are grouped into types, which enable the manipulation of their singular uses with a degree of familiarity and a set of presuppositions. And, for an individual navigating the world, there is no need to doubt this grammar as long as it remains functional. The conceptual structures of a cultural subject only command attention when they encounter a situation that resists interpretation. This is why culturally constructed worldviews assume an aura of 'naturalness', and seem to mediate the world to the observer as it 'really is'.

Two kinds of concepts

On a more analytical level, the problem can be resolved by making the distinction between two different kinds of concepts that are used to make sense of reality. Normally these have been paired and stored away in a reified form, and consequently seem to be two sides of the same coin.[4] It is nevertheless also possible for them to function separately. *Intralinguistic* concepts are defined by their position vis-à-vis other concepts of the same type, within the system of signs that are all mutually dependent on each other. They are only functional within a system of language. Let it be noted in passing that the system of language is never completely organized and homogeneous, but rather consists in a dynamic and tension-loaded totality of heterogeneous and contradictory registers of meaning. Thus, an intralinguistic concept not only is the idea behind the word, but also contains links to possible metaphoric and metonymic usage – the concept of 'heart' includes the possibility of this vital organ consisting of inorganic matter of various kinds (gold, stone, etc.) *Experiential* concepts,

---

[4] Most theories of the perceptual–cognitive process, from Aristotle through Kant to Eco and beyond, see it as a succession: it proceeds *serially* from something perceived entering into consciousness, where it is processed with the help of hard-wired or acquired machinery into a refined intellectual product of a higher order. What I would like to recall, however, is that the process is *parallel*, as neuroscience has long ago discovered (Rumelhart, McClelland and Hinton 1986:75–6). Of course, our experience lies at the basis of the world of meanings we entertain, but these meanings also organize our experience, not in retrospect, but at the same time it takes place. The world out there (as it exists for us) and the microcosm are not independent of each other, nor is one the mirror of the other, but they participate in the formation of each other while being heterogeneous and heteronomous in their organization.

on the other hand, emerge as unnamed generalizations, clusters of perceived salient distinctive features that characterize a thing at the moment, or a thing in time, or a class of things. Experiential concepts are inarticulate identifications of things in the world. They are non-verbal by definition. They point directly at something 'out there' and produce a structure of reality for the perceiver in the process. Experiential concepts should not be confused with what are sometimes called percepts, which are unstable, unprocessed and unqualified. An experiential concept is the correlate of an indexical 'this', which is repeatable and can enter into conceptual constructions of a higher order ('I am frightened of this, because of the sounds it makes, even if you say it won't bite').[5] It is the concept that appears in your mind when you are searching for an adequate word, sometimes not finding it quickly enough. Such a concept of 'dog' refers to the experienced 'dogness' of a particular animal, while the intralinguistic concept of 'dog' refers to the idea of a dog as opposed, according to its separate semantic traits, to the ideas of cats, wolves, security cameras, etc. It is also possible that the same object may become the referent for a number of experiential concepts when the context changes: what is a 'bridal veil' at a wedding may become a 'bandage' in a field hospital.

It might now be asked how and to what extent experiential concepts can be culturally contingent. This is caused by the variance in the background system (consisting of the natural environment, social practice and cultural habits) that makes some features of an object salient for its definition, and the carriers of a culture have learned to notice these features first. For example, contemporary Westerners have learned culturally that geometrical perspective is the accurate way to represent spatial images visually, while before the thirteenth century, or in many parts of the world today, this was and is not the case (see Goodman 1968; Panofsky 1991).

The same applies to all cultural concepts. Consider the concept 'home'. There are languages, such as English, Estonian, Georgian and Japanese (among others), which have a special linguistic unit to

---

[5] If our cognitive faculties have developed in the process of evolution, Pascal Boyer asks, and the functions of semantic and procedural memory are quite clear, then what do we need episodic memory for? He puts forward a number of hypotheses (2009b), but one possible explanation could be that the ability to recall specific situations is necessary for generalizing experiential concepts out of them, without which the knowledge and skills relying on the semantic and procedural memories are also unable to function. This is supported by the hypothesis that 'mental time travel' and language (as well as imagination) have evolved in concert, as a unique capacity of the mind needed for decision-making in complex circumstances (Boyer 2009b:14; Suddendorf and Corballis 2007).

designate it ('home', 'kodu', 'shin', 'uchi'), while German, Russian, Lithuanian and Turkish (among others) use constructions with the word meaning 'house' ('zu Hause', 'doma', 'namie', 'evde') to designate the same special attitude towards a particular house. The experienced concepts of 'home', however, resemble each other more in English and German culture, as opposed to Georgian and Turkish culture – the strong feeling of privacy and personal space in one can be contrasted with the caring solidarity of the relatively open circle of relatives, neighbours and friends in the other, and both types of 'home' differ from the Japanese construct of inside/outside opposition based on the idea of 'home' in that culture.

The example of 'home' also demonstrates that there exist experiential concepts of abstract ideas, inasmuch as these have a potential to be meaningful to the individual mind. Speakers of languages that do not distinguish between blue and green (for instance, Navajo) or languages that place the border between 'blue' and 'green' differently (like Japanese, in which most darker shades of 'green' belong to 'blue' – for which reason, Japanese traffic lights often use blue bulbs instead of green) obviously have a different concept of 'blueness' from speakers of languages that define colours differently. A great multitude of anthropological studies of kinship have described structurally different ways to conceptualize these relations. And the same applies also to such ideas as 'beauty', 'justice', or 'time'. Signification thus occurs when the cultural subject internally identifies a learned intralinguistic concept with an experiential one that she has distilled herself from her flux of experience, according to her cultural inclinations, making use of the choices available to her. As Clifford Geertz puts it, 'The perception of the structural congruence between one set of processes, activities, relations, entities, and so on, and another set for which it acts as a program, so that the program can be taken as a representation, or conception – a symbol – of the programmed, is the essence of human thought' (1993:94). Meanings are not simply there; they have to be enacted, produced at every single instance of their agency. They take place.

Typically, however, a subject does not produce meaning spontaneously, but in response to some other subject's claim that intralinguistic and experiential concepts do, in fact, correspond to each other. Having internalized that claim, the subject starts to act upon it, and in the process also transmits the same claim to yet other subjects, either confirming their belief that this is indeed how things are, or presenting the claim to them and inducing them to carry out a similar signifying act.

Schematically, we can sum up the preceding discussion by a transfiguration of the classic semantic triangle of C. K. Ogden and I. A. Richards (1923):

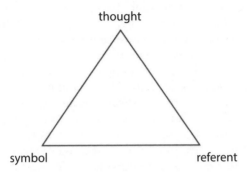

In my scheme, however, there is no 'thought'. The two types of concepts therefore place themselves on the sides of the triangle: the intralinguistic ones are derived from the system of symbols, and the experiential ones are formed by pointing at the world. Thus, instead of a triangle, we have a semantic trapeze:

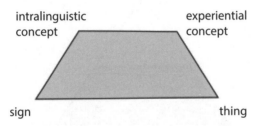

The lower side of the trapeze represents things in the material world, the upper side ideas or concepts. The left half is the sign, given in a cultural language, the right half is the phenomenon approached in the signifying act. That phenomenon always already consists of a referent and its conceptualization.

Let us designate the intralinguistic concepts with the letter A and the experiential concepts with the letter X. Although initially different, they are unified and correlated by the signifying act so that they are only experienced as separate in normal cultural practice when there is a problem in the system – for example, when a child actually sees an animal she has never seen before, but may have learned about in biology lessons at school.

The claim A = X! is the core of the signifying act. It is so intrinsic to any bestowal of meaning that it has already been taken for granted in

41

the classical theories of meaning. Even so, it is almost never realized as something absolutely unproblematic. That could happen only in two extreme cases: (1) when intralinguistic concepts so completely dominate the formation of experiential concepts that these are fully modelled on them (the Sapir–Whorf hypothesis in its strongest possible form), which is hardly likely, because learned patterns do not predate experience; or (2) when experiential concepts so completely control the signifying system that all intralinguistic concepts are their exact equivalents, producing a logically ideal language or *Begriffschrift* (Frege 1960:70), which cannot happen, because human experience is not in itself logical. The claim A = X! is thus precisely the place where the arbitrary nature of a sign manifests itself most clearly, because it is here that the connection between the signifying system and the ever-constant and ever-changing outside world is established, for an individual cultural subject, the carrier of a specific signifying system.

The place for this claim is on the top of the triangle, where the side lines of the trapeze finally meet:

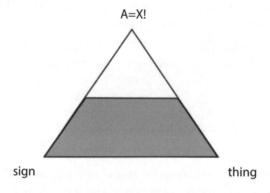

This revised semantic triangle thus has two independent entities, the sign and its reference, at its base, but its top points to the arbitrary, culturally constructed relationship that unites them in the signifying act.

Obviously, signifying acts cannot function and do not occur in isolation. Although they are the place where the cultural construction of any speaking subject's life-world actually happens, they can only perform this role as constituent atomic units of much larger processes. It is thus possible to view a cultural language as an organized set of claims of the type A = X! – of assertions that certain intralinguistically, intrasystematically constructed concepts are identical to the experiential ideas that its speakers have of things as they engage with their reality – or as a system that combines the external and internal sides of a person into an integral whole – a cultural subject.

The internalization of meaning

Socio-cultural psychologists have described the process of how elements of the life-world, in interaction with the subject, gain in their meaningfulness and may become resources for the organization of its future actions. For example, Tania Zittoun has analysed the ways in which a cultural phenomenon becomes a symbolic resource[6] (and thus rises in its degree of meaningfulness) by being used to handle new, unpredictable situations (2007:343–4). This transformation does two things to a text: it changes its 'aboutness' – i.e. it comes to be seen to speak about the subject and her life-world in addition to its own referent – and places it on the subject's personal timeline (recalls a part of her past, explains her present or helps to organize her future) and is thereby incorporated in her life-world in a more intimate way (2007:346).[7] If we want to extrapolate this 'aboutness' from cultural phenomena to any kind of signification whatsoever, we can recast it in the guise of functionality. This is what Umberto Eco talks about in his discussion of Eleanor Rosch and her surprise that, while she had identified trees and furniture as belonging to the same level of superordinate conceptual categories, on the next, basic-category level, test subjects were much better at distinguishing chairs from tables than oaks from maples (Rosch 2008:242–3). For Eco, this is not surprising

---

[6] At pains to distinguish her notion of 'symbolic resources' from cognitive schemas, Zittoun includes in this category only 'cultural elements' (cultural texts in the traditional sense of the word) and 'symbolic systems' (religious, political, ethnic discourses) that are relevant to the imaginary experiences (2007:344). It seems, however, that these limitations are too severe and partially confusing. First, the distinction between schemas as tools for the smooth organization of canonical situations and symbolic resources as tools for meeting unexpected challenges and reducing ambiguity does not always work, since the latter task can also be performed by schemas, or initially attempted by schemas before turning to other resources. Second, we should observe more carefully how Zittoun's 'elements' and 'systems' work in experiential practice: particular cultural texts frequently capitalize on the ambiguities within and clashes between different symbolic systems, and these, in turn, organize meaning on a higher level. Indeed, some of Zittoun's own examples (e.g., the identity-defining capacity of household objects (2007:319)) are not quite compatible with her definitions. But none of that undermines the validity of her model – on the contrary, this shows it can be used more broadly to describe the conditions of 'becoming meaningful' for any reifiable meaning.

[7] For Lotman, texts in such situations perform the function of codes that a person uses to decode her internal autocommunication (1992:84–6). This agrees well with a non-linear understanding of codes as organizations of schemas proposed in the next chapter.

at all, because we make our distinctions on the basis of the perceptual situations in which the shape and role of the objects in question are more salient than their other aspects. We can thus tell a banana from an apple easily, because the distinction is important for our culinary practice, but 'unless we are primitive forest dwellers who depend on their ability to recognize different species of trees, trees appear to us as furnishings of the environment that, as far as our needs go, all perform the same function (they give shade, mark boundaries, cluster together in woods or forests, etc.)' (2000:185). If the distinction made within the linguistic system thus corresponds to a salient difference between experiential concepts, then it will also make the corresponding signifying claim more meaningful for the subject, because it is 'about' her experience in her life-world. Eco concludes his discussion with an explanation of why he can tell banyans and mangroves apart without being able to recognize elms and linden trees: banyans and mangroves appeared in the adventure stories he had read as a boy, and when he later travelled to places where these trees grew, he specially went to look at them and memorized their appearance (2000:185–6).

Following Valsiner (2001), Zittoun also identifies several stages in the processing of inner experiences into functional categories, from grouping events in the immediate experience into clusters to naming these clusters, identifying them as instances of broader types, and, finally, developing overarching principles about these types (2007:347). On another axis, she distinguishes between the levels of reflectivity – of the awareness of the subject itself of the process – from a degree zero, where the subject is unaware of the shaping effect of a cultural experience, to deliberately looking for symbolic resources and reflecting upon them (2007:354). In both cases, the levels of mediation proceed from the particular to the general (which is perceived to be more objective and thereby more weighty), arriving at 'an imaginary sphere where personal, unique experiences meet culturally elaborated versions of other people's comparable experiences' (2007:348) – or, in the present terms, the signifying claim produces a highly internalized meaning. The levels of reflectivity also move from the immediate experience towards a reflective position that places the resources at a distance from the observer. But these two distances need not correlate. Zittoun suggests that 'reflective uses [of symbolic resources] are likely to be the most transformative' (2007:354), but there are reasons to doubt this: for example, a reflective use of religious texts is not very likely to cause a conversion. On the contrary – the highest degree of mediation at degree zero of reflectivity is probably the point at which a meaning is most intensely internalized.[8] This is the point where we accept a claim to be a statement about how things truly and naturally are, an item of knowledge to be henceforth used for answering questions about new things that are appearing in our life-world.

The importance of reflectivity also shows that the cultural subject, whatever its ontological status, is not merely a passive recipient of new constitutive notions, at best endowed with the capacity to accept or reject them as such, but an active participant in the exchange, able to process and adapt them in order to fit them in its own *bricolage*. In Bakhtinian terms, the subject is internally dialogical (or polylogical). And in a fundamental sense, this dialogue not only takes place between different tendencies within its personality, but also on a temporal axis. The subject comes into being at the point of convergence between its understanding of the past and of the future. It needs to project itself into future action, while simultaneously retaining a vision of itself based on its past, including past mediations of its life-world. As Suddendorf and Corballis have argued, memory as such has evolved as a tool needed to make decisions about the future (2007). In this sense, the subject also blends the textual and the practical. Its past self consists of textualized experience, while the future self will have to evolve in practical interaction with its reality.

A signifying claim can thus be meaningful for the subject in different degrees, and its exact relevance is determined in internal dialogue, where the 'I' of the present moment addresses its textual and practical counterparts, its past and its future. Engaged in constantly ongoing *bricolage*, the subject changes the 'aboutness' of the cultural phenomena around her to interpret what goes on in her own life-world, using texts and practices of different origin in different functions, according to the roles that she assigns to them, and permanently constructing herself in the process.

Claims and bids

To recapitulate the discussion so far: a sign that has entered circulation and functions uncontestedly is a reified claim of identity of two

---

[8] Gerald Duveen arrives at a similar conclusion in his development of Serge Moscovici's concepts: reflectivity is the key characteristic by which active and productive social representations are distinguished from hegemonic, closed systems of meaning (2007:548–9).

abstractions, one of them distilled from the lived experience and the other conceived within the system of language. This claim has the potential of becoming meaningful for individual persons to different degrees. This claim, and neither of the concepts which it unites, is the signified in the bipolar structure of signs in the Saussurean tradition. A signified thus comes into being only with the emergence of the sign itself and does not exist before that. Herein lies a major part of the arbitrariness of signs. Not only is there no natural or essential connection between the signifier and the signified, but the latter is itself an arbitrary construction, a claim of identity between two mental projections of different orders that correspond to the two facets of culture – the textual and the practical. It should also be noted that, although the connection is, in itself, arbitrary, it is nevertheless real. Karl Mannheim, having famously relativized social norms as historically conditioned, proceeds to assert that this fact in itself does not devalidate them: relative, contextual norms are not non-binding (1985:77). The same can be said of working significations. Each signifying claim has been made by someone, accepted by a collective and will be taken for granted by those who will afterwards be enculturated by this particular collective, until problems arise with its adequacy in its role of a cognitive tool used to facilitate our interaction with reality. The arbitrary nature of signs does not make them less real, or possible to dispose of. The members of a cultural community have accepted each of the signs they share as significant, and they need not go through the signifying act each time they use them, but if a sign is used idiosyncratically, if a word is being assigned new meaning, or a term is redefined, they evaluate the new claim and either reject it, accept it temporarily (as in reading poetry), or let their repertoire of signs be permanently altered.

The overall standard by which a community, or any one of its members, judges the validity of each single claim is what I will call 'cognitive adequacy'. In the narrow sense, a set of meanings is cognitively adequate for someone if she believes their descriptions of reality to be reasonably correct and is able to act on the basis of them. In the broader sense, however, a cultural phenomenon is cognitively adequate if the community is satisfied by the answers it gives to the questions of individual people, or the solutions it offers to their problems, or the explanations it provides to their anxieties. Such a satisfaction need not be motivated mainly – or even primarily – by rational judgement: on the contrary, at complicated historical moments, it is frequently a simple slogan carrying a fitting message that seems to explain things with more clarity than obscure reasoning.[9] The popular support given by many Germans to Adolf Hitler after a period of devastating inflation, or by many Americans to George W. Bush in the painful aftermath of the 9/11 terrorist attacks, were not manifestations of sheer irrationality and despair. In both cases, easily identifiable culprits and simple, decisive recipes to deal with them seemed, to many, cognitively more adequate than any other way to make sense of the situation.

In the process of judging a new signifying claim, people thus rely sometimes as much on their emotions as on their reason. If they do abandon their former beliefs, it happens on a more encompassing level than simply rational acknowledgement of the superiority of some other assertion – they have to be profoundly dissatisfied with the world that their beliefs construct for them in order to want to change it in a radical way. In a stable situation, however, the overwhelming majority of cultural phenomena are considered to be cognitively adequate by the overwhelming majority of the members of the community that shares them. In medieval Europe, Jacques Le Goff observes, there was no separate word for 'religion' (2005:200) – not because there wouldn't be much of it around, but, on the contrary, because religious beliefs were considered cognitively so adequate by everyone that there was no need to label them explicitly as 'religious'.

At any moment, there also exists a certain number of signifying claims that have recently entered broader circulation, whose degree of cognitive adequacy is not yet clear. In their divergence from what has hitherto been generally accepted, they present what I call a 'bid' to raise the level of cognitive adequacy of the community. Either tacitly or explicitly, they claim to present a new outlook on things, capable of explaining the world (or a part of it) to fellow cultural subjects in a more satisfying way. These bids are then evaluated; some are endorsed, others rejected. This is how the cultural process works. In a normal situation, the number of challenging bids remains within an acceptable bracket that the community can handle. If there are too few of them, then the cultural system is incapable of self-correction; if there are too many, it is in the process of rupture.

Such bids thus have to go through a process of evaluation, with

---

[9] 'There is always a moment in history when [certain] discourses obtain a general consensus not so much because they interpret the situation correctly (i.e., in accordance with the exigencies of the moment and developments dictated by the needs of the majority) but rather because they correspond to the essentially utopian desires of that majority. Such political interpretation interprets desires; even if it lacks reality, it contains the truth of desires' (Kristeva 1982:86). This 'truth of desires' is what I mean by cognitive adequacy in the broader sense.

results depending on who is the judge. For example, the sentence 'Berlin is not what it used to be' makes different sense to someone who has been in Berlin repeatedly over the years, to someone who visits the city for the first time, and to someone who only knows it from films and books. For each of the three, the sentence unfolds as a series of superimposed signifying claims that connect a slice of reality, experienced in a specific way, to a shared vocabulary and plunge the resultant signified into the process of distilling the next intrasystematic concept, which will again be joined to the next experiential concept in the next moment. Berlin-now, the reunited and vibrant capital of Germany, is experienced as a different concept from Berlin-once, a city maimed by a dividing wall, but Berlin-once is nevertheless in many ways present in Berlin-now. To someone who now visits it for the first time, Berlin-once is a concept that emerges from stories about the past rather than from direct personal experience, but these stories are also an experience, albeit of a different kind, and in itself changing in correlation with how the reality of Berlin changes in time. The discrepancies between the repertoires of intralinguistic concepts that are linked to each other by the rules that constitute the internalized worldview, and the actual experience of how reality becomes significant, are usually overcome smoothly, when perceivers make individual corrections to their repertoires. Sometimes people do it collectively, as during periods of rupture – or 'explosion' in Lotman's terms (2010b) – when previous regimes of signification lose their cognitive adequacy and collapse completely, to be replaced by others that emerge, ideally through a joint effort, after a period of trials and errors. Older inhabitants of such cities as Berlin may call streets by their previous names long after a critical mass of younger generations has validated the new map of the city. But the individual passage from one intralinguistically signified world to another could be much more painful than that, if not altogether impossible, as the contrast between the two ways to see Berlin in Wolfgang Becker's film *Goodbye Lenin* (2003) aptly demonstrates.

The endorsement of a cultural bid always works through an instance of authority.[10] In an ideal case, such authority is consensual and transparent. As opposed to the extremes defined explicitly through their relations with power, an independent symbolic authority can truly conduce people to internalize the claims it supports. For

---

[10] The term is used here as defined by Steven Lukes (2005:35). 'Authority' is opposed to 'power' in that, for whatever reasons, people accept it willingly, while power is present only where there is a conflict of interests.

example, this happens with fashion, which cannot be dictated to the market by a single central institution, but depends for its content on a group or network of competing judges of taste. Such an authority is only possible when its endorsed worldview is, at least for the most part, cognitively accurate – that is, offers satisfactory answers to relevant questions, and enjoys willing support among a critical mass of the carriers of the culture. For example, it is likely that individuals growing up in a society that endorses unfettered competition and pays little attention to either social solidarity or class distinctions are more apt to develop personal ambitions of the 'American dream' variety. If no institution or network of institutions possesses enough authority on a particular matter, the decision stays in each case with the individual. Institutions are only vested with genuine and stable symbolic authority by the choice of the people who decide to trust them, and they are able to keep their authority only until they do not break this trust. Indeed, as Jeffrey Alexander has demonstrated, it is dangerous to assume that power is linked to certain institutions or holders of positions automatically. Any symbolic power, too, must be performed or enacted, and it is possible to either succeed or fail in doing this (2011b:88–9). Alexander calls such performative success 'fusion', meaning a situation in which the 'actors' and the 'audience' are tuned, so to speak, to the same frequency, with everyone collectively accepting the content of the meaning-generating act in the way it happened during the rituals of traditional society, and such fusion still remains the goal of performative power acts, although in modern society it is considerably more difficult to achieve (2011b:33–39). In the broader context of symbolic power, such a 'fusion' is too demanding a goal. For the symbolic authority to be successful, it is quite sufficient for its endorsement of new bids to ensure their circulation. That can also happen as a result of rational decisions by single individuals to follow its lead. In some cases, it is even possible that endorsement is achieved by convention – for example, at official events that are ornamented by musical performances that nobody enjoys.

Normally, however, an authentic relationship with one's cultural environment presupposes that people are, to a certain degree, themselves engaged in the construction of their life-worlds, which includes also the acceptance and rejection of signification claims. These cannot be substantiated by authority alone. Of course, a political authority can establish itself, at least for some time, by force, also in an atmosphere of dissent, and a religious authority can ensure its prescriptions are followed through an alliance with the powers-that-be. The exact structural opposite of this is a symbolic position that defies the political authorities in principle and uncompromisingly resists anything that is endorsed by them. This would be the attitude of a radical subculture that has high requirements for those who wish to belong. People who normally wear suits have to change clothes before they can go to a heavy metal concert. If they do not, then either suits are no longer a sign for respectability or else heavy metal has lost the status of a radical counterculture. If neither of these is the case and someone still turns up in a suit among the rank-and-file audience of a heavy metal concert, this act should be read as a bid to change the cultural balance in either of these directions, even if the situation has come about entirely by chance.

From a certain point onwards, signifying claims start to reorganize and restructure experience, or at least the modes in which it is represented, even to the perceivers themselves. People let this happen if they see that the resulting situation is more fully in accordance with the surrounding reality, and resist if it distorts their relationships with things. The terrifying results of the Stanford Prison Experiment, carried out by Philip Zimbardo in 1971, show how, in the course of only six days, students arbitrarily divided into prisoners and guards developed unexpected traits of character and the ability to carry out sadistic torture on their peers in a wholly arbitrarily constructed setting. We can only imagine how much more efficient, even if invisible, similarly structured processes are that constantly run their course in the less strained environments where we lead our lives.

A bid is thus any signifying claim that promises, if accepted, to add to the overall cognitive adequacy. Normally, people start to choose between various bids to re-signify their reality only when their current, previously reified repertoire of signs fails to connect their lived experience to the cultural languages at their disposal, either because they are experiencing it differently or because they are experiencing something they have never seen before.

When discussing bids, we thus have to distinguish between individual and collective endorsement, or validation by the symbolic authority. The nature of the latter also characterizes the 'bidding space' – the structure of the cultural arena defined by the rules of who can make a bid, what the stakes and premiums are for the bidder, how and to whom the content of a bid is made known, as well as who is in the position to judge the bid and how the judgement should be legitimated. It is conceivable neither that no single meaning could and should be taken for granted by any participant of a cultural system at any time, nor that nothing can be questioned and no proposals put forward for interpreting matters differently. The cultural system of the first kind is really not a system at all, but a chaos of private languages from which a cosmos is yet to be created, and which therefore fails to provide a reliable interface with reality for anybody. The second kind, however, is too tight, incapable of evolving and therefore also of adequately responding to changes in reality, including the ones it causes itself. A cultural system must thus ideally be relatively stable, but only relatively.

Since communication is collective and private languages are not functional, a symbolic authority is necessary for the distribution of meaning to be successful, even if this authority is nothing more than a reified symbolic accord or a system of accords that functions as a front for collective endorsements of signifying bids. However, Marxist and Foucauldian critiques of symbolic authorities make it clear that institutions of symbolic authority normally tend to assume more functions of power than just that. It is indeed possible for the holders of power to control the cultural system by controlling the bidding space – by determining which areas of our mental universe are open for contestation and what kinds of criteria can be used to judge the resultant bids. But the extent of that control is a matter of struggle and negotiations. For example, on the one hand, Angela McRobbie has shown how the cultural roles created for women by popular media are being undermined by their consumers in their own bids for autonomy (2000); on the other, however, Joanne di Mattia demonstrates how 'postfeminist' popular culture, seemingly adopting the new values of self-reliant and empowered women, in texts such as *Sex and the City*, continues to perpetuate the old stereotypes of gender, promoting the idea that the life of a woman cannot be accomplished without a man (2003).

The relation of a new signifying bid to the symbolic authority is always more complicated than a simple proposal for innovation or challenge to the existing order, and involves several simultaneous pretensions. Making a bid to improve the accuracy of the cultural interface between ourselves and our reality functions on another level as a bid for control, or participation in its exercise. The Church did not persecute heretical scientists just because their views were, in the opinion of the persecutors, not in accordance with strict orthodoxy, but because the collective bid of natural science to replace this orthodoxy as the primary explanatory discourse also claimed for the sites of rationalist learning a position comparable to that of the Church in the social arena. This is the reason why major shifts in the organization of knowledge and radical changes in the political order are likely to coincide. When political institutions fall, a lot of open positions appear simultaneously in the temporarily less-regulated bidding space of culture, where the old regime had been guarding its interests, and it is for the emerging symbolic authorities to decide what the new ground rules will be and how the bidding space should be reorganized. Michel Foucault's *Order of Things* (2002b) shows how this has taken place during the leaps between discursive formations in European history, and Stephen Toulmin has analysed in his *Cosmopolis* (1992) the differences between two competing epistemological bids, those of Montaigne and of Descartes, showing how the Cartesian turn foregrounded some and downplayed other aspects of the humanist legacy, thereby shaping European modernity into a form that was in no way predestined for it. Another and perhaps even more suggestive example of an unsuccessful, but promising, bid are the short-lived reforms of Wang Anshi (1021–86), who tried to reorganize the Chinese field of knowledge by opening up Confucian discourse to natural, technical and medical science. The result was a rapid and stunning technological progress that quickly made China the most advanced country in the world of that time (Cotterell 1990:171–2). Wang Anshi could make his bid also because the ideology of Confucianism was, at that moment, itself on the verge of significant reforms – the first great Neo-Confucian masters Zhou Dunyi and Zhang Cai are his contemporaries (though not ideological allies). However, the guild of conservative scholars, led by the eminent historian Sima Guang along with Su Dongpo, one of the finest Chinese poets of all times, challenged Wang's bid as a threat to ethics, always (at least on paper) the primary prerequisite for a career in public service, so that after Wang's political demise scientific and technological research in China quickly faded out. Although historical speculation is always useless, we have, in the case of both post-reformation Europe and eleventh-century China, good reason to believe that, were the bidding space structured differently, the alternative bid could well have been accepted, which in turn might have given the general course of events a different direction. It also shows that an increase in cognitive adequacy, which should in principle be the main criterion for accepting a signifying bid, is not necessarily the one that determines which decisions are actually made. Similarly, commercial concerns may override a bid that might undermine the existing politico-economic structures;[11] political programmes that appeal to

---

[11] Economic reasons for making conservative choices may also proceed from less voluntaristically shaped circumstances – so-called 'path dependence' (Vega-Redondo 1994) – such as the costs of learning and installing new systems, or the comfort of habit (Patterson 2004:92). For example, the added value of a software upgrade may be less noticeable than the trouble it takes to adjust to it.

the irrational fears and hopes of the electorate are often more successful than well-balanced and carefully calculated action-plans; and aesthetically as well as intellectually undemanding, but easy-to-sell, products of popular culture do better than their more sophisticated rivals on the market. All of this means that cultures frequently opt for choices that, in hindsight, will not prove to be justified.

Summary

In this chapter I have argued that cultural meanings result from a signifying act or a series of them, in which experiential concepts distilled from reality are linked to intralinguistic concepts, defined with the help of other concepts of the same kind. The meanings that come into being this way are both irreducibly personal and shared in communication, because they are tied to collectively used signifiers and personally lived internal realizations at the same time. These meanings are claims, though not consciously experienced as such, because they rest on an arbitrary connection, which is valid neither outside the signifying system nor outside the experience of the signifying person. Our description of the world thus always rests on a bundle of assumptions, the external forms of which we share with our peers, but only as individuals do we relate to them in their full extent. In cultural interaction with our environment, we express ourselves, voice our experiences (both physical and mental), and though most of our self-expression is compatible with the assumptions of other people about how things are – that is, we reiterate claims that have been made before – all of us also make claims that are new in content. These claims may be the kind that presuppose some changes in our organization of knowledge, promising, as a rule, to increase its cognitive adequacy (understood in the broadest possible sense, as pertaining to its informational, intellectual, ethical and aesthetical content, although any single claim can also affect only one of these aspects). Such claims become bids. If endorsed, they indeed bring about a certain amount of change in the cultural system. Of course, it is not sufficient that the bid be endorsed by just a small group, or in some cases even the majority of people sharing the cultural system – there is always a symbolic authority in play whose opinion ultimately matters. It is also up to this symbolic authority to make the rules for bidding, that is, to design the bidding space – there is no culture where all people can suggest all kinds of changes to the existing system – but the bidding space may be more open or more closed, usually in correlation with how society in general is organized.

Thus we can see that our cultural expressions, once launched into circulation, acquire a life of their own. They become texts, and one way to model the cultural environment is to see it as a space where texts are produced, circulated, interpreted and preserved. An effort to develop such a model of culture as a textuality will be undertaken in the next chapter.

— 3 —

CULTURE AS TEXTUALITY

In the previous chapter, I argued that cultural phenomena – multiple simultaneous instances of meaning assignation and reception – come into being at the intersection of two heterogeneous streams of concept-formation, the linguistic and the experiential. Cultural subjects define the terms they use for speaking about reality linguistically, and they connect them to abstractions they derive from their individually lived experiences. These two registers correspond to two different ways of describing cultural phenomena and cultural systems. On the one hand, these can be viewed primarily as textualities, that is, ordered sets of texts of different status that are related to each other and come with pre-arranged modes of interpretation. On the other, they can also be looked at from the experiential point of view and seen as practices, actions in which the carriers of the culture are involved and which use and produce cultural texts as side-effects. The first approach, characteristic of semiotics and textual theories, conceptualizes cultural phenomena as things, objectifies them; the second one, adopted by anthropology, sociology of culture and much of cultural studies, treats them as events that can engage people, objects and sites and that proceed according to generally – but not exhaustively – describable rules. Although it is possible to produce informative analyses of cultural situations with the help of both approaches separately, neither is in itself sufficient, and both of them are necessary for a comprehensive and coherent view of the analysed phenomena, because both these aspects are relevant for the cultural world on all levels. Texts have a higher degree of stability and are able to survive greater changes in the environment, when previous practices are transformed or forgotten. Even within a relatively stable cultural environment, practices may have to rely on normative texts (recipes) for their transmission and perpetuation, and they depend on surrounding discourses for their cultural status. Accordingly, all aspects of those other cultures to which people have no experiential access – all those of the past and most of those separated by space – are only available at any given moment through texts and in a form already shaped by their encompassing textuality, which they, in turn, also put to the test and thereby define.

This chapter will concentrate on the textual aspect of culture, while the practice aspect is discussed in the next one. I will present here a model of how cultures, seen as textualities, can be described. The term 'textuality' is not used here in a semiotic sense of the world itself seen as a web of significations, but for a heuristic conceptualization of the cultural environment as an ordered space of texts – a space where texts are produced, interpreted, preserved and transmitted – or, from another angle, a description of the cultural process in which the relatively stable products of meaning-related activities are in focus, rather than these activities (practices) themselves. Obviously, it is not possible to theorize in any depth on all texts of all kinds at once, so I will be addressing only macro-level issues that work in a comparable way in all areas of textual production and interpretation.

We can start by dividing all texts into two main status categories – *base-texts* that are a part of the definition of a cultural community and are, at least in some ways, shared by the majority of its members and can therefore actively participate in the generation of new texts, or *result-texts*, that have just entered circulation within the cultural community. Some of the latter have short life spans, like fads that stay in fashion for one season only, but others may eventually become base-texts themselves. Between these two there is the *operational memory* of the culture, a shared (and internally contradictory) mental space of the cultural community and its various subgroups where texts are produced and processed. The textuality is also inevitably linked to the *cultural institutions* that control the production, circulation and preservation of the texts, including both physical repositories and educational, legal or commercial bodies whose actions affect the textuality and shape the destiny of each individual text in it.

Before proceeding to discuss these four elements of the model in more detail, I would like to dwell for a moment on the notion of 'text' itself. Although it is going to be treated as a 'thing', or as a material object throughout the following discussion, we should nevertheless remain aware of its abstract and indefinite nature. In a semioticist manner, the term 'text' will refer to all transmissible products of signification, regardless of the cultural domain and channel of transmission, more

56

or less in the same way as Ulf Hannerz uses the term 'externalisations of meaning' (1992:4) or Wendy Griswold defines 'cultural objects' (2008:12–14). Thus, it is not only novels, paintings and symphonies, nor even laws, ceremonial scripts and food recipes, but also patterns of urban planning and even teachable ways of looking at a landscape (e.g., in military tactics or artistic photography).[1] The texts need not have a fixed material shape, as indeed texts of oral folklore or dance performances do not, and their channels of transmission may cause considerable variation across their versions in time and space, but this is not necessarily to be thought of as distortion, if it is not done wilfully and without respect for the text's integrity. A text neverthe-less has to be separable from any of its individual manifestations, in a similar way to how philosophical logic makes a difference between propositions and sentences: 'propositions are what get asserted by the utterance of sentences; and they are what enter into logical relations with each other' (Grayling 1997:14). Propositions, in other words, are types, and sentences their tokens. Similarly, a text – a literary work, for example – is a type, and its many editions, the numerous physical copies of each edition, as well as its translations, are its tokens. Yuri Lotman has even suggested that, in the case where an author has been unable to decide between textual variations, the 'text' is an abstraction that contains all the variations, and its varia-tive editions are all incomplete (1992:96). But from the point of view of the texts' functionality, it is unclear why one should privilege the author's intention and not just admit the general fluidity of a signifi-cant amount of texts over time. One could also ask what relationship to the text the external, physical elements of its material appearance have – in the case of a literary work, for example, its typeface, format, kind of cover, presence or absence of illustrations, etc. – on the one hand, they do not affect the verbal form of the text, but, on the other, they certainly have an influence on how the book is read. An array of works that have similar physical appearance may be grouped together on that basis, and a particular type of edition or framing may date a text in the recipient's mind.

If the work happens to be a play, then we can also include in the set of its tokens all of its different productions on stage, and each individ-ual performance of each production. It is clear that all the tokens of the type are far from identical and it is a matter of judgement whether

---

[1] Let me add that I do not agree with those who 'insist that the whole world is nothing other than a text needing to be read and deconstructed' (Harvey 1996:87). The cultural layer is indeed always superimposed on the reality it mediates, but it is not itself a part of the reality outside any observers' input.

each of them is true enough to the source to be actually called a token of the same text. The borders of straightforward productions of a play and more or less creative adaptations is certainly vague, and it is similarly difficult to set the criteria for acceptable deviations in translations. For instance, if we do not allow for changes in poetic form, Chinese poetry becomes untranslatable, because there are very few languages on earth that can loyally reproduce the tonal and monosyllabic character of the original. At a certain point, a recontextualized interpretation may have placed itself so far from the original that it is justified to talk about a new, independent text that can mark its descent from another text without being its token. In fact, in some cultures, translations of poetry have been viewed as original works of the translator that are only based on another text by another author – for example, Catullus's 51 *Ille mi par esse deo videtur* is actually a translation of Sappho 2 *Phainetai moi kēnos isos theoisin*, in which the significance is conspicuously altered by the fact that the speaker of the love poem has changed from a woman to a man. Similarly, one should read Ezra Pound's 'Cathay' as a collection of his poetry, and not of the Chinese originals it is an idiosyncratic adaptation of. Translations aside, even within the field constituted by one particular text, the differences between its tokens may be huge – a classical text known from a relatively late manuscript may be re-evaluated when an earlier manuscript is discovered, as happened, for example, with the *Daodejing*, the Chinese classic philosophical text attributed to Laozi, when a different and probably less edited version of it was found during the excavation of a noblewoman's tomb in Mawangdui in 1973 (Penny 2008:xv–xx).[2] By analogy, it could be argued that, although the same basic script is enacted in all the households that celebrate Christmas, O-Bon or Bayram in the same way, the individual token performances of the same ritual-type are wildly different both in how they appear on the surface and in how they become meaningful for their participants. But this still does not bar us from reading them all as variations of the same text.[3]

---

[2] Indeed, whereas earlier authors such as Gerald Bruns still opposed the 'open' text of a manuscript in a copying culture to the 'closed' text of a printed book (1982:44), Philip Cohen then argued for a change in our approach to literary cultures precisely because all of their texts are unstable (1997:xxii), and Jerome McGann has proposed a theory (2001) of the textual that not only takes into account the manuscript and the printed text, but the cybertextual domain as well, seeing all these as varieties of the same basic mode of text circulation.

[3] In religious studies, the suggestion of Lawson and McCauley that we should read religious rituals as texts generated in a cultural language that can be analysed in a Chomskyan manner (1990) has found considerable support, and it is interesting to note

All of this shows that, unlike a logical proposition, a text is never self-identical, and the type–token bipolarity is always ambiguously present. We should even presuppose it in cases where we know of only one single manifestation of the text in question. Roland Barthes has famously opposed the notion of a closed, self-identical, immutable 'work' to the (then innovative) concept of dynamic, innately heterogeneous, contestable texts (1977). From the current perspective, it seems, however, that if either of these is a heuristic mental construction, it is surely the former, not the latter. Images of static, closed and self-identical texts are being constructed by symbolic authorities and perpetuated by educational and ideological institutions, but they have no counterpart in reality, as deconstructive and subversive readings of canonical texts have repeatedly shown. In fact, as Dominick LaCapra has pointed out long ago, canonical texts only stay canonical because they have 'complex ideological, critical, and at times possibly transformative implications', not only for their own, but also for subsequent, cultural contexts (1989:140). In a sustainable cultural system, the static images of self-identical works are not very productive, because they will be abandoned sooner or later if the text-types continue to elicit meaningful new responses from the members of the textual community, or they will push their referent-works out of circulation, because the corresponding texts will lose their relevance for the people. Chekhov's plays stay on stage because they have something to say to each new generation. There are also authors whose works do not speak to us, and this is why we cease to read them.

Another dimension is added to the innate plurality of a text if we consider that texts come into being not at the moment when they are produced – or, to be more exact, launched into circulation as bids – but at the multitude of moments when they are received and interpreted by their addressees. Post-structuralist literary theory has convincingly made the point that the meaning of a text is generated by the reader, or the collective of readers, and it is therefore not self-identical even when the physical text they read is (Barthes 1977; Eco 1979). It is nevertheless possible to argue that the meaning is always a part of the text, if we envisage the text itself as plural and consisting of all the singular instances of being actualized in someone's receptive mind. Words on the page of a dictionary have meaning in

in this context how Sherry Ortner has argued that cultural schemas are, in fact, embedded narratives (1990:62–3) – not to mention all of the recent work applying methods of narrative study to analysis of social practice (see, e.g., Thornborrow and Coates 2005).

the linguistic sense, but they become meaningful only when they are contextualized and joined into sentences. The word 'linguistic' here refers to all possible cultural languages and systems of encoding, and 'text' to any cultural expression or utterance. Although this chapter possibly privileges cultural phenomena in verbal form, the limits of a textuality are never confined by a singular signifying system. Texts pictured as discrete linguistic entities are in fact just points of entry to structured, but unbounded, territorialities of meaning that can be enlarged by all subsequent interpretation bids that are accepted by the symbolic authority.

When we call a text by a name like 'Hamlet' or *bœuf bourguignon*, we do not refer to an object with distinct borders, but to a textual field, in a similar way to how, when we point to a famous debate, we are speaking about the different opinions expressed therein and the streams of thought that have led to them, as well as the streams of thought generated by them. But although the ontological status of texts is fairly vague, it is nevertheless meaningful to speak about them as discrete entities that are related to each other, forming groups, sets and systems that can be relatively stable over long periods of time, because different tokens of the same types can occupy the same positions in such structures. These systems, or textualities, are always necessary as environments in which the interpretation of existing texts and the production of new ones can take place.

Any such textuality only exists in relation to a community – a group of people who are fluent in the relevant cultural languages and share the norms of interpretative behaviour. But while we will talk about self-conscious groups of culture carriers in the next chapter, the communities related to textualities cut across space and time and embrace people who are not necessarily related to each other in any other way than by sharing a certain amount of texts. Pierre Bourdieu has, for different purposes, analysed the sales figures of different books over time and shown that, while the sales of Beckett's *Waiting for Godot* were vastly inferior to those of prize-winning popular novels at the time of its publication, it has accrued a constant and growing number of buyers over the years and thus proved itself to be a profitable long-term investment (1993:97–9). This also tells us that the readership of Beckett's play is stretched out in time. The growth of its sales over years marks the growth of the text in status in its relevant textuality and its becoming meaningful for more and more people in the textual community. (These two developments are not the same thing, but they certainly enhance each other.) It is, in principle, possible to define textual communities by single texts and practices. All the people who have gone through a culturally coded visit to a Finnish sauna form the sauna community, and all the people who have visited a Japanese *onsen* (hot spring) form the *onsen* community. All the people who follow football form the worldwide football community. In the same sense, all the books I have read or bought or know of through reviews or have just heard mentioned also include me in a certain role in their respective textual community. But it is obvious that there are very strong overlaps in such single-text nano-communities. The sauna community is led by Finns, as is the *onsen* community by the Japanese, so we can expect familiarity with other Finnish/Japanese cultural texts among a large percentage of their respective memberships, and people who have read Aristotle and Hegel are likely to have read Plato and Kant as well. Therefore, it is much more productive to talk about larger textualities and textual communities, because they allow for a more generous scope of conclusions and let us construct more complex textualities, wherein texts are related to each other. However, a certain amount of care is always needed: for instance, the football community that consists of all football fans worldwide probably does not have much more in common than an interest in the game, and though it can be a trigger for conversation between two people who do not know each other, it leaves very little space for generalization about its actual members beyond their football-related activities – something, of course, that, to a lesser extent, applies to all cultural communities of all kinds.

In the contemporary Western cultural system there is no clear demarcation line between communities (although this is by no means a rule for all times and places). We can see, for example, that many recent films with claims of universal appeal presuppose from their worldwide audiences a certain degree of familiarity with American popular culture.[4] This can as easily happen in arthouse cinema (both American and non-American) as in new popular productions, which indicates that the presumed audiences of all these films are expected to share the consumption habits of popular culture. Indeed, while it is easy to theoretically imagine an insurmountable abyss between highbrow and popular culture – and many symbolic authorities have

---

[4] Let us note in passing that a similar presupposition from a Chinese or Russian film-maker would limit the international viewership of the film to the partisans of these cultures. American directors can, nevertheless, be confident that American popular culture has secured itself a certain position in any contemporary textuality. On the other hand, the majority of the recipients of American popular culture are actually people with no experiential understanding of US society and its realities – who know 'Wisconsin' and 'Wal-Mart' only as elements of texts.

historically promoted such a view for their own ends – this has almost never actually corresponded to cultural realities. This does not, of course, eliminate the difference between larger and narrower cultural competences – a randomly picked person who has seen films by Jean-Luc Godard is more likely also to have seen *The Simpsons* than a randomly picked person from among the watchers of *The Simpsons* is to have watched Godard. Thus, the percentage of readers of Beckett who also read the prize-winning popular novels of their time in all likelihood remains pretty much the same; however, it is more than just probable that the overlap between the readerships of bestsellers of 1960 and of 2016 is minimal. It is therefore impossible to assert that a given set of texts corresponds to a given group of people who have read them, but it can more confidently be assumed that textual communities with fuzzy boundaries continue to exist over longer periods of time.

One should thus remember that, though it is helpful to imagine a community that specifically relates to the textual system under scrutiny, there is not always an actually definable group of people out there who would constitute this community in real life – unlike communities based on simultaneous cultural practice. (It can be argued that the communities of genre fiction fans or other subcultures are held together by practice, not texts.) Textualities are also background systems that help us to see how different modes of expression and interpretation evolve in time, what kind of factors affect the status of a text and let one text both contain and be contained by others. Textualities are the frameworks within which intertextuality takes place, the sites of coding, decoding and recoding, of the production and disqualification of rules, norms and habits that govern both expression and interpretation. The organization of textualities follows degrees of cognitive salience, foregrounding the texts that actively shape our behaviour at the expense of those which constitute our passive knowledge. But everything that can be observed within a textuality and approached from the side of the linguistic can also be seen from the angle of practice, and then it will look different. The textual and the practical are two sides of the same cultural coin.

Base-texts and result-texts

Any fixed entity that emerges in the cultural process as a result of expression and is open to interpretation is a text. This definition includes not only novels, paintings, symphonies, ballets and films, but also liturgies, cities, carnivals, dinners, bullfights, weddings, suits and gardens – all these are texts inasmuch as they can be decoded, interpreted, translated into another cultural language. The temple of Angkor Wat is not simply a sacred building, but also a text that recounts with remarkable precision the version of the history of the universe it endorses (Mannikka 1996). The gardens of Versailles can be decoded as the manifestation of an order that came to be read by republicans as tyranny (Girardin 1979). We can read about the ways of cooking food (Lévi-Strauss 1983) or the system of fashion (Barthes 1990). It is possible to look at the systems of other cultures from the outside, as it were, without being experientially familiar with them, but a cultural subject always and necessarily has to be able to read a certain amount of domestic texts in order to function normally in her own culture. By 'reading', I do not mean here a complete perusal with all details committed to memory. Most educated Westerners are familiar with the main narratives of the Bible and can recognize more than a couple of dozen quotations, but few people other than dedicated Christians or scholars of religion have an actual knowledge of the whole book. The knock of destiny in Beethoven's Fifth Symphony takes just a few bars while the rest of it is mostly for aficionados, and the menus of Chinese restaurants in most Western cities are embarrassingly alike, as well as poorer than anywhere in China. A textual system is not a chronologically ordered museum or a well-catalogued library, but rather like a chaotic antique shop, where invaluable gems and complete junk can easily stand side by side on a shelf and necklaces of glass beads be accidentally wrapped into the pages of some rare manuscript. But there is no other way for it to function as a living organism, being able to adapt to circumstances, to reorganize itself without losing stability, and to generate unprecedented new expressions for which a proper place within the system does not yet exist. Nonetheless, this is what textualities constantly do, and also the reason why no symbolic power is ever able to impose itself on a textuality to the degree it might wish, without paralysing the system in the process.

But, precisely for the same reason, it is impossible for a textuality to be completely chaotic. A cultural system is much more functional if a critical mass of its carriers is familiar to a certain extent with, for instance, the Bible, rather than being divided into more or less equal fractions that know, respectively, the Qur'ān, the Vedas, the Bible, the Kojiki, the Popol Vuh, the bsTahGyur, the Sundjata, the Kalevala and the Talmud, but have no idea of any other text on this list. (All of these texts or their antecedents have proved themselves to be able to stand in a similar central position, higher in status compared to most other texts in their home textualities.) If such fragmentation occurred, the cultural community would disintegrate into many mutually incompatible textual communities. This is indeed one of the charges levelled against the idea of multiculturalism, or the right to inherited cultural identity, even though promoters of multiculturalism (see, e.g., Kymlicka 1995; Modood 2013) do not at all endorse such fragmentation.

In any textuality, texts always differ in status. Some occupy a more central position than others, and familiarity with them can be presupposed of any functional cultural subject. These are what we can call base-texts, those that define a textual community and form a part of the necessary cultural competence of its members. The varying degrees of familiarity with the base-texts also structure the community – those more familiar with Einstein's theory of relativity (which is a base-text of contemporary Western culture even if only a small minority of its carriers actually understands it) than with the Bible are more likely to have a degree in physics than to be actively practising Christians. For most people who belong to neither subgroup, these two texts are probably at more or less equal distance, and there are also a number of religious physicists who belong to both. A structured scheme of a consistent society correlates with the map of distribution of cultural competences in it, and this correlation reinforces the social relations as well as cultural differences. David Chandler has remarked that ancient Cambodian society could be roughly divided into two groups – those that knew Sanskrit and were not engaged in rice cultivation, and those that did not and were (1983:22). In such situations, people are likely to construct and maintain their distinctive social identity around their cultural distinctions, which would suggest to the Sanskrit-knowers that they should think of themselves as superior to the rice labourers because they know Sanskrit, instead of acknowledging that learning Sanskrit is a privileged duty they have assigned themselves after subjugating the rest of society into agricultural slavery.

Base-text status also entails at least some cultural productivity. Lotman has suggested that, in order for complex signifying systems to function properly, it is necessary for them to have a history (1992:101), i.e. a pool of antecedent texts on which new expressions can rely. But this need can also be described differently: a cultural system does not and cannot have a history, because the texts that circulate in it are always a part of it in its present state, even if it were 'no longer the present of the past that speaks to us, but its pastness'

(Lowenthal 2002:xvii). Their actual age is much less important than their cultural status, but sometimes the latter is upheld by the former – it is difficult to perceive a text as a 'classic' if it is not yet old enough. Any new text can attain sufficiently popularity for there to be no need to explain it when you want to refer to it, but in the vast majority of cases its fame will fade with time. Franco Moretti has pointed out that, of the literary texts in circulation roughly 150 years ago, only 0.5 per cent are still there (2000:207). For Moretti, the aspect of a text that ensures its continuous popularity is some specific and successful innovation of the literary form, of which the author of the text herself need not even be conscious, but there are other kinds of productivity that could also do the trick, from original wit to a representative way of capturing identity-maintaining historical circumstances, etc.

In order to stay in the operational memory, a text will have to support the creation of new meaning. If it is able to launch some of its elements – singular signification claims – into the linguistic repository of signs, it becomes a part of the background for further signifying acts. Access to it will therefore be necessary for future cultural subjects. A critical mass of ongoing allusions to a text is conversely also necessary for retaining it in circulation while the texts containing these allusions stay in circulation themselves. These allusions should also be critical for the interpretation act, not mere trivia. If the base-text is structurally involved in the production of new result-texts, then it cannot be replaced by any other, including its own clones, i.e. texts that mechanically repeat its structure and consist of building blocks that mimic the original. This is seen more easily in popular culture where the traffic flows are more intense. The works of Elvis Presley and the Beatles have unquestionably become base-texts, while those who have become popular by emulating them have had much shorter life spans.

Another feature of the base-texts is that they have to be endorsed by the symbolic authority. The ability to generate new meaning is neither an innate characteristic of a text nor a guarantee of high status in the textuality. Cultural history abounds with examples of texts with immense signifying potential that were not received well by their times (though they have been rediscovered, unlike a probably existing multitude of other such texts of which we know nothing), and also with cases of relatively meagre texts that were elevated to high positions by some symbolic authority for extended periods of time. From British eighteenth-century poetry, those who have survived till today, Robert Burns and William Blake, were considered marginal in their lifetime, unlike Edward Young, the great favourite of his contemporaries, who is now almost completely forgotten. And from the fiction of that period, it is the subversive Henry Fielding who speaks to the present more than Samuel Richardson, the torchholder of the times. Of all these, Blake still continues to influence current authors both with his automythological poetic language and pre-airbrush fantastic style of painting, and quite a few lines by Burns are in circulation on the base-text level as well. But the symbolic authority can bestow base-text status also under pressure from political power. There was a period in the history of Russian linguistics when every book on the subject of language had to quote an article by Joseph Stalin on that subject (1972). Nonetheless, this status is always lost as soon as the power backing it is no longer there.

The endorsement by symbolic authority is normally manifested in a privileged position in distribution and perpetuation. Texts taught at school are not selected at random, but, so to speak, on a need-to-know basis. Schools of all kinds have to make sure that their alumni have at least the minimum of necessary cultural competence in order to function in their textual environment, and, of course, they have to impose on their graduates the subjectivity standards of their timespace. Therefore, the knowledge of base-texts comes with attached interpretations, privileged ways of reading, and these may change quickly even if the texts themselves retain their status. But it is possible also for the symbolic authority to change the selection of texts in order to retain its own credibility. The argument over which texts make up the cultural heritage of the Americans – is it the European (white male) tradition or something else? – is well known (see, e.g., Rosaldo 1993:xxi–xxii). On a similar note, the unflexibility of the French system is reported by Alain Gerbault, who notes that in history lessons in French Polynesia the children have to learn that their ancestors, the Gallians, were blonde and had blue eyes (see Weil 1999:431).

Normally, of course, the simple act of base-text status being bestowed by the symbolic authority is not in itself sufficient to produce a change in reality, to make the text function properly in its new productive role, and it takes time – about a generation – until the effect becomes permanent. This endorsement by the symbolic author-ity is, nonetheless, the main threshold of distinction between base- and result-texts. Familiarity with base-texts can be assumed, and if someone does not live up to the assumptions, it is her problem, but no one can expect a fellow carrier of a textuality to know all result-texts (except when that person is a part of a cultural institution that demands this of her). Those who launch result-texts into circulation should expect them to be interpreted according to the rules upheld by base-texts. These norms may sometimes also include the requirement to challenge the tradition in an original way. A genuinely innovative result-text, however, seeks to displace these norms and therefore acts as a bid to reorganize the textuality on the structural level. Simultaneously, this is a bid for higher status. If the text succeeds, it will also retain a certain position in the textuality; if the achievement becomes permanent – and the newly proposed norm is endorsed as a part of the textual system – the text that introduced it will attain base-text status.

As we have seen, in a stable cultural environment the status trajectory of a text is traversed slowly and gradually. But there have been cultural situations in which new base-texts have assumed their position very quickly. The *Kokinshū* the first imperial anthology of classical Japanese poetry, was assured of its base-text status even before compilation, through a decree issued in 905 by the emperor, which set up a committee of poetic authorities to accomplish the task, and after its completion it immediately became the standard for all subsequent poetic practice, as well as for the interpretation and judgement of texts that had appeared previously: the structure of the anthology ingeniously established a thoroughgoing codal parallelism between the annual cycle of nature and the development of a love affair, and *all* texts in circulation, including those that had been written previously, from then on came to be read in that interpretational paradigm (see Raud 1994:44–55 for a more detailed discussion).

Generally, however, the status trajectory of a text moves in the opposite direction, by first achieving high status in a subculture, or textual subcommunity, and emerging from there into the general domain. The first exhibition of impressionists in Paris (1874) was not favourably received by the symbolic authority that had flatly rejected the work of the group until that time (indeed, the name 'impressionists' was initially coined by Louis Leroy in order to ridicule them – see Harrison, Wood and Gaiger 1998:573), but aroused considerable enthusiasm in those artists who were dissatisfied with the standards and codes of artistic representation then in force. In Bourdieuvian terms, the group they formed engaged the ruling one in a struggle for symbolic domination and eventually won, replacing the former aesthetic by their own (Bourdieu 1993:106–8), but it is perhaps more appropriate to see the process as a gradual infusion of a subcultural aesthetic into the general one. The scandals related to the innovative texts of the time, such as *Les Fleurs du Mal* by Baudelaire and *Olympia* by Manet, gradually brought new ways of expression to the attention of the broader public and assured them a certain form of circulation, albeit with a negative label. Once they had penetrated the overall bidding space, however, they had the possibility of addressing a larger, non-subcultural audience and, step by step, acquired higher and higher status until they finally became base-texts. Nonetheless, this did not completely replace the standards of the aesthetic, but only redefined them. The new constellation of base-texts included both the old and the new ones and neutralized the opposition between them, instead of acting on it. For someone not closely allied with the conservative or the innovative camp, the base-texts of both remained relevant. What was accomplished though was the marginalization of a large proportion of result-texts that had entered circulation simultaneously with the innovative ones, but adhered to the old standards.

The difference between the base- and result-texts is still not limited to the endorsement of the one by the symbolic authority – and not of the other – but concerns the relation of each category to the cultural institutions in general, and their behaviour in the spaces of the operational memory as well.

The operational memory

The operational memory of a textuality is the imaginary space in which its base-texts are continuously (re)interpreted and result-texts produced. These two processes are distinct, but not separate: all the result-texts of a culture take a significant proportion of their building blocks from the pre-existent texts, and the analysis of these texts is what extricates those blocks for the purpose. Strictly speaking, in the operational memory it is not important whether a text is a base-text or a result-text only recently in circulation. Each text is operated upon in a similar manner, and the results of the operation are immediately available for subsequent use. For a text, to be in circulation means to be in the operational memory, but of course a hierarchy of relevance can be discerned here as well. Some texts are constantly accessed and processed or called upon as resources for the interpretation of others, but some are conveniently stored away and either remain available for a smaller part of the cultural community or lie dormant until their possible re-discovery at a later date. To use the analogy of a library: some texts are on open shelves, some are in stacks that are closed to the general public, and some are in repositories, to be ordered specially. The system of how texts are ordered is itself a part of the operational memory, and it is constantly changing. As can be seen, it imposes another kind of division upon the bulk of texts. The hierarchy is closely related to productivity. This is a feature which is not in strict correlation with the status of a text on the base-result axis. On the one hand, there are many base-texts in each culture that are not especially productive, hardly ever accessed, but nevertheless stable in status; on the other hand, there are result-texts that have just entered circulation, but have hit a nerve and therefore immediately become immensely productive, spawning a multitude of clones and imitations for a brief period, to be thereafter more or less permanently moved to the archives. The similarity to the distinction between episodic and long-term memory is obvious.

However, for the present purposes, I am going to use the term 'memory' not in the psychological sense, but rather more in the manner of information technology, in which memory is not the sum total of recollected data available to the computing unit, but the actual space in which computations are performed. Similarly, we can speak of accessing texts that are stored in repositories, retrieving them into the operational memory, and analysing them in it. But there are natural limits to the usefulness of this analogy. The operational memory of the culture is physically located in the brains of its numerous carriers, which is why it cannot be a self-identical thing, and never completely and contiguously present in one place. Each of its instantiations is an unrepeatable variation and includes elements that are not present in any other one. Obviously, the actions of all these individual brains become relevant only in the self-expression of their owners. This, too, does not take place in a vacuum, but in specifically ordered sites, from writing desks to lecture rooms to theatres or cafés where regular customers meet for gossip. More productive texts are simultaneously accessed at various points of this network, and multiple – quite possibly contradictory – interpretation bids emerge as a result. Nevertheless, the individual sites of the operational memory are joined into a huge web by communication channels which are also not pure and transparent. Interaction within that web keeps each of these sites active, and when communication is cut off, they lose their impact on the whole. Communication channels include, of course, not only person-to-person interaction, but also exposure to new texts and participation in shared cultural practices. These sites are themselves socially constructed and regulated by specific institutions, through which symbolic authorities participate in production – for example, by foregrounding certain interpretations at the expense of others. Though the institutions are more than just technically involved in the workings of culture as a textuality, I would nevertheless like to postpone a more detailed analysis of their role to the discussion of the practice-centred model of culture, in which their function is similar, but much more prominent. For the time being, it must be said that, in spite of what a symbolic authority might want to achieve, the institutions of a society can never have total control of the operational memory of a culture and keep the processes of meaning production in check. No culture can completely define and prefigure the ways in which each of its individual carriers thinks and acts. Accordingly, the messages emitted from the interpretive network are also not always organized by strict and systematic principles or supporting each other in content. But neither are they random – they have been produced at a site in the operational memory, launched as bids and at some point endorsed by some instance of symbolic authority. Quite obviously, the operational memory of a culture is not a neutral space which texts can enter and leave unaltered. On the contrary, it would be more appropriate to say that each text is somehow affected by each retrieval. When Pascal Boyer writes about external memory aids, he could equally well be describing the workings of textuality as such: 'We often assume that external storage is just that, a form of "storage" in which information that may otherwise be in our minds can be downloaded, then retrieved in similar form as need dictates. . . . However, information is not a static property of the strings of symbols, but a property of the processes they trigger in the interpretation device' (2009a:307).

To recapitulate: the operational memory of a culture is a virtual space, a network that unites various individual sites of text processing with each other and with the storages of the texts in circulation. It has a structure that is acquired by each carrier of the culture in the process of enculturation. This structure can be described in general terms as an order of *knowledge*, *codes* and *standards*.

Organization of knowledge

By *knowledge*, I mean the totality of linguistically shareable information that can be available to an individual carrier of a culture. That it *can be* available does not mean that it actually is relevant for her: histories of Iran are on sale in many bigger bookstores in the Western world and can be found in public libraries, but only a few of us ever acquire and peruse them. The fact that they are there, however, makes their content knowledge. We may choose to learn or not to learn the Amharic language, but it is available to us, unlike quite a few languages worldwide that have not yet been studied and described by linguists. Thus, each cultural system operates at every moment with a distinctly limited body of knowledge – however vast, and however rapidly its borders might be expanding.

All knowledge is textual in origin, and therefore learned, but different from *skills*, which are learned practical abilities and not necessarily linguistically shareable – one cannot learn to play the violin only with the help of a textbook. But knowledge is also detached from its textual base – a unit of information becomes knowledge at the precise moment when it is naturalized by the collective of 'knowers': in other words, when it no longer matters where exactly it has been learned. I may know that René Descartes coined the dictum 'I think, therefore I am' and I may know that it is to be found in chapter 4 of his *Discourse on the Method*, and both these are items of knowledge precisely because it is irrelevant whether I learned this in a philosophy lesson, read it in a textbook or noticed it while reading Descartes myself. Knowledge, as the term will be used here, is also indifferent to truth – every cultural community is, at each historical moment, in possession of a certain amount of knowledge about the natural world, for instance, but this knowledge can be changed when their beliefs are convincingly proved to be wrong. The people of the Middle Ages in Europe *knew* that God exists and that the Day of Judgement could arrive any minute. This knowledge gradually became a belief with the same content for those who held it.[5] As Mannheim has famously argued, knowledge is always ideologically biased (1985:60–70). Even the allegedly value-neutral truths uncovered by natural sciences are unavoidably incorporated into ideological constructions and thereby transformed into knowledge. When, one day, the question arises of whether and how much subjectivity should be allocated to human clones and artificial intelligence, the answers will depend on what will then be the ideological basis for the description of these phenomena. Different perspectives assign different degrees of relevance to different items of knowledge. But, as Mannheim also advises, there is no need for despair: whoever is conscious of her inescapably ideological nature and accepts the condition, learning to live with it, is also less

[5] My use of the words 'belief' and 'opinion' is idiosyncratic. A belief, for the present purposes, is something that can legitimately be both held and doubted in a cultural community. In contemporary Western society, the existence of God is a matter of belief. However, the domains of beliefs and knowledge are separate. Beliefs cannot be held of things that are in the domain of knowledge. But one can have opinions on them. These opinions are correct if they correspond to knowledge, and incorrect if they do not. Thus, children have the opinion that Santa Claus exists while most grown-ups do not. The domain of opinions also includes value judgements.

vulnerable to the effects of the ideological bias and able to transcend them (1985:78–84). A culture that possesses mechanisms for constant adjustment and revision of its knowledge – that is, a culture with a sufficiently democratic bidding space – is certainly better equipped for its tasks than one that persists in all of its inherited follies.

The difference between the linguistic and the experiential also cuts through the spaces of knowledge. A distinction should therefore also be made between two kinds of knowledge, which we could label 'encyclopaedic' and 'thesauric', in analogy with two kinds of dictionaries that we use.[6] Encyclopaedic knowledge is textual and consists of explanations of what something is. For instance, 'Athens is the capital of Greece' is a piece of encyclopaedic knowledge. A word, a sign, any unknown unit of signified reality enters our sphere of encyclopaedic knowledge when it is explained to us. Somebody who learns that 'the first modern Olympic games were conducted in Athens' needs to know encyclopaedically what 'Athens' is in order to place the event on a mental map of the world. Thesauric knowledge, in turn, is to an extent practical and provides us with the signs to designate the meanings that we operate with. Greece is a country, and a country normally has a capital. Therefore, 'the capital of Greece is Athens' is a piece of thesauric knowledge that tells me, among other things, where I can find various government offices in Greece, if I have to go there on official business.

It should immediately be noted that the bodies of encyclopaedic and thesauric knowledge that we use are not complete mirror images of each other.[7] The encyclopaedic definition of 'Christopher Smart' is 'an English poet'. However, the thesauric definition of what an 'English poet' is, for most people, comprises Shakespeare, Byron, Browning and perhaps a few others, but Smart would probably appear only in

[6] I use these terms differently from Eco, for whom 'dictionary' means the repository of primary lexical definitions, but 'encyclopaedia' and 'thesaurus' are used synonymously for the storage of broader cultural knowledge (1976:98–100, 1984:3). 'Thesaurus' is understood here in a sense closer to what is meant by the term in information science, where it is a tool for the retrieval of information. A typical definition is presented by Uri Miller: a thesaurus is 'a lexico-semantical model of a conceptual reality or its constituent, which is expressed in the form of a system of terms and their relations, offers access via multiple aspects and is used as a processing and searching tool of an information retrieval unit' (1997:489).

[7] Indeed, the discrepancies between encyclopaedic and thesauric knowledge in the same people can be striking: Justin Barrett and Frank Keil have shown that religious believers can have an encyclopaedic understanding of God as an omnipresent and transcendent being capable of attending to everything at the same time, while in their practical (thesauric) explanations God becomes distinctly anthropomorphic, active only at a particular moment and place, one at a time (1996).

a more or less exhaustive, encyclopaedic definition of 'English poets'. It is, of course, possible that, for a dedicated researcher or editor of Smart's works, Smart is 'the Poet', as Shakespeare is 'the Bard' for many, but such a thesaurus is clearly very idiosyncratic. Thus, speaking about the more general thesaurus of a culture, one cannot say that such thesauric definitions are valid. If they fail to be used in cultural practice, they are simply wrong. In a modern Western city full of sushi bars, *nattō* is not a part of the correct thesauric definition of 'Japanese food' although technically – encyclopaedically – this is what it is, and for the Japanese it has a peculiar significance. Japanese schoolchildren are occasionally assigned a specific task of approaching foreigners with a list of questions about their impressions of Japan, and one of those is whether they have tried *nattō*, fermented soybeans the Japanese eat at breakfast from a very early age, but which do not normally appeal to Western tastes. Thus, for the Japanese, *nattō* is very much part of their thesauric definition of quintessentially 'Japanese' food. The same kind of arbitrariness also characterizes encyclopaedic knowledge, its stronger truth claims notwithstanding. The ancient city of Samarkand, the capital of Timur's descendants and one of the major centres of Turk and Persian culture in North Central Asia, has never in its history been part of Russia, but for those Westerners to whom 'Russia' and 'the Soviet Union' used to mean the same thing, it did not matter, and Russia was – in their encyclopaedias – the country where Samarkand was situated, an opinion that was shared neither by Russians nor by the Uzbeks and Tajiks of Samarkand at the time when the Soviet Union existed.

Thesauric knowledge is also changing quickly: thesauric definitions of 'famous rock musician' or 'fashionable colours', for instance, change every few years, if not more quickly. Encyclopaedic definitions may be timed but thesauric entries only rarely are – a conscientious theatre director might be interested in finding the correct thesauric answer to, say, 'a mid-eighteenth-century Italian composer' in order to be able to accompany a production of Goldoni with a piece of music that would be identified by more enlightened spectators as distinctly belonging to this particular cultural setting.

It is also evident that thesauric knowledge is constantly needed for cultural practices and navigating in the world, while encyclopaedic knowledge serves to explain the world from its linguistic outside. The knowledge acquired in encyclopaedic form is transformed into thesauric in practical use, and those bits of thesauric knowledge that are no longer used in practice move back to the encyclopaedia.

As mentioned above, it is also necessary to distinguish between a personal encyclopaedia and a communal one. All my dubious beliefs form a part of my private encyclopaedia, and my idiosyncratic opinions belong to my personal thesaurus. In these, the beliefs are true until corrected, and not distinguishable from knowledge. For instance, I have met a grown-up person with a very limited knowledge of music, for whom Beethoven was the name of a dog, as in a popular film. If idiosyncrasies form a small part of my knowledge, I might be somebody interesting to debate with, but if such opinions come to dominate my worldview, I would be weird, marginal, or even locked up. The conformity of my personal thesaurus to the communal one is a token of my cultural competence. It is, however, not impossible to imagine that the number of people who think Beethoven is a dog may steadily grow until one day their belief substitutes in the communal encyclopaedia the belief that Beethoven was a composer. But the beliefs and opinions of a whole community might equally well look weird to another community whose encyclopaedia and thesaurus are different. The French have historically gained enough symbolic power to convince others that cheese is to be eaten as dessert; thus, while tapioca pudding remains predominantly in the culinary encyclopaedia for the majority of eaters, a dessert of cheese has moved into the thesaurus.

Taking a cue from Foucault (2002a:145–8), we can also speak about *archival knowledge*. As the term is used here, the archive is actually a variety of the encyclopaedia, which contains the kind of knowledge that is generally irrelevant, and therefore inaccessible to the majority of the carriers of the culture, though preserved and processed by a small group of specialists. Indeed, it is possible to imagine (although not to carry out) a determination of the relevance of an item of knowledge by assessing the proportion of those members of the community in whose personal encyclopaedias it exists. It is only items scoring well enough that can be thesauric, while anything with a poor result is on its way to becoming archival. The relevance of specifically subcultural thesauric knowledge for the whole community can be hypothetically measured in the same way.

Subcommunities based on archival knowledge may be professional, such as scholars of medieval dialectology; or regional, such as a village community that remembers details of local lore; or religious, such as the priests of an esoteric tradition living in the midst of a generally agnostic culture. Needless to say, for the members of such a subcommunity their knowledge is not archival at all, but fully encyclopaedic and partially thesauric. However, what characterizes archival knowledge for the rest of the community is that it is not productive, nothing especially worth learning. The choice by a carrier of the culture to join such a subcommunity, and to identify herself actively through it, establishes a difference between that person and the rest of the general community, which may be marginalizing (as in the case of the esoteric religion), or socially counterproductive (as in the case of the village), but also neutral or at times even enhancing in status (as in the case of scholars). It may not be a matter of simple decision though, because archival knowledge can be protected by the subcommunity of its keepers from all outsiders. A local community may keep its secrets from those not born into it, and an esoteric tradition may impose severe initiation rites, just as scholars usually require proof of ability from neophytes in the form of a dissertation. These measures may be essential for keeping the knowledge intact, but, given its general irrelevance, they also lessen its chances of return to the general encyclopaedia.

Nevertheless, such a return is possible. When the currently accessible encyclopaedic knowledge is found to be lacking, cultures frequently turn to their archives in search of solutions to the problems they are facing. Particularly in East Asia, a large number of cultural innovations have habitually been proclaimed by their proponents to be returns to the old, forgotten ways. A resurrection of local archives can be a part of an identity-construction project in various contexts ranging from nationalistic power-play to the design of touristic attractions. And a wave of religious activism can seize a substantial part of a pragmatic society, as the new religious movements of Japan clearly demonstrate.

The main difference between archival and subculturally encyclopaedic knowledge is thus its current degree of *relevance*. Subcultural knowledge is more readily accessible to the general community and may have a more direct bearing on its lives, while archival knowledge is frequently accessed through specific and rare points of entry. Even if higher degrees of competence in subcultural knowledge are generally attained only by the members of these respective groups, pathways to elementary proficiency are more readily available. With archival knowledge, this is not the case – and not necessarily because of the restrictions its keepers have imposed, but because there simply is no need. This is because the borders of general/subcultural/archival encyclopaedic knowledge are regulated by an economy of demand and supply. Paradoxically, the democratization of access to knowledge can even limit the availability of certain kinds of it: in the present times, for example, when specialist literature can be ordered by its readers through internet bookstores, normal bookshops no longer carry much of it, and, though it stays available in principle, it is no longer accessible for the sympathetic layman who is not informed enough to know the right authors or titles and to search for them on the web. This fosters a compartmentalization of knowledge, supported by the intensity of the information flows in each particular sphere of specialization, and pushes towards the archive quite an amount of knowledge that recently used to have quite decent – though not spectacular – scores of relevance.

This indicates also that items of both encyclopaedic and thesauric knowledge are by no means evenly or normally distributed according to their relevance. On the contrary, the structure of the spaces of knowledge is itself an eloquent characteristic of a culture. We can imagine more homogeneous and stable cultural situations in which there is a strong thesauric core of knowledge shared by the absolute majority, and the amounts of encyclopaedic knowledge are shared according to the curve of normal distribution, but it is also possible that most of the thesauric knowledge in another situation is divided between parts of the community (for example, the linguistically different communities of a multi-ethnic state), which means it is culturally split. If, in such a case, there is a sufficiently big proportion of highly relevant encyclopaedic knowledge and social competence shared between the thesaurically different groups, it can be assumed that the general level of education is high enough for thesauric differences to be resolved and for sufficient mutual understanding to prevail between them as a result. But if the relevance of encyclopaedic knowledge is low, then the community in question remains stable only if it is elitist and authoritarian – for example, a small group of sophisticated aristocrats governing a culturally different population of peasants; it will then consist of groups that see most things differently and have little understanding of how others see them.

But this indicator alone tells us little about the situation if we do not take into account *concentration*, another parameter describing the spaces of knowledge. For instance, if most encyclopaedic knowledge scores poorly in relevance for a cultural community, this may be because all of it is specialized – that is, mostly everyone has a decent education in a certain area, but knowledge is shared only in small groups – engineers have no idea about history nor doctors about economics. But it may also be that knowledge is concentrated – that there is a small elite in possession of the bulk of encyclopaedic knowledge, leaving everyone else in ignorance. This is the kind of difference that separated medieval Europe from medieval China. In Europe, different kinds of sophisticated cultural knowledge were available

76

to the people in courts, monasteries, universities and cities, while in China there was basically only one predominant, not marginalizingly subcultural, gateway to higher degrees of knowledge, which was the Confucian education system for officials. In Europe, the diffusion of different kinds of cultural knowledge supported the emergence of different positions of social self-consciousness, which, in the long run, led to ideals of democracy based on mutual respect between these positions. In China, however, the concentration of knowledge in the possession of an enlightened, open and merit-based elite supported authoritarian power, which has kept a transformed descendant of the elite in the position to rule over less-educated masses up to our times. It is also clear that the concentration of knowledge fosters a strict regulation of the cultural bidding space, and vice versa. But such a structure can remain remarkably stable over long periods of time and even survive several social revolutions unless it becomes cognitively inadequate, as the case of China again testifies.

To recapitulate: cultural knowledge is organized in two basic forms, encyclopaedia and thesaurus, and encyclopaedic knowledge includes a subdivision of the archive. Comparing these categories to the aspects of our command of foreign languages, we could call thesauric all that we can express ourselves, encyclopaedic all that we would understand of what others are saying without external assistance, and archival all that we would only understand with the help of a dictionary. Thesauric knowledge is manifested in cultural actions; encyclopaedic knowledge in more passive, interpretational practice. In other words, encyclopaedic knowledge mediates the texts that already exist and that remain relevant; thesauric knowledge is involved in the construction of new texts or conscious alteration of existing ones. Both encyclopaedia and thesaurus can be found on two levels: the individual – or the cultural knowledge of one particular person – and the communal – the shared knowledge of a cultural community. The communal encyclopaedia consists in the sum total of all the individual encyclopaedias of the community, although only minimally shared parts thereof belong to the archives, but with the thesaurus it is more complicated: the communal thesaurus comprises only the thesauri of those members of the community who are allowed to act in the bidding space and to launch new texts into circulation. The communal knowledge is also characterized by levels of relevance – which shows how widely particular items of knowledge are shared within the community – and concentration – which shows how big a proportion of the community has wider access to cultural knowledge. The higher the levels of relevance and the lower the concentration, the more cohesive is the community. In reality, the distribution of knowledge is always characterized by some structural irregularities, explicit or spontaneous limitations of access, trends of specialization, correlations between central or marginal social positions and layers of specific knowledge. However, empirically, none of these traits can be precisely measured and we can only make conjectures about them on the basis of secondary evidence.

Standards and codes

In practical use, the circulation of texts is strongly regulated by what I will call 'cultural standards', the general understanding of what is what. No culture can manage without them. What standards do, both in textual interpretation and in practice, is to define the levels of acceptability of something as what it claims to be. For instance, after we have become cultural animals, we never eat anything that has not previously been signified for us as food. But the standards of what food is may differ greatly, and be related to other domains of cultural activity, as Claude Lévi-Strauss has demonstrated in his discussion of the cultural significance of raw and cooked food (1983). Nonetheless, it is clear that any new cultural claim must match the standards of acceptability in order to be launched as a bid. And further standards will affect its fate after that. Just like everything else, standards are by no means permanent, though they are relatively stable, and some standards are more stable than others. Thus, for instance, the majority of cultures hold that the killing of other people is not permissible, but there are possible sanctioned exceptions, such as during wars and in applying the death penalty, and not all human beings (for instance, those of different faiths or allegedly inferior levels of civilization) are necessarily included under 'other people'. A campaign to abolish the death penalty or to remove the difference between the members of the community and outsiders would be a bid to change this standard.

Each standard contains a threshold of acceptability, and these are in many cases arbitrary, established by tradition rather than rational debate. Much higher levels of public drunkenness and domestic violence are tolerated in Russia than in Sweden, and a hideous legitimizing discourse for wife-beating has even been created in Russian culture – possibly to help the victims to come to terms psychologically with what they cannot change – namely, that beating is a proof of love. This, inevitably, has also affected the standard of what can be considered 'love'.

In the textuality, these thresholds are fixed and challenged in acts of normative theorizing – for instance, when free verse displaces rhymed poetry, the threshold for considering a certain kind of text to be poetry also changes. But while this change may affect the synchronic world of practice almost completely – for instance, allocating realistic painting styles to a marginal position within the world of art – in the diachronic world of textuality the result of such a change is the redefinition of the domain in general. After every new redefinition, 'art' includes everything that passes the new threshold – that is to say, both what was art previously and what counts as art now. It is only very rarely that a change of standards significantly affects the very status of a larger amount of base-texts, although it can drag down their level of productivity. A complete rupture is nevertheless not impossible – it may, for example, be a by-product of a violent revolution. A cardinal rearrangement of standards entails an active and aggressive position on the part of the symbolic authority, which is again possible only when the bidding space is either rigidly regulated or violently contested.

The threshold of acceptability can, moreover, be arbitrarily placed at various points on a gradient that is in itself shared. We can have many different and simultaneously acceptable positions regarding eating the flesh of other living beings. At the one extreme, there are people who can eat everything that moves. The ban on eating human meat is nonetheless very common – almost a global standard. Then there are those who do not eat particular kinds of meat – such as Jews and Muslims, for whom pork is forbidden by religious norms – or those who do not eat red meat, or those to whom only fish is acceptable, until we come to vegetarians and vegans. The standards of eating can be connected to other regulations, such as fasts and feasts, or proper ways of killing the animal, or preparation. The bidding space of food can be strict and narrow, when only slight amendments to traditional recipes are considered proper, or open and democratic, as in contemporary urban spaces, where the food cultures of all parts of the world can be found side by side. Some of these competing cuisines subculturally preserve their internal regulated character even in this cosmopolitan setting, while others enter into fusions and produce new variations unheard-of in their places of origin.

Although, on the whole, conceptual gradients dissect our realities more adequately than binary oppositions, the case of standards is a partial exception. Anything we judge by them either passes the test or does not. It is a partial exception because in different circumstances the level of acceptability may vary. For instance, a person

79

may consider a lurid joke acceptable to tell in some companies and not in others, and even in those others the joke may become acceptable when the mood gets sufficiently informal. So, in a sense, we can imagine a gradient of acceptability for the joke, but at each point of the gradient the standard delivers a yes/no value. (If we think to ourselves that a joke is 'maybe acceptable', this means we have not tested it yet, or we may be about to venture on a bid to change the standard for this particular situation.) In this way, standards can perform the role of triggers for acts and attitudes (such as indignance when someone tells an unacceptable joke) and, more importantly for the present perspective, they can also function as triggers for codes. If we have recognized something as poetry, we start reading it with the help of the poetic codes at our disposal. And vice versa, when we have judged something to be inedible, it is no longer important whether it is spicy or mild. In this way, standards operate actively on the flow of signs at each instant of cultural activity, in order to activate new codes (when, for example, we recognize a discourse as ironic) or to deactivate them (when a situation is no longer funny).

This has brought us to the actual moment of extracting meaning, and to the problematic of *codes*. Semiotics and discourse linguistics have provided us with various theories of codes and decoding,[8] and recently cognitive science has augmented these with tentative descriptions of underlying biological processes (Feldman 2006:43–82; Reyna 2002:126–35). Most of these theories share a number of presuppositions regarding what interpretive codes are and how they function. First of all, they are envisaged as analogous to lexicons, ideally existing as ordered lists of more or less strict correspondences of elementary units similar to the arrangement of entries in a dictionary. The recipient is supposed to dissect the message into single elements, such as the letters in the alphabet, and structural principles of organization then guide her through a process of serial scanning to the appropriate point on the code-list where the equivalent meaning of the item is stored. Second, codes are presumed to be objective rather than personal, to exist in an ideal form as self-identical wholes. Degrees of individual competence in them are another matter, but ideally their mastery can be more or less complete. Individually stored versions can be incomplete and contain mismatches or errors, but these particularities are deviations and have no effect on the code as

---

[8] There are numerous theories of codes (Eco 1976; Fontanille 2006; Greimas 1983; Groupe Mu 1982; Jakobson 1985; Lotman 1970 – to name but a few), and they all differ from each other in some respect, but nevertheless seem to agree on the basic presuppositions outlined below.

such. And, finally, the decoding process is characterized by tension and contradiction between different codes – which offer different equivalents for the same sign – rather than their smooth interaction. Contradictory codes may be involved in the process of interpretation just as it is possible to look up the same word in several dictionaries. But this only happens if the first and primary code fails to fulfil its function, as may sometimes happen, for example in reading poetry or texts that are self-contradictory to begin with (Lotman 1970:86–87; Riffaterre 1978:3–6).[9]

I find this understanding of codes problematic and would like to suggest that we should abandon the dictionary metaphor altogether. It is true that the material of a large number of codes can be ordered as if in a dictionary, according to some structural principle or other, as verbal signs normally are. However, this order, following the dictates of a meta-rule superimposed upon the code from outside of it, is not the natural configuration of the units that make it up. A serially ordered dictionary privileges encyclopaedic meaning, while the practical use of codes is predominantly thesauric. The interpretations of the utterances received from the environment do not stop at deciphering, but most of the time generate new expression. In encoding, it is signs that are searched for, not their meanings. And although there are some codes (such as those that real dictionaries describe) that fit the metaphor comfortably, there are also others that do not.[10] Among these are, for example, the codes that are used to interpret visual images, and their obvious incompatibility with the image of a dictionary has prompted some researchers to look for differently constructed modes of processing meaning (Whyte 2006). But though these efforts can be successful and convincing, it is rather deplorable if they have to be ever more frequently undertaken merely as alternatives to a

---

[9] Many theorists do not share this view, beginning with Roland Barthes, who proposes that we analyse texts with the help of several simultaneous and mutually supportive codes, and has provided for us examples of how to do this (Barthes 1970). However, Barthes's analyses show that he used his codes rather arbitrarily; it would not be too difficult to devise some other set of codes and deploy it differently. And that, in my view, is precisely what each interpreter of each text is constantly doing. It is therefore both impossible and unnecessary to try to describe and define the sets of codes we use in our interpretive practice to the degree of precision most theorists are seeking.

[10] Victor Burgin, having denied that there is a signifying system common to all photography, goes on to posit 'a heterogeneous complex of codes upon which photography may draw' (codes of gesture, lighting, etc.) and stresses that photography signifies *on the basis of* these codes, because the consideration of these codes would never exhaust the signification (1986:72). Photography signifies, but without a system; it has codes, but they are placed at arm's length. However, this appears more broadly, and therefore we should open up the notion of codes so that it could also be used for all cultural languages without reducing their specificity.

general explanatory paradigm that still stays fixated on the verbal and thus contributes to the fragmentation of cultural theory as a whole.

Another problem arises in connection with the postulation of codes as somehow existing independently of the processes that take place in individual minds. One can, of course, posit the existence of a *langue*-like code – in fact, a meta- or archicode – that is separate from, and only manifests itself in, the personal and individual codal apparatuses that each interpreter uses for making sense of the textual flows that address her. But this should not be done for more than purely heuristic reasons. In practice, codes do exist only as particular variations in the minds of particular individuals, each one slightly – or not so slightly – different from every other, but with a significant overlap that makes communication possible. The notion of the archicode is dependent on our understanding meaning as a purely intralinguistic phenomenon, but, in the present sense of meaning as the identity claim for an intralinguistic and an experiential concept, the idea of archicodes as objectively existing realities makes no sense. Each user of a code has her own dictionary, so richly illustrated with personal pictures, video clips and voice recordings of varying quality that it would be equally justified to call it a systematically arranged diary or memoir.

To avoid this, I suggest we redefine codes and decoding in such a way that our concepts are no longer dependent on the dictionary metaphor, and simultaneously include everything meant by the current, but sometimes too loose, usage of the term 'cultural codes'. This can be achieved by combining the text-oriented code theory of semiotics with the practice-oriented schema theory of cognitive anthropology. We are used to thinking of codes as systematically organized assemblages of singular and minimal interpretive devices, but these items need not necessarily take the shape of idealized and stable dictionary entries, nor do they have to be organized according to one principle only. We can think of them as something akin to cognitive schemas, linked to each other through a multiplicity of methods.

The idea of schema reaches back to the philosophy of Kant, who used the term to denote various tools for grouping reality on a much more basic level (1781:140–6) and this notion has also been discussed in philosophical literature (Dufrenne 1966:156–9; Eco 2000:66–75), but it is mainly in cognitive anthropology that it has evolved (via psychology) into an efficient conceptual tool, broadly signifying an open and structured semantic field clustered around a representation, a recipe, a script or an abstract concept. Schemas are 'cognitive structures ... primarily used to organise experience, ... abstract representations of environmental regularities' (Mandler 1985:36–7), each of them is 'an organized framework of objects and relations which has yet to be filled in with concrete detail', able 'to relate terms from different domains to each other' (D'Andrade 1995:124). In actual research practice (which necessarily presents its results in a verbal form), schemas tend to be 'of' certain words, or concepts, although this is not what they are in psychological reality. Claudia Strauss and Naomi Quinn have presented a convincing argument for why such flexible units of stored knowledge perform much better in the role of codal units than fixed entities could: because in the actual practice of interpretation meanings are themselves always flexible and inconsistent, even if shared between persons. Strauss and Quinn also show how this connectionist model is in accordance with the findings of neuroscience (Strauss and Quinn 1997:50–4).

What also has to be stressed is that, even if we speak about the transmission of schemas in learning and cultural interaction, they nevertheless only exist in human consciousnesses in individual, personal and not necessarily static form (Strauss and Quinn 1997:59). In this sense, they have a close counterpart in the linguistic term of *frames* (Fillmore and Brown 2006). Frames are personal, just like schemas, and they are also flexible, prone to being altered or recast in the process of use. The difference between schemas and frames, as I see it – apart from their disciplinary provenance – is that frames are functions of words, and schemas more broadly of practice: insofar as linguistic communication is also a form of cultural practice, frames are a subcategory of schemas.

But through their connection to a verbal substratum, frames also seem, at least on the surface, to possess something that other kinds of schemas do not appear to have. Namely, we can order frames of specific words in just the same way that we order the words they are frames of – in a serial sequence organized according to a set of arbitrary, but internalized meta-rules, such as an alphabet. Schemas, on the other hand, are usually depicted somehow just as being there and becoming activated for the interpretation of a situation whenever needed, but otherwise lying dormant in a huge, seemingly unorganized pool.[11] For the interpretation of highly complex cultural

---

[11] This is the approach criticized by Orlando Patterson: 'Note that software (culture), hardware (structural enactments) metaphor includes a critical feature of all cultural processes missed, or downplayed by analogous images such as "schemas" . . . namely, the fact that they are all rule-based' (2004:79). But Patterson then goes on to extract from this a much greater degree of coherence of cultural models than seems reasonable. Revealingly, he writes: 'The fact that people are often contradictory, confused,

phenomena, this view seems far too simplistic.[12] Indeed, on the one hand, there are phenomena that can be approached with quite a few different series of schemas; on the other hand, when one has chosen a certain schema, it is likely that other schemas in the same series will become active for the interpretation process as well. These *series* of schemas are what we could call codes, and they are not just small clusters of a few related schemas each, but can be very large, complicated and multiply organized systems containing schemas of many different kinds (verbal, visual, emotional, etc.) that both operate inside particular cultural languages and form connections between them. I would, however, refrain from distinguishing between codes according to the form and provenance of the units they contain (verbal, visual etc), because in actual interpretation practice we make use of them simultaneously, even if the text addressed uses only signs of one certain kind. And that, too, is not the paradigmatic case. Without mentioning film, or performing arts, alternative ways of encoding can be a part of single-form texts as well: surrealist poetry can contain very ambiguous visual metaphors, and religious painting can use strictly decodable symbolics.

Which particular codes are in use, out of all those available, depends both on the nature of the 'incoming' flow of signs – or, more precisely, what the standards have told the interpreter about it – and the situation within the interpreter's consciousness, i.e. on which codes have just been active, the general mood or tuning of the interpretive apparatus. For instance, after being tuned to something funny for a sufficient period of time, one may find it difficult to switch to a more serious mode in an instant, though the standards may signal that the issue at hand demands a more solemn attitude.

However, such codes are not organized according to a systematic principle, a meta-rule. Rather, they form rhizomatic structures more akin to hypertexts: each schema in a code may simultaneously be linked to an infinite number of others, and by different principles of

and downright incoherent in their views and rationalizations is not inconsistent with a conception of cultural models as rule-based and coherent. My word-processing software is very coherent – except when it occasionally crashes. It is what I do that is too often contradictory' (2004:79–80). But it is precisely in these 'crash' situations – or what Lotman calls 'explosions' (2010b) – that culturally significant and innovative meanings are produced, and, unlike software, cultural codes are still able to express and convey them. A cultural model that would treat such situations merely as anomalies would not be very useful.

12 As Lotman has pointed out, frequently and in different contexts, complex forms of communication always rely on the tension that appears between multiple, and not necessarily mutually compatible, codes used during the interpretation process (1970:33–7; 1992:36, 100; 1993:370; 2010a:105ff.).

association.[13] Thus, we can easily imagine a fairly large set of heterogeneous schemas assembled by what we could call 'the romantic code', ranging from ideas about appearance, clothing, mood, spatial organization, interior decoration, to behaviour in critical situations or speech patterns, and not all of these are necessarily compatible with each other. Life in primitive circumstances on a desert island is romantic, but so is a luxurious dinner by candlelight in a top floor restaurant overlooking a great city. Nevertheless, both schemas belong to the same, distinctly identifiable code that is itself distinct from, say, the code of efficiency and pragmatism, and tensions between these two codes can well be exploited in a text – for example, a romantic comedy about a successful businesswoman. A code can also simultaneously exploit schemas of different kinds and efficiently combine them. Accordingly, verbal impressions of a picture or a piece of music can perhaps best be formulated with the help of the same code.

Summary

By way of conclusion, let me now try to outline a brief sketch of the interpretive process. First of all, I hold that interpretation is not the mirror image of encoding – that is, the deciphering of a message according to transparent rules and with the help of self-identical, organized codes; rather, it is the construction of a representation, a meta-representation of the message out of the materials the interpreter has used for constructing her own cultural subject.[14] All texts of any kind can become meaningful for the recipient only as flows of signs that appear in time; a novel is read or a film is seen as it unfolds in a temporal sequence, just as a tourist finds her way in a new city over a period, during which her interpretive faculties are active. At each moment, the incoming flow first passes through the cordon of standards, which characterize it in yes/no terms (poetic, decent, beautiful, edible . . .); the appropriate means for interpretation are selected by the first standards that tell the interpreter what kind of a text she is dealing with (these can be changed during the process – for example,

[13] This brings to mind how Giorgio Agamben describes Aby Warburg's huge, almost Borgesian, library, and particularly the way that Warburg used to reorganize it whenever his research approaches changed, transforming it into 'a kind of labyrinthine image of himself' (1999:284) – this is how any cultural subject constantly reorganizes the codal resources at her disposal.

[14] '[E]ven banal conversations require that listeners construct by inference an optimally relevant interpretation of utterances, which cannot be directly decoded from what is said' (Boyer 2009a:311–12).

when it is found out that the text is of a different kind from what it claims itself to be). The standards then trigger codes. If a text qualifies as poetry, the poetic code(s) at the interpreter's disposal are obviously the most appropriate for its decoding. It can happen that the interpreter does not have the necessary codes, or, again, her standards may not be able to characterize the text with sufficient precision. For instance, a reader with very conservative tastes may fail to register a poetic text as poetry because it does not rhyme and its lines are not isometric – even if it is a translation from an ancient Greek classic. On the other hand, some codes may be active even if the text does not actively require them – for instance, a feminist reader is always alert to the modes of representation of gender relations, regardless of their level of relevance in the construction of the text.

Just as Lotman frequently stresses, there are always several codes in operation at the same time, and the results they yield may support or contradict each other.[15] The ambivalence and tension created by the latter case may stay within the interpretation or be discarded, for instance when all the other codes, including the highly personal ones, support a certain kind of meaning and only one suggests something different. The codes also mediate thesauric knowledge, which includes the interpreter's expectations of how things ought to be. This mediation helps us to come to terms with the world of the text – for example, to expect the fantastic rather than the ordinary in a fairy tale (there are not very many animals in them who cannot speak at all) and to tune our thesaurus to the appropriate wavelength. Whenever the text still seems to be at odds with our thesauric knowledge, we have to resort to our encyclopaedia, possibly an external one if the internal one is of no use. But this inevitably changes the way we relate to the text. An encyclopaedic intervention interrupts the smooth textual flow, in the same way that a joke ceases to be funny when it has to be explained.[16] When a text is accessible to the interpreter only rationally, it becomes less meaningful in other ways. This

---

[15] Although Lotman has, to my knowledge, never explicitly distanced himself from the dictionary-type understanding of codes, his explanatory practice occasionally fits much better with the rhizomatic theory of codes proposed above, for example when he speaks of texts that become codes, such as the building of a church regarded by a believer as a religious and philosophical, not an aesthetic, structure (1992:86), or when he talks about the creation of the deciphering code during the process of interpretation, using both what is there in the text and the personal cultural resources of the interpreter (1970:35–6).

[16] Pieces of non-thesauric knowledge (encyclopaedic, archival or even invented by the author) can be marked as such and introduced in the text as well, but this does not take the interpreter out of her thesauric world.

is not a problem with texts that have nothing to convey apart from rationally decodable content, but these only make up a small part of any cultural environment, and even they cannot escape treatment by personal, emotionally loaded codes during the interpretation process – for example, being seen as excruciatingly boring.

One part of what emerges as the result of this process is knowledge, which will either be discarded after that particular textual flow stops or be stored in the encyclopaedia, such as the events of a narrative we are now familiar with. Another result of the process is an impression of the text, the psychological state it induces together with the ideas (signification claims) it has provoked in the interpreter. Most of these are reiterations of what she has previously experienced, because otherwise she would not be able to receive the text at all. However, what makes particular texts meaningful is the small proportion of signifying claims novel to their recipients – unexpected tropes, bold philosophical assertions, adjustments of aesthetic standards, or precisely captured nuances of reality that are rendered significant in representation. Or, in other textual worlds, appealing combinations of tastes, skilfully presented views in architectural space, inspiring images of holiness and so on.

Innovative texts make bids to change their recipients as cultural beings. These go beyond the simple inclusion of some new items of knowledge in our encyclopaedias. Such a bid suggests an adjustment of a standard or a code, or possibly even of thesauric knowledge. The success of the bid depends on its force, on the one hand, and the flexibility (or, from another perspective, the capacity of resistance) of the interpreter, on the other. We might try an exotic dish and find it rather tasty, but not something we would include in our regular diet of 'proper food'; we might listen to a sermon without converting; or read Nietzsche for the encyclopaedic knowledge of what his thought is like. But someone might see a documentary on global warming and decide to change her consumption habits as a result, which ruins her family life, because her children would not agree to the change of standards, or she might see an unlikely combination of colours so tastefully applied in somebody's clothing that she also has to modify her own notion of style.

The reception of texts as bids unavoidably affects their status. A book that changes one life will forever hold a special place in that person's biography, but a book, such as the Qur'ān, that changes the lives of a multitude of its recipients shortly after its launch into circulation will immediately acquire base-text status in the emerging or reformed community. More often, however, the process is slower

87

and less dramatic, just as the bids are themselves more modest in nature. A historian stumbles over a document in an archive and publishes it. Another historian finds that this document sheds new light on a chain of events previously interpreted quite differently and writes an academic book about it. One reviewer agrees, another one is sceptical, so a debate ensues that arouses public interest. The new interpretation bid is rewritten as a more popular account, and so persuasively that most readers are convinced by it. In the next edition of school textbooks, the new interpretation has replaced the old one and risen to base-text status. Or maybe not. People endorse cultural bids that they find convincing in their promise of higher cognitive adequacy, but quite frequently they also endorse some bids because many others whom they trust have endorsed them, or because they have been backed by the symbolic authority (which may amount to the same thing). In this way, many books are bought because of the blurbs on their back covers.

Quite a lot of interpretive activity proceeds very smoothly, without much active effort, because the elements of the received text are easily decoded within the available cultural competence, but those texts that actually contribute to the cultural subject are themselves also demanding. And, as research has indicated, people are indeed more interested in texts that put their coping potential to the test rather than those that can be understood too easily (Aitken 1974; Silvia 2005). Thus, though Bourdieuvian sociology frowns upon assigning intrinsic value to texts, it is nonetheless possible to evaluate particular texts according to their correlating qualities of significance for their recipients and relative resistance to interpretation. The higher these qualities, the more potential the text has to succeed as an innovative bid and rise in the status hierarchy of the textuality.

It should also be added that the interpretive process goes on almost constantly, even if most of the time it is not consciously fixed on a particular item perceived as a cultural text. Apart from perceiving her reality constantly in an already-textualized form, evaluating the things that surround her according to various types of standards, the cultural subject is also continuously engaged in – sometimes more, sometimes less – structured external and internal conversations, and a large proportion of her acts are more or less distantly related to her sense-making activities, or cultural practices. It is to these that we now turn.

— 4 —

CULTURE AS A NETWORK OF PRACTICES

As carriers of a certain culture – that is, as members of a sufficient number of cultural communities with a sufficient amount of membership overlap – we live our lives in constant cultural activity, producing, receiving, interpreting and disseminating meanings that organize our life-worlds and are themselves structured by the conditions that obtain there. However, to think of this process as taking place in a self-sufficient textuality might easily create the impression that all this activity derives from the tangible products of previous similar activity and nothing else – that texts engender new texts and this is all there is to it. It is, therefore, important to supplement the text-centred model with a practice-centred one, in which the textual is subjugated to the practical – where the whole cultural system is described as a loosely structured and tentatively ordered, but at the same time dynamic and internally contradictory, network of practices of various kinds. Writing and reading books are, in this view, indeed important elements of the practice of literature, but it should be kept in mind that the latter is not performed in the same way at all times and in all places. There are, for example, obvious differences between the production and reception of stories told by the campfire and of a mindblowing experimental novel. But writing and reading are, by far, not the only elements involved in the totality of literature as a cultural practice: in the present world, this is managed by an entire publishing industry with agents, editors and copyright lawyers. There are hardcovers before paperbacks, book fairs for publishers and conventions for genre fiction fans, literary festivals, prizes, readings, signings and pre-Christmas sales campaigns. There are internet bookstores and e-books, and ever new gadgets that promise to take your library anywhere, and different incompatible formats that they use. There are both official and unofficial writers' websites. And then there are public awareness promotions with poems on Tube station walls as well as literary columns in newspapers and quality magazines. But this is still not all there is to know: the generic division of literature is more fragmented than it used to be before, with fantasy fans hardly ever reading a crime story or sci-fi readers peeking into a historical novel, and a highbrow audience frowning upon them all. In some places, the traditional forms of poetry with rhythm and rhyme only survive as qualities of lyrics for pop music – and are thus not considered to be poetry at all, which has to be sophisticated *vers libre*, read by other authors and professional critics only. A similar range of variations characterizes the people involved in the practice of literature as authors, readers or those engaged in supporting activities, such as editors and publishers, a certain type of people as a dominant in each segment of the literary field or type of activity – but with no absolute boundaries, with each type of literature perhaps having a different role in the lives of those engaged with it. An understanding of how all this works is by no means necessary for someone who simply addresses a text as an available element in her own textuality. Most texts are usually interpreted at their 'face value', itself a cultural construct. But in order to understand its circumstances, genesis and background, one can't really do without a grasp of its surrounding literary 'field' (Bourdieu 1993) as a site of practice.

Although there are many different ways of characterizing a practice, there are two basic forms of it, analogous to the distinction between base- and result-texts: the conventional and the productive. On the one hand, cultural practices are meaningfully encoded situations and relations, or scripts of social procedure, on which members of a community typically concur. On the other hand, they are the situations in which new meaning is produced and distributed through the interaction of people among themselves and with their environment. Conventional practices may be repeated mechanically and without calling their structural principles into question,[1] while productive practices always contain open positions by definition: positions to be filled by their participants with new, or at least wilfully chosen, meaningful elements.

A cultural practice is thus any repeatedly occurring activity that requires the participation of one or many carriers of the culture (or,

---

[1] Claudia Strauss and Naomi Quinn relate the story of a woman who always cut the end off her roast before putting it into the oven and, when asked why, explained that this is how her mother did it. The mother explained it in the same way, but when the grandmother was questioned, it turned out her pan had been too small (1997:112).

more precisely, members of a certain practice-based community) and involves the production, exchange, interpretation and dissemination of meanings. Cultural practices range in complexity from simple rituals of getting acquainted to the production and worldwide distribution of, for instance, a film that perpetuates a certain interpretation of history, metaphorically commenting on the present at the same time. Cultural practices also typically involve the enactment of previously existing texts or the production of new ones, which allows us to see them also through the prism of textuality. But they can as adequately be described on their own, with texts simply as an external resource, comparable to the material instruments the practice needs, or as more or less secondary by-products, the empty dishes and bottles that remain after the feast. This is precisely the view that I will heuristically adopt in this chapter in order to bring the intrinsic mechanisms of cultural practices to the fore.

The practice-centred scheme that I am going to present describes each cultural practice in terms of eight characteristic features that form four pairs, which characterize its cultural role, its social position, its materials and its maintenance mechanisms. The cultural role of the practice is defined, on the one hand, by its *function*, that is, the tasks it performs within the whole cultural system – its assigned segment in the available array of meanings and the actions it is to perform with the help of it – and, on the other hand, its *goal* – the tasks it proclaims to be properly its own, which may or may not coincide with its function. The social position of a cultural practice can be characterized both by the type of people regularly engaged in it – its *carriers*, their relation to power, their gender, their education, their expected life trajectory – and all typical forms of social relations they have. But it is also important to know what the *status* of the practice is in their lives and beyond it – is it prestigious, or perhaps frowned upon, considered to be childish or requiring proof of proficiency, organized collectively and under someone's supervision, or performed on certain occasions only, or carried out in private and whenever one feels like it? The *materials* of the practice are both the resources and objects needed for it – a large amount of vocabulary for poetry and a fir-tree, some candles, certain meal ingredients and a set of presents for a traditional family Christmas – and the *rules* regarding what to do with these things, and how. Finally, what I have called the mechanisms of maintenance of a practice comprise the channels of its *distribution* – the ways in which it is made available to its participants, both performers and recipients – and its *transmission*. Keeping in mind that, with the majority of practices everywhere, there are rules to be learned and also values to be internalized, it is not a matter that can be left to chance. This is why the maintenance of more significant cultural practices is usually the responsibility of some (usually specially designed) cultural institutions.

None of these aspects of a cultural practice should be seen as a static, unchanging set of conditions. On the contrary, all of them together give us a picture of the cultural system as a dynamic bidding space, which structurally regulates the emergence and development track of new cultural forms. The description of a practice necessarily contains an overview not only of the mechanisms it uses to perpetuate itself, but also of its methods of self-innovation. Change – or more precisely, an attitude to change – is relevant to every aspect of every cultural practice, however conventional, if indeed it is to be considered a living cultural form.

This is by no means the only possible or productive way to model cultural practices. For example, Bernhard Giesen has elaborated a model of practices based on the analysis of rituals (2006b), in which the meaningful repeatable practices of daily life are qualified as 'everyday rituals', while wearing certain items of clothing is an 'aesthetic ritual'. Another model is suggested by Norman Fairclough, who dissects any (social) practice into action, relations, persons, materials and discourse (2003:25). Jeffrey Alexander, in turn, has developed an influential model of cultural pragmatics that views social actions as cultural performances, efforts to create a common, 'fused' space of meanings (2011b:28ff.). Such performances are divided into elements in a different way. For example, Alexander conflates textuality and practice in the same scheme and views the influence of power relations on a performance somewhat differently. Social power, which has direct bearing on the instance of the performance, is featured as one element of the model, while a large part of reified power relations have a bearing on the situation through what he calls 'background representations', 'patterns of signifiers whose referents are the social, physical, natural, and cosmological worlds within which actors and audiences live' (2011b:29). These representations are obviously themselves also shaped by power relations and contribute to reproducing them. For my purposes, this element is closer to the concept of 'base-texts', discussed in the preceding chapter, as their production and diffusion takes place according to a different logic. On the level of practice, these texts/representations naturally also affect various other elements of the model – the goals and the status of a practice as well as the trajectories of its carriers – but in each case their influence is seen in a different way. The role of social power, too, is twofold.

Less visibly, it affects the structure of the bidding space, while asserting its presence more directly through cultural institutions.

On the other hand, Alexander views the arrangement for the performance – the *mise-en-scène* of the particular situation of performance, 'the arranging, and the doing, of actors' movements in time and space' (2011b:84) – as a separate element of the model. This, too, is not merely an aesthetic category, but involves a number of choices that may contribute to the success or failure of the performance to convince its audience of what the actors would like them to believe. The presence of this element in Alexander's model also points to the differences between our strategic approaches. What Alexander has produced is an efficient toolkit for looking at *single instances* of a cultural practice – a hands-on approach for analysing, say, the reasons behind a political candidate's rise or fall as a result of their performance in a series of TV debates with their opponents. In Saussurean terms, he is looking at these phenomena on their *parole*-level, at how they are carried out in reality. My aim, however, is to look at the more abstract *langue*-level and to elaborate on the 'conditions of possibility' of a practice, in the sense Foucault ascribes to the term[2] – in other words, to create a model for describing how and why TV debates in general come into being in a particular socio-cultural context. Needless to say, all these approaches (and other possible ones, with their own specific goals) complement each other, rather than cancel each other out.

The cultural role: functions and goals of a practice

The use of regulated, but deviant, linguistic forms – in other words, poetry – is a cultural constant, but even a brief look at what kind of tasks poetry has historically had to perform in different cultural systems makes it plain that there is no connection between the form of a cultural practice and its actual manifestations. It is true that poetry has had functions that are very widespread, and apparently independently so: for instance, religious rituals have typically made use of hymns and incantations in poetic form, from Vedic hymns and Avestic *gathas* to Jewish psalms or Japanese *norito*. It is also true that the use of rhythm and wordplay has produced mainly folkloric

---

[2] 'In any given culture and at any given moment, there is always only one *episteme* that defines the conditions of possibility of all knowledge, whether expressed in a theory or silently invested in a practice' (2002b:183).

poetry in many cultures for teasing, making fun of or ridiculing other people in ways bordering on the socially unacceptable. But neither of these functions is universal. For instance, poetry (or at least what is considered to be poetry in the cultural system) has no place in Islamic liturgy and, although a large body of religious Arabic poetry exists, it is predominantly associated with the Sufi movement, which is not the most orthodox form of Islam. And though humorous and subversive poetry may be more universally spread, it is very seldom that it gets institutionalized in such a form as during the Umayyad caliphate, when poets performed in public their nasty *hidzha* or *naqida* poems, spitting insults at each other, each other's female relatives and tribes, and occasionally extorting money from rich citizens by threatening otherwise to ridicule them with one of these venomous satires (Beeston 1983:409–12). In most cultural systems, such poetry is occasional and considered to be a low, depraved form of literary expression that does not live up to the more proper forms of the practice. These, again, are infinitely diverse. Poetry obviously requires a certain amount of skill, and a little passive experience makes it possible even for laymen to distinguish between tolerable and really bad examples of it. Therefore, its practice is frequently the domain of experts and specialists, and the link between linguistic and musical rhythm has also been exploited. But even this is not universally so – in East Asian cultures, for example, learning to write poetry has traditionally been a part of aristocratic education. Otherwise, attitudes towards poetry have varied considerably: for example, it has been considered a craft (as the Greek etymology of the word from *poiein* – 'to make/produce' – shows) as well as the result of supernatural inspiration (for instance in pre-Islamic Turk societies). Its functions have varied accordingly. The Confucian worldview, for instance, considers it to be the indication of the quality of politics in a country, and accordingly a source of metaphorically coded precedents in policy-making, as well as a textual base for diplomatic references (Holzman 1978:34). In Islamic cultures, it was for a long time considered the only appropriate form of 'high' textual self-expression. In ninth-century Japan, it initially even had two separate domains of functions: poetry in Chinese was written only by men and was performed on public occasions, while poetry in Japanese, written by both sexes, was for a time restricted to courting practice and private correspondence, and re-emerged in the public sphere only gradually. In Greece, there was a system for correlating poetic forms and the occasions to which these were suited, with local variations (Taplin 2001:43), and in medieval Europe we also witness a complicated system of generic distribution of functions over the hierarchically structured socio-cultural field. Although, from our perspective, the broadly contemporaneous practices of the skalds, the wandering minstrels, the Minnesingers, the troubadours, the *fabliaux* performers, the authors of the *Roman de Renart* and Gregorian chorals can be grouped together as 'medieval poets', they themselves did not necessarily even conceptualize their own activities as varieties of the same general practice. These examples should make it clear that the *functions* of formally similar practices may vary considerably across cultural systems as well as within the confines of each separate one. It should even be asked whether it is at all possible, or necessary, to construct taxonomies of practices and subpractices according to the different functionalities they have – and from whose point of view this could legitimately be done. Perhaps it is permissible to use our own categories for evaluating the practices of the cultural Other, with appropriate qualifications. For instance, to stay with the example, certain types of texts can function as 'literature' for us, even if they may not have been 'literature' in their context of origin, and vice versa. This is what we inevitably do when we approach a differently structured cultural system: we look for phenomena we know from our home culture and that we suppose to have universal equivalents. However, it is also possible to adopt a different perspective and to insist that we cannot judge the practices of a cultural Other according to our own standards at all. In that view, it is senseless to obstinately group together phenomena that would belong together in our own culture in spite of their obvious divergence in the one we are investigating, especially if we want to remain conscious of the historically contingent nature of any taxonomy of cultural practices, including our own. From this position, most poetry and certain kinds of prose could form a totality in a different cultural system that structurally more or less functionally corresponds to what we call 'literature', but other kinds of prose (which may seem even more 'literary' to us than the others) would be grouped together with manuals of etiquette and other texts helping the reader to learn the practice of sophisticated urban life, as was the case in the Abbasid caliphate (Marzolph, van Leeuwen and Wassouf 2004:470).

This is not a purely academic problem of genre theory, because we are dealing with practices with different functions. It will certainly not do to group together texts that result from completely different practices only because they seem similar to us, seen across the distance between us and their source context. Therefore, in addition to a generic taxonomy of practices (writing and disseminating prose is a different practice from writing and disseminating poetry – not to mention drama), a coherent analysis should also posit a functional taxonomy, and these two can relate to each other differently in different cultural systems. Generic taxonomies, such as the classification of literary genres, are not necessarily affected by such taxonomies of other practices (although there might be a correlation between subcultural types of poetry and subcultural types of music and so on). Functional taxonomies, however, are always directly connected to the entire cultural system. The task of value education, for instance, can be the primary function of a great many cultural practices, and at the same time more or less the only thing linking them to each other. In this respect, the hierarchical system of functions is even more characteristic of a cultural system than the various formal, generic taxonomies of its different practices. When we say of a cultural system that it is dominated by a strong ideology or that it is hedonistic, we imply that most of its dominant practices perform certain functions of discipline or pleasure production, and this also tells us something about its literature with all its subpractices. These can either follow, oppose or markedly ignore the dominant function, each option having its own significance. The overarching importance of the functional taxonomy does not mean that the generic taxonomy of a practice would be less autonomous – its internal rules, usually inherited or borrowed, are only to an extent shaped by the functions the practice is responsible for in the whole system.

This leads us to the next question of how functions of cultural practices should be described. It is immediately evident that in many cases the primary function of one practice is to facilitate another, structurally independent practice – saying, about a certain kind of literature, that it is 'educational' means that it is produced for the purposes of enculturating new subjects, which is itself a practice distinct from literature. What 'education' is can also be understood rather differently across various cultural systems, but let us assume for the purposes of the present example that it entails the transmission of values. Now, values are meanings inscribed in different cultural codes that inform, among other things, political decision-making. But to say that the function of a certain kind of literature is to influence the political decisions made in the future would definitely be too far-fetched. At a certain point the functions of each particular practice dissolve into the more general dynamic of the whole socio-cultural system; meanings launched into circulation from within the practice emancipate from it and are no longer tied to their point of origin. It is through the vector leading to that point that a function of the practice is realized. We should also notice that the array of functions that a practice may have can include various agendas for different types of participants – some go to chess clubs to hone their skills, others to meet like-minded people.

If our aim were to construct an all-encompassing typological edifice for all the past, present and future cultural systems of all intelligent societies, we should now have to compile a list of necessary and possible functions that cultural practices might be responsible for, which could then be put into correlation with all types of meaning-production and dissemination. But this is an impossible, as well as completely senseless, task. The changing social and natural environment constantly poses new challenges to people, and they ideally respond by modifying their cultural behaviour towards greater cognitive adequacy. Problems that did not previously exist need to be solved, and new types of cultural practice with new corresponding functions may emerge in the process. Different ways of seeing and doing things are considered adequate under different circumstances. That said, it is nonetheless also possible to list quite a few functions that have to be addressed in any cultural system – namely, the biological and social constants: pleasure, pain, desire, fear and other emotions, self-preservation, illness, death, violence, domination, solidarity, need for explanation, need for self-expression, and so on. On the one hand, one or a couple of these are most likely involved in any practice people are regularly engaged in, but to be satisfied with only this list (as some early functionalist anthropologists were – see Malinowski 1960:171ff.) would be unnecessary reductionism. Reality is eminently more complicated and different factors interact and influence each other in a variety of unpredictable ways.

For example, it can be said with confidence that the spread in Japan of the cult of Jizō Bosatsu (Kṣitigarbha Bodhisattva), a relatively marginal figure in the Indian Mahāyāna Buddhist pantheon, is caused by the sexual economy. This bodhisattva is believed to take care of dead children in the afterworld, and initially acquired his popularity for the consolation effect in dealing with infant mortality – a function he had never had in India or China (Kitagawa 1966:84). Bereaved mothers started to clothe the statues of the bodhisattva with garments that had belonged to their dead babies. This, in turn, was a borrowing from such 'neighbouring' metonymic practices as pouring water on holy statues on hot days (for example, you are expected to do this to the statue of Kūkai on Mount Kōya, at the Oku-no-in temple), or touching the parts of the body of a healing statue that you have problems with yourself (for example, the Pindola statue in front of the Tōdaiji temple in Nara is credited with the power to heal you by proxy if you do this). Another thing to keep in mind is the Shintō spatial practice of demarcation of the holy: a rope would mark off an area or even an object, like a large stone, as more intensely divine, and the clothing of objects also took on that function. As a result, we can find in some Japanese cemeteries or on temple grounds sometimes quite large numbers of stones and also old statues with unrecognisable features that are wearing strange clothes (including Mickey Mouse T-shirts) or just covered with some cloth, and the intent of those who arranged them this way is also not unambiguously clear.

Another issue to be raised in this context is the status of 'child': Jizō also takes care of aborted foetuses, which is why his popularity has never faded even after the rates of infant mortality in Japan have dropped considerably. In the traditional Japanese understanding, infants are, in their first years, still closer to the status of the foetus than of a human being – for example, they are not entitled to proper burials. Abortion, which has been legal or semi-legal and widely tolerated in traditional Japan, thus results in a death that is culturally equivalent to the death of a newborn or a very young child. However, the mother bears no moral responsibility for it. These dead children of both kinds (*mizuko*, or 'water-children') are treated in the same way and mourned in the same kinds of ritual (Harvey 2000:334–41; LaFleur 1992). This strange ambiguity shows how an earlier code of conceptualization (meant to handle infant mortality) has been mobilized in the service of a new sexual economy. The time when aborted foetuses started to acquire the status of dead infants coincided with the establishment of a strongly 'moral' regime in the society, which punished adultery by death, but, in order to cope with the inherited liberal attitude towards sex and the flourishing new urban culture, developed a discourse on prostitution complete with a spatial arrangement that made it socially acceptable. Illicit sexual liaisons were not only condoned for men, but even served as a source of a sort of secondary symbolic capital, *iki*, knowledgeability about the ways of the world. On the other hand, such activities were also bracketed off from mainstream society and transferred to licensed quarters, where a counter-society (called 'the floating world' or *ukiyo*[3]) established itself with its own rules and regulations. However, unlike in many other cultural systems, this counter-society was not one of outcasts. Since most prostitutes were daughters of indebted farmers, sold to the

---

[3] The meaning of the word changed along with the growth of the cultural status of its referent: the Japanese word *uki*, if written differently, can also mean 'loathsome' and this was what the permanent inhabitants of that world initially thought it was.

licensed quarters by their parents, their lifelines acquired the status of filial sacrifice. These girls had allegedly willingly given up their possibilities in mainstream society in order to help their parents in their financial predicament (Burns 2005:30). Consequently, they had acted as perfect Confucian daughters and were not to be spurned. Under the circumstances, it was obvious that a mechanism was needed to handle the predictable growth of abortions, both by manipulating their meaning for the mothers and by accommodating them in the cultural system at large.

From this example it can be seen not only how a practice, as a response to a certain socio-cultural need, branches off into a heteronomous textuality on completely other terms, but also how separate functions (coping with infant mortality; maintaining a sexual economy of a certain type) may be confounded into one whole through the conceptualization of all the things involved. This leads us to ask whether it is completely justified to refuse ourselves a position of perspective from outside the cultural system in question. We may not share its cultural codes and beliefs – we may distinguish between a foetus and a child and also think that clothing a statue with children's clothes has no effect on the well-being of a certain dead child. But this means we are already using our own categories to characterize the functions of the Other's cultural practices after all.

I think the problem is solved by separating the function of a cultural practice from its *goal*, or the functions it proclaims to be its own within its cultural system, using the coding mechanisms available to it on its own terms. This makes it possible to say that, while the goal of the Jizō cult is to ensure the protection of higher powers for the dead children/foetuses, the functions of this practice are much more rational, such as enabling people to cope with personal loss, especially for culturally disendowed mothers. No one will ever come to understand the cultural Other if they impose their own conceptual schemes on it throughout, but the postmodern refusal to see connections unseen by the Other itself will not take an analysis very much farther either. What is needed is a sufficiently clear view of the practice placed within both the source and the target cultural systems, making the one intelligible to the other.

But it is not always easy to identify the goals of a practice within the cultural system that operates with different categories from our own. There are, of course, some practices that proclaim their goals explicitly in the texts they produce or use; nevertheless, in the majority of cases they have to be inferred from the reception of the practice – if sources are available to that end. It is also never obvious that the actual effect of the practice on its participants coincides with the intent of its producers, or even that the sources describing it can in fact be trusted. For example, the intended recipients of political brainwashing may have learned to answer as expected when the brainwashers test them, although they survive in 'doublethink' and do not themselves actually believe in what they are saying. Nevertheless, for an outside observer, their utterances may seem to be legitimate testimony. And even the performers of the brainwashing may themselves also be involved in the practice only half-heartedly, not believing in its necessity, efficacy or content. For many Soviet schoolteachers, the reason for conducting a 'political information hour' was, in fact, just to avoid possible persecution, and they had learned to be indifferent to the effects these activities had on their pupils. The description of the goals of the cultural Other is thus a tricky exercise, one that becomes more challenging as the difficulty in interpretation of its codes and conceptualizations increases. To go on with the story of Japanese Edo-period sexual economy – it produced a considerable amount of literature, ranging from fiction to guidebooks, newsletters and manuals of behaviour for newcomers to the world of the licensed quarters, as well as moralistic critique, both sincere and ironical. These texts were, naturally, integrated into the more general textuality of the times and influenced by it. Thus, the generally 'light' character of much of this urban culture also carried over to the pleasure quarters' textuality a specific kind of parody, the *mojiri*, which consisted in changing a few characters in a word or phrase so that the entire meaning was subverted. Such parodies were sometimes based on long and obviously well-known texts and their typeface frequently looked very similar to some well-known edition of their subtext. This also happened to educational texts for young ladies. The parodies look like instructions in good manners and high morals (with a lot of orthographic errors), but in fact promote sexual pleasures and criticize the openly hypocritical, but nevertheless strict, moral norms of mainstream society. The *Onna Daigaku Takarabako* ('The Treasure Box of Great Learning for Women') by the Neo-Confucian scholar Kaibara Ekiken (1630–1719) becomes *Onna Dairaku Takarabeki* ('Great Pleasures for Women Who Open Their Treasure Boxes'), and so on (Tsukioka 2007). Similarly, many prose works by Ihara Saikaku (1642–93), one of the greatest writers of the time – for example 'Five Women Who Loved Love' (1686) – while condemning the actions of its heroines on the surface, are almost openly in sympathy with them and not the social norms that oppress them. Proclaimed false goals may thus be a practice of evading castigation in an overregulated cultural bidding space. But it may also serve other purposes – deceiving the participants of the practices (like all kinds of performing magicians, healers and miracle workers) or hiding their primary goals under secondary ones, proclaiming entertainment, but aiming at indoctrination, as, for example, Hollywood action films frequently do.

All of this poses more problems when we are dealing with a cultural system distant in space and time. But the distinction between the functions and the goals of a practice is just as relevant in the analysis of the practices of the contemporary Western cultural system and may yield interesting and informative insights. For example, Jonathan Friedman has pointed out, as a function of European nineteenth-century theatre and novels, the creation of a conceptual space 'wherein the individual could fantasize privately about alternative identities' (1994:26), thereby facilitating the spread of individualism and the transition of the whole society to modern forms. This is something that can hardly have occurred to the participants of the practice as a goal of their activities, although it was, indeed, an important function of the practice, something that has now been taken over and amplified considerably by the technological opportunities of cyberspace.

The last issue to be dealt with concerning the cultural role of practices is the question of change. It is quite common that, as a result of the changes in the external world, a practice ceases to fulfil a certain function, but is nevertheless carried on, out of inertia or because it has acquired a new function, perhaps without the performers even realizing this has happened. In such cases, the goals of the practice may remain stable, at least for a time, or are maintained for appearances. For example, the cultural function of Christmas has long ago ceased to be religious and is now mainly commercial, but also the reason for a short winter break in most social routines. Nevertheless, there survives a value-based discourse on Christmas, and various Christian institutions try to claim the holiday as properly their own (having historically expropriated it from pagans celebrating the Winter Solstice just as big shopping-centres are now expropriating it from them). The contemporary form of Christmas is also actively practised in cultures which have a very vague and superficial relationship with Christianity, such as the urban centres of East Asia, where a Western-type shopping hysteria with all the global décor elements precedes the New Year celebrations, which are then performed in the domestic traditional way.

It can thus be said that multifunctionality and the propensity to acquire new functions – what Jonathan Zittrain has called 'generativity'[4] – can provide a practice with ongoing importance and guarantee its survival in the system, all change notwithstanding, while practices that have a strictly outlined and very particular function will presumably cease to be performed when the cultural need for that function disappears.

The social position: the carrier and status of a practice

Every cultural practice is performed by some people for the sake of either themselves or other people, but only a limited amount of practices is potentially available to each participant of the whole network – there is no 'linguistic communism' (Bourdieu 1991:43–4) in any language, natural or cultural. In traditional societies, the distribution of speaker- and performer-positions is more rigid, since the network of practices is strictly correlated to the hierarchies of social stratification and their internal orders are mutually reinforced, in both directions. In modern democratic societies this is not necessarily the case. But, following Alexander (2011b:29–31), we can still usually distinguish between two types of participants, active and passive. I will call *performers* those participants of a practice who have at least some decision-making power and who are responsible for the success of the whole endeavour, and *recipients* those who have to follow the rules imposed on them, even if their participation entails considerable activity. For instance, in a disco, the ticket-buying dancers are the recipients, and the managers and the DJ are the performers, although most of the former move around considerably more spectacularly. However, the traffic of meanings between performers and recipients is not necessarily one-way, and the boundary between them may be fuzzy, sometimes even allowing the same person to be in both roles at the same time – for example, in group therapy, where the therapist and the members of the group are all performers and recipients, each in their own way.

Performers and recipients do not necessarily share the same characteristics. Some social groups, such as priests, itinerant actors, scholars or Bohemian artists are primarily defined by the things that they do. Success within these groups may bring with it social rewards, which

---

[4] 'What makes something generative? There are five principal factors at work: (1) how extensively a system or technology leverages a set of possible tasks; (2) how well it can be adapted to a range of tasks; (3) how easily new contributors can master it; (4) how accessible it is to those ready and able to build on it; and (5) how transferable any changes are to others – including (and perhaps especially) nonexperts' (Zittrain 2008:71).

means certain talents can open up possibilities of upward mobility for anyone. Other activities may be considered prestigious or base mainly because of the social status of their practitioners, and that induces aspirers for this status to engage in these practices, thus perpetuating and investing in their high status, as Bourdieu has shown (2007:174–7ff.) The phenomenon of the *parvenu*, ridiculed in all ages, shows the salience of the distinction between social and cultural status. As long as the practices of the people who have acquired economic and perhaps also political power remain of low status culturally, they will not be able to overtake or even to influence the symbolic authority, and they have the choice of either succumbing to the current order and adopting the high-status practices, or making a collective bid strong enough to displace that order and establish their own practices as dominant. When the Tabgachi Tartars conquered the North of China in 386, their power base remained rather fragile until one of their leaders, known to posterity as Xiao Wen-di of the Tuoba Wei dynasty, decided on a cultural switch. He forbade the speaking of the Tartar language, the use of Tartar clothes and, most importantly, forced the wild nomadic chieftains to settle down and established them as Chinese officials, offering them material benefits in exchange for the adoption of Chinese customs and language (Cotterell 1990:137–9). In a generation, the Tabgachi culture had become extinct, but the Tuoba Wei dynasty – henceforth the most dedicated supporter of the most orthodox Confucianism – ruled for 149 years, which was quite an achievement in these troubled times. The Arabs, on the other hand, tried to maintain the domination of the simple and largely pre-Islamic values of the desert at the core of their life-world, even after subjugating the much more sophisticated cultures of Egypt, Syria and Iran. This generated a long-standing internal contradiction in the Islamic world: long after the Iranians, in particular, had internalized the creed of Islam, they continued to make fun of the simplistic Bedouin practices of their conquerors, because they were convinced of their own cultural superiority and, by analogy, came to be inspired by their own pre-Islamic cultural tradition (Dols and Immisch 1992:322; Kennedy 1986:101). The inability to separate ethnic ('inward') cultural values from a uniquely 'outward' ideological base thus contributed to the instability of the caliphate.

Of course, similar processes also regularly take place within cultural systems, among the users of broadly the same set of cultural languages. Thus, the generic and functional taxonomies of a practice and its variations have to be related to the hierarchy of carriers as well, which, similarly to that of functions, is also open towards the rest of the cultural system. Of course, a cultural hierarchy of practice carriers need not, and normally does not, mirror the social hierarchy of the persons involved. A king (such as Louis XIV) can participate in a ballet production and let himself be guided by a dancing instructor, and a military dictator (such as Ashikaga Yoshimitsu) can take lessons in poetry from someone ahead of himself in that practice, but not necessarily in anything else.[5] The position of a person in the hierarchy of practitioners is defined primarily by factors internal to the practice, and the potential for external factors to interfere with it is in reverse correlation with the 'serious' status of that practice.

We can thus say that, in addition to the division into performers and recipients, the carriers of a practice differ from each other in the degree of those qualities that mark them as possible practitioners in the first place. It is usual that a cultural practice requires its participants to have certain qualities or skills in order to be properly performed or received, and normally also some inclinations (a contemplative and peaceful lifestyle goes better with the practice of religious chant than that of punk music). In addition to such intrinsically grounded qualities, the system may also impose on the practice additional rules that cannot be explained by the nature of the practice alone: some practices may be gendered, others linked to age groups, yet others only available to communities defined on the basis of some other practice or a set of features, as subcultural practices usually are. As a result, the carriers of a practice can be described as a set of ideal types with a number of distinctive features in common, differing from each other by the degree to which these features are present in particular individuals.[6] It is also possible that different qualities are needed for a higher position among the ranks of different types of practitioners: less analytical reason may be needed to be an actual cre-

---

[5] It is, nevertheless, possible that sometimes the nerves of a political leader cannot cope with the tension. When Emperor Uda was both a participant in and a judge of the Teijin poetry contest in 913, he is reported to have said on one occasion that, although everyone could see his adversary's poem was actually better, it was not fitting for an emperor to lose and he therefore proclaimed it a draw (McCullough 1985:244).

[6] Even those qualities that seem to be binary, such as gender, can actually be measured by the degree of proximity to the ideal type commonly accepted by the community. Judith Butler has argued (1999) that gender as a cultural category is always 'performed' through the emulation of certain standards. Moreover, the definitions of 'masculinity' and 'femininity' vary considerably across timespaces, and the position of someone engaged in a 'male' or 'female' practice depends on how close that someone is to the ideal of the 'real man' or 'real woman' current in her cultural system. It should be noted that these models are not always adopted uncritically, but have to become meaningful for the subjects who perform them.

ative performer than to be an evaluator (a critic, a judge, a teacher), and support activities (organization, management, etc.) require again quite different capabilities. The latter two, especially, connect the practice to other social and cultural networks, although the creative performing types also tend to overlap, and alliances between people are based on their worldviews (for example, radical versus conservative) rather than in-guild solidarity.

The qualities that describe the carrier of a cultural practice are of three main types: *personal*, such as talent, skill, sensitivity, diligence, amenability to the corresponding lifestyle, etc.; *social*, such as membership in status groups, relation to the power pyramid, economic circumstances, interpersonal networks, etc.; and *educational*. The first two can also be separated into what Alexander calls 'primordial' qualities (2006:195; 2013:125) – that is, qualities that people have by virtue of belonging to a group and that cannot be learned by outsiders – and acquired qualities that result from life-choices. The educational qualities also include, in addition to relevant training and success in qualifying tests, everything that a performer is supposed to have gone through during her formative years. For instance, a Japanese *renga* poet was supposed to have travelled widely in order to be a 'true master', while a 'true artist/poet' at the turn of the twentieth century in Paris had to be poor and preferably suffer from tuberculosis or some other serious disease.

If needed, the practice also develops procedures for testing the level of these qualities. Medieval craftsmen had to present a masterpiece to their peers to be recognized as full members of the group and universities require of aspiring scholars that they defend a dissertation and thereby prove their ability to pose problems, analyse sources, critically evaluate other scholars' work and present their ideas with a required degree of lucidity (or, depending on the academic culture, the absence thereof). It is remarkable that while academic defences have a long history, the qualities initially tested by them were quite different, converging on oral rhetoric and the capacity to convince listeners, something that people aspiring for faculty positions at universities now have to do by other means. For instance, in seventeenth-century Germany, the defenders were not required to write their dissertations themselves, but had to argue the case presented in a text that could just as well have been written by someone else (Fasolt 2004:96).

These test mechanisms have an important role in establishing the degree of openness of a practice, along with social constraints pertaining to status. A practice may be very democratic and open to everyone, at least as a recipient – such as pop music or television – or open, but strictly hierarchical: every child can draw (and there can be exhibitions of children's drawings), but only acknowledged artists get their paintings shown in art galleries and evaluated accordingly. But there are also practices that are half-open, available only to group members, though a provisional or temporary membership is anyone's for the asking. This, for example, is the way of hobby circles that are always eager to welcome new members, but these, in turn, have to abide by the organizational rules of the group. And then there are those practices in which every participant has to be a performer, at least on the minimal level. Some sports, such as ski-jumping and *sumō* wrestling, can be meaningfully followed by people who have never tried either in practice, but others, such as chess, make no sense if one has not tried to play the game oneself. In tenth- to twelfth-century Japan, composing poetry was a necessary survival skill for all courtiers because of its functions in social life; thus, every recipient of poetry was also a performer. But, while entry-level chess is available to anyone who knows the rules and has access to a board, a set of chessmen, and a potential partner, one either had to be born as an aristocrat or become a priest in order to join the circle of Japanese classical court poets. Such limited access was at once a corollary of the high status of the practice and a way to maintain and reinforce it. Even long after the court aristocrats had lost their political power to the emerging samurai estate, their monopoly on poetry, among other things, ensured them the position of symbolic authority for a long time.

But, although the cultural status of a practice strongly correlates with the social status of its carrier type – making the practices of aristocrats aristocratic, so to speak – this is not the only and absolute rule that positions a practice in the status hierarchy of the cultural system. First of all, it is possible for a thoroughly unaristocratic practice to be taken up and cultivated as a fashion by a number of the more fortunate, and thus to acquire, at least for a time, higher prestige. Waves of primitive rusticality have swept through sophisticated and very urban cultural environments repeatedly and all over the world, achieving their apogee perhaps in the circle of the Swedish Queen Kristina after her conversion to Catholicism, abdication and move to Rome in 1654–5. There, she gathered around her a significant intellectual entourage, which evolved into the Academia dell'Arcadia after her death in 1689. The Arcadian poets formed a community in which their social background had no role, assumed the personae of pure and simple-minded shepherds with virtual identities, address-ing each other with invented names (Marrone, Puppa and Somigli

2006:65), and thus credited the imagined 'low' and popular culture with a high status – imagined, because it obviously did not mimic that of real-world shepherds. They had behind them, of course, a long tradition of pastoral poetry reaching to Theocritus and Virgil that was an important part of 'high' literature. But the practice of erotic folk poetry, presumably sung by prostitutes, in the South Chinese court of Liang Wu-di (before his conversion to Buddhism around 515), in which the emperor took an active part, is a clear case of status ascription, emphasized by the peculiar symmetry of the two poetic anthologies compiled and sponsored by his sons. While the emperor was still promoting hedonistic and sensual practices, his more soberly inclined Crown Prince Xiao Tong produced the *Wenxuan*, an anthology of poetry and prose promulgating more serious values, an effort that actually came to establish base-text status for everything included in it – but this happened much later, the initial official reception of the *Wenxuan* being significantly cooler. And after Liang Wu-di had had his change of mind, his younger son Xiao Gang, who had taken up his father's early sensual tastes, became responsible for the *Yutai xinyong*, and the development of 'low' folk celebration of carnal pleasures into the markedly 'high' palace style (Chang 1986:146–57). This anthology has been denigrated by later scholars as a contrast to the *Wenxuan* – undeservedly as to the quality of its poetry, but understandably if we take into account the Chinese narrative of power. Whatever the historical practice, the Confucian value system has never propagated any values that oppose the aristocratic to the people – on the contrary, those in power owe their elevated status to the 'mandate of Heaven', or the assumption that authority naturally gravitates to those who are the most responsible, the most ethical, in every way the best possible rulers. And if they, or their descendants, misuse the power delegated to them, mutiny against them is not only permissible, but even commendable. This doctrine had a lot of practical use during the period in which short-lived dynasties followed each other in quick succession, and the separation of elite cultural practices from general ones certainly did not contribute much to the longevity of one's ruling house. In fact, the Liang dynasty came to its end with Xiao Gang's rule. In the present context, this is an example of how the status of a cultural practice is a fragile and a delicate thing, and must be carefully balanced within a larger framework of discourses.

But there may be various other reasons why the presumable correlation between the social status of participants and the cultural status of the practice do not coincide. The power elite is not always linked to symbolic authority, and in cases where two are opposed to each other, it is the symbolic authority that wins the arguments about cultural status (while the power elite wins most other arguments). The Soviet Union had a tremendous ideological industry that ruled over all possible varieties of cultural practice, but never managed to endear its product to its recipients. In such areas as the film industry, the control was almost complete, both because the amount of resources needed made independent ventures impossible, and because the prospective audience for film was the biggest imaginable compared to that of all other forms of cultural expression. This is why control was considered to be even more necessary than elsewhere. However, even here, in spite of the multitude of shelved films and good scripts that were not allowed into production, the state had to achieve a certain *modus vivendi* with the most talented film-makers, as soon as it realized that it needed an international reputation. Even so, one of the artistically most appreciated Russian film directors of the period, Andrey Tarkovsky, after long deliberations finally left the country. And in other spheres, wherever the state could only control the institutions of distribution, not production, its chances of attaining the status of symbolic authority were even slimmer.

Of course, just a rather limited number of people actually had access to illegal underground (*samizdat*) publications, and information about semi-official or underground art exhibitions or concerts was spread only through trusted informal channels. However, the void created by censoring out the independent creative impulse was not filled with the officially endorsed cultural production, because it simply did not touch any nerves at all. This situation had several interesting effects. For example, it created a rather peculiar attitude to classics. Although these were censored as well by publication policies – darker, pessimistic or simply too complicated books, such as some works by Dostoevsky, were not published in sufficiently large editions – classic writers enjoyed a much wider readership in Soviet Russia than their equivalents in other countries, simply because there was not much else to read. Similarly, in genres such as music and ballet – where experiments would hardly in themselves lead to ideologically dubious semantic content, but were nevertheless incomprehensible to the censor and possibly conducive to further independence in thinking – classical forms were enshrined and celebrated as the 'correct' traditional forms of cultural practice, which allowed institutions such as the Bolshoy to prosper, but seriously impeded the development of new ways of expression, again forcing a large number of creative personalities into emigration (which led to ever tighter control on contacts between creative people and their

108

counterparts abroad). Another effect of the situation was a heightened awareness of cultural imports. Whereas, in most large cultural communities (such as North America, France, India or Japan), domestic cultural products are more important for the people than imports, in the Soviet Union it was the other way round. The circulation of global popular and commercial culture was restricted and delayed, and 'complicated' or experimental texts were also carefully filtered, but this only increased their status as a source of prestige for those who had access to them. And, in addition, this paradigm made impossible the emergence of a 'Soviet' identity that would be shared by all the nationalities of the new empire, however fervently the authorities would wish for this to happen. For minority cultures, the importance of both classics (in their context, their own) and foreign cultural imports enhanced centrifugal tendencies. These were only strengthened by the Russification efforts of the late Brezhnev era, as well as its economic failure, which eventually led to the break-up of the Soviet Union and the liberation of Eastern Europe. Culturally, however, there was almost nothing to break up, because the cultural common ground was very narrow.

It is thus important that we do not confuse the status of a practice with the status of its practitioners, either outside the practising circle, in the social hierarchy at large, or inside the practice, where bids are constantly launched by newcomers to redefine the field on their own terms. The status of the practice itself is an expression of its position in relation to other practices, not only in the public view, but also personally, for each single member of the cultural community. The latter is again difficult, if not impossible, to assess. On the one hand, people, especially the more occasional recipients of a practice, tend to adopt the general view of things and possibly assign a higher status to a practice (such as the opera) that they do not engage with very actively, as opposed to other practices (such as soap operas) to which they dedicate considerably more of their time or resources. For an obsessed mind, pornography can be extremely meaningful, but bids such as de Sade's to raise it to a high status have been exceptional and largely unsuccessful. It also goes without saying that subcultural status paradigms of cultural practices need not coincide with mainstream ones (i.e. the ones shared by most other subcultural communities within the same cultural system) – indeed, the assignation of a higher status to some specific non-mainstream practices is precisely what defines a community as subcultural. We can also view lifestyles as sets of cultural practices loosely hanging together and mutually reinforcing each other's status. Something yuppies start doing will quickly be picked up by wannabe yuppies, regardless of what they thought of it before.

To sum up: each cultural practice is performed and received by certain types of participants who can be characterized by their social background and constructed identities (gender, ethnic and so on), educational experience and personal qualities, and different varieties or degrees of these may be required for different kinds of participation. Each cultural practice also has a certain status within the whole cultural system and in the life of its every participant, and this status generally correlates with the social status of its carriers, although not strictly. The status of a practice as such is also different from the status of its product (texts) or its performers, whose hierarchy within the practice is not necessarily relevant to their status as representatives of the practice. The status as such is a kind of intrasystematic meaning and is achieved as a result of a typical signifying act: a certain position vis-à-vis other practices is claimed for certain activities in reality, and either endorsed or rejected by the cultural community. Altogether, the configuration of carrier types and status tells us a lot about the practice as a bidding subspace – who is entitled to make new bids for meaning, for status and for the position of symbolic authority within the practice-community. A cultural system can also be evaluated along the axis of liberality. A rigid system allows only appropriately tested and acceptable people to participate in each cultural practice, strictly in line with their status; a liberal one makes most of its practices available for most people, at least at entry level, and lets them try to persuade each other of the meaningfulness of what they do as well as they can.

Materials and rules

On the whole, there is much less to be said about the materials of a cultural practice, because it is intuitively clear what these involve, from the physical objects needed for carrying out the necessary activity to the technologies, as well as other intellectual resources, without which it wouldn't work. Seen from within the practice-centred model, the relevant base-texts of a culture form a part of the materials needed to practise it. More broadly, anything meaningfully present in our life-world is a 'material' for some elementary form of cultural practice. Although most of the examples in this book of how cultural mechanisms operate are predominantly drawn from such practices as literature, arts or religious traditions, this is only because in them the structures of meaning have attained much greater degrees of complexity and their discussion is more informative. This does not mean that the arrangement of furniture in someone's living-room and a walk in the forest observing plants and birds are cultural practices in some fundamentally different or inferior way. Only those things that may physically exist, and even in some ways be engaged with a distant segment of a cultural system, but that are never ever named to the subject or by the subject, and accordingly never enter any of her signifying claims, are not present in her life-world. When they are, they have already been touched by cultural practice. Thus, exotic landscapes and smiling foreign children can rightfully be called materials for the practice of travel photography. Denis Cosgrove and his followers have shown long ago that nature, unobserved, and landscape, observed, are two different things, because the latter is constructed in cultural practice (Cosgrove and Daniels 1988).

In this sense, and in the spirit of de-ontologizing cultural phenomena, the materials of a practice also include the languages, natural and cultural, that a performer needs for self-expression. The mastery of Latin or classical Sanskrit was a skill that any speaker of, respectively, a medieval European vernacular or a prakrit language in pre-Islamic India needed in order to participate in the cultural practices of a certain status, but both languages were also 'foreign', acquired ones for all of their users. Since the semantic fields of concepts do not overlap between languages, nor the lists of salient categories (grammatical gender, number, etc.) that are expressed with grammatical means, we can say that the use of a language is, on a very primary level, already a cultural practice. This view is primordially reflected in the beliefs in the magical power of naming shared by many animist cultures in different places of the world. Such a view of language also forms the basis of Yuri Lotman's concept of 'secondary modeling systems', i.e. those cultural practices that we learn in addition to our natural languages and superimpose as rule-sets on their usage (1970:16). This hierarchy of rules is an issue for discussion: for instance, the North American semioticists, with their belief in a more basic and non-verbal conceptual structure, consider natural language itself the secondary modelling system, and cultural languages therefore tertiary (Sebeok 1994:124–7). In this case, I would rather agree with Lotman, because the idea of large-scale pre-verbal conceptual systems simply confuses our personal, private modelling of the world with the systematic character of learned sign systems. Moreover, I would be inclined to include such cultural languages as musical scales, or conventions of visual representation, in the ranks of

111

'primary' modelling systems, together with natural languages that are similarly learned and thus not so very natural at all.

Another important category of materials is the technologies available for performing certain tasks. Technical achievements ranging from the domestication of fire and the invention of writing to image manipulation software and communication satellites play a tremendous role not only in how practices are managed and meanings distributed, but also in the very structure of the meanings themselves. Jack Goody (1987) and Walter Ong (1988) have analysed the influence of writing on textual practices and shown how memory aids have transformed them to the core. Similar shifts have been caused by many other technological innovations, and quite often they have increased the chances of cultural bids that make use of them. Therefore, it is also important to note who has access to such technologies and how their use is regulated in a particular historical situation.

Speaking about the resources a participant in a practice can use, we should also include her personal memories and life-experience, although these can never be adequately described, even if only in the broadest terms, which risks the substitution of generalized narratives for actual lives and thoughts. For the description of the carrier type, we need to know the educational requirements, assessed, as it were, from the outside, but the materials of the practice include what the participant has extracted from her education and can actually draw upon. One may perceive one's education as useful and relevant for one's activities, or as outdated and unpractical. And one's way of seeing things is doubtless moulded by the circumstances of looking. We can imagine the tremendous difference between the internal 'meaningfulness' of a dissertation on the metaphysics of Aristotle written in the peace and quiet of Cambridge and another one a person would write, for example, in the atmosphere of Berlin in 1989 or Greece in 2015. Nevertheless, such conjectures are necessarily speculative, in spite of their obvious importance for the personal formation of the individual practitioners in a particular timespace.

In any case, the concept of the materials of a cultural practice should be understood as broadly as possible, so that each single segment of our life-world can be treated as a material, however minimal, for a practice that we are involved with, however passively. Of course, there is an overlap of materials between practices – the same actual things can be a part of many different practices – and this explains why these things can be meaningful for us in several different ways. The classic contrast between a stone in an art museum, perceived as a work of art, and a more or less identical stone in a geological museum, perceived as a sample of rock (Eaton 1983:101), is a case in point. A thing is assigned its place in our life-world by a cultural practice, such as enshrinement in a museal space, which is itself a signifying act (and a bid that only works if endorsed by us), not a natural realization of its intrinsic essential qualities.

This brings us to the question of rules. Here again, the example of natural language as a cultural practice can serve as the prototype of distinction. Its vocabulary and conceptual structure form the materials of speaking, while the grammar, whose structure inevitably highlights some semantic relations and downplays others, forms the core rules, augmented, in the practice of speech, by the pragmatic rules that regulate which patterns are appropriate for which kind of situations. Without these rules, speech would be impossible. Nor would any other cultural practice be imaginable without a set of rules that facilitate the transmission of larger bulks of meaning structured into utterances and messages. But it is equally difficult to fathom a practice with absolutely rigid rules and no exceptions. Even the most traditional and guarded practices, such as religious liturgies, change significantly over time, and many such practices that implicitly carry the claim to have been transmitted since time immemorial are known to have been recently invented (Hobsbawm and Ranger 1983) or significantly altered during the course of their development. This is because a mechanism for breaking the rules usually exists within the framework of the rules themselves. We can call them meta-rules, second-level rules on how first-level rules could and should be treated if their validity is called into question.[7] A good example is the relatively quick succession of representational styles from the middle of the nineteenth century till after World War I, on the basis of which Bourdieu has elaborated his theory of cultural economy (Bourdieu 1993:45–61, 238–53). When academic painting is challenged by impressionism, which in turn is subverted by cubism, fauvism and pointillism, and these by futurism, and then Dada and abstractionism, we are only seemingly dealing with a process of radical rejection of all former principles and repeated efforts to build up a new aesthetic from a clean slate. In fact, each of these styles does to its predecessor

---

[7] At the origin of hermeneutics as a self-conscious discipline, Friedrich Schleiermacher divided texts into classical (innovative in form, but not so much in content) and original (innovative in content, but not so much in form), positing two extremes: common small talk (not innovative at all) and ground-breaking texts, innovative both in content and in form (1998:13). The latter cause a break in reading practice, because we have to approach them without support on either side, and without such meta-rules we could not understand them.

113

the same thing that the predecessor did to its own, and more or less in the same way. Each style emphasizes the rights and power of the artistic individual over the represented material in a slightly more radical way. The requirement of increased radicalism is a meta-rule: it is difficult to imagine what would have happened if a new group of painters had proclaimed a return to Ingres, say, during the period between the high tides of cubism and of abstractionism. Most likely such a project would not have met with much success in the avant-garde circles, even if someone had proposed it. Obviously, this would have been a violation of the meta-rule, since such 'returns' were not the thing to do at that time. Although the pace slowed down, the same meta-rule continued to work in the modernist paradigm even afterwards – indeed, giving the impression that this is how culture always works. But in traditional East Asia, for instance, most innovations have been 'returns', and they have followed a meta-rule of their own: the development of the practice has been divided by the standard-bearers of the new trend into three distinct periods – the 'old', the 'middle' and the 'present', with the middle representing decline and corruption of what was well in the 'old' times, to which the 'present' must now return – needless to say, in a radically different form.

Returning to the story of the modernist meta-rule: it was finally displaced by the postmodernists, who – instead of rejecting the previously valid first-level rules of representational practices in order to offer their own, more radical answers to the same questions – started to doubt the radicality of radicalism itself, and, as a consequence, caused something akin to paradigm change in science (Kuhn 1962). This, of course, also affected the first-level rules quite significantly and made previously unacceptable modes of representation valid again, but under new meta-rules in which irony replaced radicalism. Similar paradigm changes can be observed in the history of any cultural system, usually as responses to changes in the outside world that need to be addressed with more cognitive adequacy. For example, technological advancement can make some problems obsolete and cause others, and different forms of social oppression solicit different cultural reactions to them. Usually, however, such paradigm changes are complex affairs with multiple causes, each of which is a part of a larger process, trigger to a chain of transformations, so that causal relations between the end result and its initial reasons are not necessarily obvious. They are more likely to occur during ruptures, but not impossible in stable situations either. Typological narratives, such as the Marxist theory of economic determinism that ascribes changes in the cultural system to shifts in the mode of production, fail to account

114

for all significant variations in cultural phenomena. But historical evidence suggests that changes in cultural paradigms are not predictably derivable from what happens in any other sphere of life, and the kind of reaction that a certain type of alteration in our environment (for example, the removal of technological barriers to information traffic or a sudden increase in population density) may provoke in a particular setting will always depend on a multitude of heterogeneous local factors. Something that is considered a welcome development in one place may be met with caution and even hostility in another. This also applies to global paradigms as they realize themselves in local settings. There has been a lot of debate on alternative modernities (Appadurai 1996; Feenberg 1995; Gaonkar 2001; Knauft 2002), the various socio-cultural forms that modernization has produced in different parts of the world, all shaped by the environment in which, and the terms on which, the principles of modernity have been implemented. The general conclusion that can be drawn from these discussions is that it indeed makes sense to speak of modernity as a cultural paradigm, but not in too rigid a form. Its actual manifestations may vary to a considerable extent. Many of its features may seem natural and essential from a Western vantage point, or so tightly linked to each other that one aspect necessarily causes the rest – for example, that the liberalization of the economy brings along the liberalization of the political system. But when different modernities all over the world are taken into account, it becomes apparent that these features are, in effect, independent and contingent, simply happening to co-exist in the Western local setting (Raud 2007:v–vii).

At least three levels of rules for a cultural practice can thus be distinguished. The first level consists in the actual rules that govern its regular performance and must be learned by new practitioners, with some positions open for new signifying bids. The second level of meta-rules settles how and for what reasons these rules can be broken in an expectable and acceptable way. On the third level, there are the rules of the cultural system that regulate the process of paradigm change, themselves unaffected by it.

Cultural institutions

The fourth and final pair of characteristics of a cultural practice addresses the ways of its distribution in its own timespace and its transmission to posterity. Both these aspects have been extensively researched by anthropology and cultural sociology. These two tasks are carried out in most timespaces by specific institutions: entities with a distinct socio-cultural status, at least some continuity and usually also a spatial shell. But cultural institutions, too, need to be de-ontologized and not thought of as concrete places run by people in charge, according to clearly articulated rules. These institutions comprise the whole Bourdieuvian field, including both the sites where the products of practices are made available – such as theatres, libraries, churches, concert halls, websites, galleries, fashion shows, museums, festivals, stadiums, amusement parks, shopping malls, discos, etc. – and the sites where people acquire the necessary qualities to become performers of these practices – such as universities, terrorist training camps, artists' studios, monasteries, gyms and dōjōs, prisons, conservatoires, etc. But in addition to these, the role of cultural institutions is also performed by the sites and channels through which information is exchanged and discussed, such as publishing houses, television, cafés, marketplaces, public baths, secret societies, newspapers, salons, internet forums, gentlemen's clubs, billboards, etc. Many of these, such as concert halls and universities, are perceived to be cultural institutions by the community; others, such as prisons and public baths, are not, because they serve some other primary function, although it is in prison that a member of the criminal cultural community can become most quickly fluent in the argot, internalize the thieves' values and behaviour codes, and learn to read tattoos – in other words, acquire the cultural competence expected from a fully fledged member of her group. Cultural institutions can have a solid existence in time and space – for example, in the form of an old opera-house with music-related elements built into the décor of its walls; or come into being only for several days a year, like a periodic festival; or exist mainly as a network of people, like the brotherhood of stamp collectors who can gather in any available space and turn it into a philately club for the time they are there. Some institutions, such as art galleries, allow their recipients considerable freedom of movement; others, such as theatres, pin them down to one place; some, such as sculpture parks and television, separate the performer and the recipient so that there can be almost no interaction between them, even as applause or booing; in others, such as monasteries or cafés, there is no clear boundary between different kinds of participants. Nevertheless, all cultural institutions share a few common traits: it is through them that the performing of the practice is organized; they are where result-texts are disseminated and new performers prepared for their task; it is through them that cultural subjects are constructed and maintained.

116

There are quite a few aspects that need to be accounted for in order to describe the institutions of a cultural practice. Institutions can be competitive and operate just like businesses in a market, but they can also have a monopoly in their domain. They can be open and liberally organized, or closed and strictly hierarchical. They can be traditionalist, or favourable to change and innovation. They can be dominated by the internal development logic of the practices they mediate, or embody principles of their own that they impose on the practices, such as economic rationality or patriotic sentiment. It is also necessary to outline who the stakeholders in these institutions are – whether they are independent in the formation of their views, or represent the interests of some other institution. The mechanisms of how decisions are made and judgements passed, rules established and changed, or the qualifications of performers certified, are similarly important. More than any other aspect, the outlook and build-up of the institutions determines the structure of the bidding space and thus sets the conditions under which the cultural process evolves. In this sense, cultural institutions can be thought of as 'points of passage', as defined by Kevin Hetherington (2001:71): both spatial and virtual points where materials and performers meet to engage in the practice, and from where the products of their activity – the texts – are launched into circulation. The territory formed by these points, as well as the possibly imaginable trajectories that connect them, form the cultural system of our life-world, in each particular place endowed with meaning for the subjects who move around in it, and, as a whole, in generally sufficient correlation with what happens in the physical world to ensure its functioning on a level good enough for its inhabitants.

This means that the network of cultural institutions is at each point also linked to the other hierarchies discussed here – the taxonomies of function and form as well as the position on the social ladder, the schemes of status of cultural practices. The health of cultural institutions obviously depends on their relations with the centres of power, although through their regularly successful bids to represent the symbolic authority they are not completely at their mercy. As Pierre Bourdieu has shown, the success of cultural institutions depends on their skill at manipulating what he calls 'symbolic capital' – a good investor in this has to be able to notice emergent and soon-to-be-dominant trends while ignoring fashions that will soon be considered vulgar. Symbolic capital can be invested in a beginning performer, and, if that bid is endorsed, the investment will bring dividends to the institution by further raising the status of the discoverer of the new bright star (1993:75–7). But the Bourdieuvian field has only one pole of symbolic authority, that of the 'high' culture, which, according to him, is able to structure the whole system. Not only are bourgeois entertainment and cheap mass culture for the proletarians of the mind allocated a lower place in the hierarchy, but also their carriers themselves are endowed with an understanding that their place is lower. This may have been so at the high tide of modernity, but is by no means a universal rule. Take, for example, the contemporary Western cultural situation, in which the block of 'high' culture has been fractured, some of it becoming 'parade' culture, publicly showcased and lavishly funded, and some of it marginalized into almost sectarian pursuits, while a part of symbolic authority has been claimed by the entertainment industry, which frowns at snobbish and highbrow experimental practices with disdain. Indeed, 'Cultural snobbery consists of an ostentatious denial of snobbery. The principle of cultural elitism is omnivorousness – feeling at home in every cultural milieu, without considering any as a home, let alone the only home' (Bauman 2011:14). Symbolic capital is thus circulating in the form of many different currencies, which are not freely convertible into each other, and historically this kind of situation is actually to be met more frequently than its modern opposite.

However, the links between institutions and the configurations of other practices are not necessarily status-bound, or not only that. It is easy to see how different sorts of available materials are linked to different types of performers through different institutions: avant-garde theatrical groups that perform avant-garde plays with distinctly avant-garde directing styles are likely to appear on different stages from more traditionalist ones, and in this case it is the choice of stage that signals the aesthetic alignment. In a cultural system that uses several natural languages, such as medieval Europe or Japan, different languages are allocated to different types of practice even by the institutions that maintain them, and though it is perfectly possible for a performer of these practices to be involved with different varieties of them, it is a part of required cultural competence to be able to choose the language correctly.[8] Of course, just like all other rules, these can also be challenged and changed by a new bid, if the condi-

---

[8] In the extreme case of Javanese, the language contains two almost completely different sets of vocabulary and grammatical markers, *ngoko* and *kromo*, to be used at different levels of politeness. A linguistically competent speaker of Javanese should not only master both *ngoko* and *kromo*, but also be aware of when either one of them is to be spoken: *ngoko* is used between close friends, wives and husbands, talking to children, whereas *kromo* is used between strangers and in formal situations (Siegel 1993:15).

118

tions allow. The practice of painting was once carried out primarily with oil paint, but never with excrement, and dead human bodies were not used as material for sculptures, but now that the work of Anton Henning and Günther von Hagens has been established as art, this is no longer so. Similarly, when the poet Ki no Tsurayuki decided, in the beginning of the tenth century, to write his diary in Japanese, he had to assume the persona of a woman, because men's diaries were written in Chinese at the time – while women did not write diaries at all and only began to do that after Tsurayuki's bid had been accepted in the cultural system.

We can see that cultural institutions are upheld and defined by idiosyncratic rule-sets that they assemble from rules generally available for regulating the respective practices. There are also second-level rules that all institutions must follow lest they be criminalized – such as, in our times, copyright – and tertiary rules that have to be kept if they want to exist at all – for example, the representation of extreme violence has to be achieved without physically harming the actors. These rules are also not universal and have not been followed at all times. Quite some time has passed since the Roman gladiatorial fights, but the debate about whether animals can be killed for artistic purposes is rather recent. But most of the rules that cultural institutions follow in their activities contain options and open positions, which they can fill according to their own preferences, either going with the mainstream, choosing a niche or launching a bid for a completely new approach. By making these choices, cultural institutions assume a role in organizing the territory, and also communicate their agenda to prospective performers as well as the potential recipients of their texts.

It is necessary to distinguish carefully between the rules of text production or performance – of how the materials of a practice can be approached, arranged, treated, manipulated and transformed – and the rules that govern cultural institutions, although in the case of larger and synthetic practices that involve the participation of a large number of performers with different tasks – such as triumphal marches, opera or film – there is an area of overlap, where organizational possibilities define the limits within which aesthetic choices can be made. Institutions may also exercise ideological control over the purity of the product and try to impose on the performers a worldview that they represent, but this either works as a structural principle, bringing to the institution only those performers that share its convictions, or entails a strong bid for controlling the whole territory and embodying the symbolic authority, thus bringing the bidding space to a standstill. This latter option is seldom successful, at least not for a longer period of time.

In general, however, cultural institutions are constrained by three kinds of rules, each regulating one area of activities – dissemination, preservation and transmission. The task of preservation is named separately because this is what links the activities of dissemination and transmission, although there are no institutions that are only involved in the preservation of cultural phenomena, without providing access to them, or fostering the competences needed for their production and reception. In fact, archives and repositories can function as the sites of both, and even closed and private art collections are available to closed and private circles of visitors. The rules of preservation are also the rules by which the cultural value of texts is judged on a very basic level, because things without any such value do not have to be preserved. From the vantage point of purely cultural practice, the criteria involved in making the either–or decision are standards of quality – whether a text is potentially successful enough in circulation – and the degree of variation from the norm – whether a text is not too eccentric to begin with (quite possibly most decision-makers in various timespaces consider this, too, to be an aspect of quality). In general, it can be said that the decisions regarding preservation are made by the symbolic authority, but at each point of a long chain of critical junctions this role of authority is internalized and performed by different individual people, from the author who decides whether to publish a poem or burn it, to the editor who decides to accept or reject it, the readers who decide to like or dislike it, the librarian who decides to acquire or ignore it, and the professor who decides to analyse or not to analyse it in her seminar.

The rules of preservation thus act as meta-rules for dissemination and transmission, and they also form the linking point of the network of practices to the textuality, because these rules also affect the distribution of knowledge into thesauric, encyclopaedic and archival. These are the rules that the symbolic authority embodies, and through which both the continuity and the innovation capacity of a cultural system is ensured. Individual cultural institutions can bend these rules in one direction or another, sometimes risking becoming repositories of worthless junk – but junk that may one day re-emerge as collections of highly valuable antiquities or sources of important historical knowledge.

The rules of dissemination and transmission, though both influenced by the rules of preservation, regulate two clearly separate domains of cultural activities – or what can be called their synchronic and diachronic axes. The rules of dissemination include, on the one hand, the legal and economic aspects – the rules that regulate the exchange of the cultural product for material benefits as well as establish the rights and obligations of various parties involved in the process – and, on the other hand, the workings of the established channels of text dissemination. We know, for instance, that paintings can hang in both museums and art galleries, and that while many museums charge for entry, art galleries do not – but that one can buy a painting at a gallery, while in a museum this is not possible. Nevertheless, it is quite usual for art galleries to organize exhibitions for which they really do not have realistic hopes for sales. But if a gallery were to start to charge for entry to such exhibitions, it would lose its visitors – with the possible exception of if it is showing the works of an artist with such a reputation that it would, effectively, change the gallery into a small museum for a short period. The rules of dissemination may also have no bearing on the economic aspect of the practice at all. For example, in many countries, theatres normally have cloakrooms while cinemas do not. As a result, one has to dress for the theatre, but can go to the cinema quite informally and on the spur of the moment. On the other hand, in a cinema one can eat and drink openly and is even encouraged to indulge in particular foods. Someone eating popcorn at the opera, however, would certainly be frowned upon. These differences persist though the cost of tickets, the length of performances, the intellectual challenge and the prestige of the texts distributed may be comparable.

While the rules of dissemination are to some extent relevant for all participants in the practice, the rules of transmission pertain only to performers. In effect, these rules construct the people affected by them as performers, ensuring that they have all the qualities needed to meet the requirements of the carrier type. In order to maintain the continuity and vitality of a practice, three main kinds of things should be transmitted: the relevant knowledge, the necessary skills and the corresponding beliefs and values. These also form hierarchies, because certain skills and certain units of knowledge have to be acquired in a certain order. One cannot immediately start with the details, without having some basic training first. The growth of knowledge, the development of skills and the formation of views are also linked to each other, so that, for example, some parts of knowledge can only be transmitted to those who have proven they have internalized the necessary values or acquired a necessary skill. A large part of the qualities cannot be transmitted explicitly, externally, but only appear as a result of the internal development of the practitioner. For example, in order to transmit an attitude of unquestioning respect for one's seniors and their authority, it will not do to constantly repeat this principle – it has to be built into the structures of the transmitting institution itself, as well as into the way the procedures of the institution make sense to the recipients of the transmission, so that they either fail and drop out or emerge transformed as the result of their training. It is usual and customary for all cultural practices to have a model set of social relations between teachers and disciples, colleagues and rivals, settling their acceptable forms of communication, degrees of tolerated opposition and critique, and other norms of behaviour towards each other as well as their broader social network, all predicated on a basic attitude towards their craft. Needless to say, these rules change when the practice evolves. For example, historically, the fellows of Cambridge University had to live in the college (in practice they did not always do that, but the requirement was officially abandoned only in 1809) and give up their income if they got married (Gascoigne 2002:12–13). Given their dense relations to the clergy, this must have made the atmosphere of the university somewhat resemblant of a monastery, with all the consequences this arrangement may have had for the social relations between the faculty and students, as well as the construction of academic knowledge that they jointly pursued.

Régis Debray has pointed out another important difference between cultural transmission and simple communication, consisting in that transmission also entails a transformation of the thing transmitted (2000:7–8). The knowledge, the skills and the views do not simply have to be accepted by each new generation of performers; they also have to become meaningful for them. In the process of transmission, the cultural practice is constantly reconstructed, even if it is carried on without alterations. Those of its parts that are accepted by the new generation without questioning form the backbone of its traditionality and maintain their position until someone comes along who launches a serious bid doubting their adequacy. There are practices in which innovation is avoided as long as possible, and others where it is encouraged for its own sake, but in both it is governed by the rules of transmission, and those specify what you have to know and be able to accomplish in order to qualify as a reformer. These rules can be successfully broken only by someone who manages to challenge the whole institution, perhaps overthrowing its internal hierarchy as a result, or establishing a new, competing institution to carry on with the reformed variation of the practice. Histories of religious movements, schools of academic knowledge or institutionally established artistic practices provide a multitude of examples.

122

Summary

The model of culture outlined in this chapter sees a cultural system as a network of practices, most of which branch into generically or institutionally defined subpractices. I have identified four pairs of aspects by which a form of practice can be characterized in a limited timespace: its functions and goals, its typical participants and status, its materials and rules of production, and the institutions engaged in its dissemination and transmission. We have seen that each of these aspects entails its own, relatively autonomous principles of organization and depends on a multitude of factors that are independent of the internal set-up of the practice. The particular forms that these principles are embodied in, however, are linked to each other at various levels and the practice emerges in its unique shape as a result. It is, of course, possible to point out other aspects of a culture in order to ensure a more complete description, but I believe these eight to be sufficient for the purpose of comparing similar practices across cultural boundaries and between periods.

We have also seen that, in principle, everything about a practice can change, but there are different thresholds of transformation: there are positions whose content can be largely irrelevant (a church may start using electric candles instead of wax ones, even if the light of these is slightly different); others that are open and will be filled by new successful bidders (the replacement of traditional church music by new styles of composition has occurred periodically over the centuries); yet others that challenge some structural principles and change the paradigm of the practice to some extent, retaining its continuity (after a heated debate, Protestant churches opened their ranks to female priests in the 1980s); and yet other kinds of change that break with the past and claim ground for a new practice, allegedly able to replace the institutions of the old one and perform their functions better (every Christian sect believes its founder to be superior to Martin Luther, though few prove to be as successful) – and, of course, it is possible that a certain practice will be abandoned, in the way that the Christian cultures of Syria and Egypt came to be superseded by Islam. As has repeatedly been said, I also believe that a description of cultural practice, based on this model or any other, may be informative to a certain extent, but is incomplete without a complementing description of the corresponding textuality. Although a practice can be viewed and treated as a stand-alone cultural phenomenon, each practice both produces new texts and relies on pre-existing ones, just as the textuality is dependent on the practice. Thus, even if heteronomous mechanisms are at work in both models, their effect on each other is nevertheless of the defining kind, and therefore a sufficient description of a cultural phenomenon can only be achieved through the simultaneous use of both models concurrently.

— 5 —

CASE STUDY I:
THE METAPHYSICS OF LOVE
AND THE BEGINNINGS OF
ITALIAN VERNACULAR POETRY

In the next two chapters, I will present two separate attempts to systematically apply the terminological apparatus developed in this book to actual cultural phenomena. One of these is historical, namely Italian poetry of the thirteenth century; the other is more recent, the art scene of Eastern Europe after the fall of the Iron Curtain. Both case studies should be read primarily as exercises in method, not as contributions to specialist debates, interfering with which I have consciously sought to avoid. As I hope to show in the final chapter, the two models developed earlier allow us to make broad generalizations about how cultural change occurs as well as to highlight both similarities and differences in the cultural processes taking place at various historical moments and parts of the world.

This chapter is dedicated to the beginnings of Italian vernacular poetry, which, though resting on an already rich heritage, is an important turning point in European cultural history, changing the paradigm of literary expression and paving the way towards the Renaissance, and from there to modernity. While still retaining many characteristics of high medieval culture, the literary movement known as the 'new sweet style' is one of the first sites where features of modern subjectivity begin to manifest themselves. This is why the importance of the work of Dante, Cavalcanti and their peers reaches far beyond literary history proper and deserves to be analysed also for its impact on the whole European socio-cultural process.

Italian political landscape in the thirteenth century: the bidding space

It has been customary since as long ago as the time of Hippolyte Taine (1866:93–5) and Jacob Burckhardt (1936:85–8) to point out the role of social and political fragmentation behind the extraordinary cultural upsurge and vigour of the Italian renaissance, which allowed for a multiplicity of political and cultural spaces to coexist at the same time and, accordingly, was able to offer each creative personality a choice between different environments suitable for their self-realization. However, the fact is that such a politico-cultural fragmentation had not been a new phenomenon since high Middle Ages: the division of power between a Rome-based Pope and an emperor with German roots never created a clear-cut political system with a promise of longer stability, and that, in turn, allowed the cities of Italy to assert themselves as local centres with substantial autonomy and self-confidence. In fact, as Mario Ascheri observes, they had no choice: there were plenty of matters not regulated by Roman, Langobard or canonical law that nevertheless had to be decided, such as rights of immigration, validity of contracts concluded elsewhere, how to manage debts, and so on, which is why the city had to exercise sovereign powers within its limits – and this produced a high level of civil self-confidence, so that citizens, regardless of their social provenance, came to identify themselves with a particular city rather than the Empire or any other unit (2006:54–6).

Indeed, the cities, with their level of civil participation, territorial coherence and political identity came to represent a fairly different form of political structure from the other authorities of the time. Their organizational qualities may seem natural from our point of view, but in the context of surrounding political realities they were an anomaly. We are accustomed to thinking of France, Italy and other medieval political entities as if they were earlier forms of the current nation-states with which they would have a distinct continuity (and this is a view that the national histories of those countries tend to encourage), but, in fact, if we need to look for an equivalent of medieval power structures in today's world, a limited liability corporation comes much closer. The title of king embodies the controlling interest; shares in a corporation, however, may be owned by individual small stockholders (feudal vassals) or also by other corporations. Thus, for instance, during a quarrel between John Lackland and Philip II, John was summoned to the French court by Philip as his vassal, because of his fiefs in France, and when John replied that, by privilege, he, as the Duke of Normandy, was not compelled to go to Paris, he was summoned there as the Duke of Aquitaine and Count of Anjou instead (Warren 1978:74). Of course, the hostile takeovers of the time were accomplished on the battlefield, not in stock exchanges, and present-day CEOs do not have to give their daughters away in marriage after a successful merger has taken place, but the way in which large territories passed from one kingdom to another as a result of negotiated alliance deals while nothing much changed in the places themselves, and the way the allegiances of military leaders shifted according to such agreements is much more resemblant of modern corporate practices than of political process. We should also not be misled by the excessive need to control territory. Most of the time this was not done in order to reorganize that territory politically, or to alter the identity of its inhabitants, but simply in order to claim the fruits of their labour: land was the main source of income, and the people who lived on it were, in a way, a part of the deal. Most probably they had a strong sense of belonging and local identity, but that is all we can assume; the inhabitants of cities, on the other hand, were conscientious citizens ready to protect their status, as their military valour has repeatedly proved. And this was not a result of common ancestry and a long sense of roots – indeed, quite the contrary. As Jacques Le Goff has shown, migration from the country to cities was one of the major processes that happened in the Christian world from the tenth to the fourteenth centuries (Le Goff 2008:59), so we may assume that in most cities a large part of the population had a fairly shallow local history. Moreover, Italy in the twelfth century was a melting pot of various ethnic groups (Montanelli and Gervaso 2004:139), all of them with their own habits and customs, which were slowly growing closer to each other. It is thus reasonable to assume that the self-consciousness of city people was, in a sense, more modern, and future-oriented, and amenable to change.

In addition, Italy had its own complications in the form of two parallel and non-overlapping power-systems of comparable strength. The political processes in all other areas of Europe were, of course, also influenced by the strength or weakness of the Pope, but nowhere else was that influence so directly felt. Compared to most kingdoms, the Holy Roman Empire was much less stable and plagued by constant intrigues, but neither was the Holy See more balanced. There were occasions when there were two more or less equally legitimate popes with different political sympathies elected at the same time (such as Victor IV and Alexander III), or two crowned emperors, such as Otto of Brunswick and Frederick II after the latter's coronation in 1215. Mutual excommunications or declarations of the invalidity of the other's credentials rarely had any real effect; results were produced only by decisive action. Quite understandably, the situation was eminently suitable for other types of political authorities to assert themselves – even if only locally – and to navigate through the tides sometimes relying on one quarrelling giant, sometimes on the other.

It is frequently said that the two major political parties of the time in Italy, the Guelphs and the Ghibellines, designated the supporters of the Pope and of the emperor, respectively. In fact, the situation was more complicated, and the content of the labels often indicated opposing someone rather than support (Fumagalli Beonio Brocchieri 2009:39–40). The alignment of a city with either party was usually for opportunistic reasons and had nothing to do with long-standing political sympathies. Families, however, were more stable in allegiance, so if a house had been Guelph, its heirs did not befriend Ghibellines easily, although this, or even intermarrying, was not altogether impossible – thus, for instance, after a (Guelph-favouring) peace between the parties was imposed on Florence by Pope Clement IV in 1266, the poet Guido Cavalcanti of the White Guelphs was 'given in marriage' (Petrocchi 2008:4) to the daughter of the leader of the Ghibellines.

Indeed, there was no natural side a city could have taken in these struggles, because, while politically the emperor might have been a threat to their independence, culturally he was no doubt their ally. It has been said that, though the first notarial acts in Italian dialects were written as early as around the year 1000, the clergy was extremely reluctant to relinquish its hold on the intellectual resources of society, which is why the Italian vernacular was so slow to develop (Montanelli and Gervaso 2004:295). The change came with Frederick II: while German-based emperors before him had not contributed much to the rise of the vernacular high culture, Frederick's court in Sicily had made it not just possible, but highly prestigious. A large part of the cities' cultural outlook owed, in general, a large debt to the lifestyle of court nobility: particularly in Italy, Jacques Le Goff writes, it was customary for aristocrats to have residences in cities, and the wealthier citizens came to imitate their building style, so, although towers and similar architectural elements were not used by them for defence purposes, they were a sign of prestige (2008:59). We may assume many other cultural phenomena migrated similarly over status boundaries, and were also correspondingly transformed in the process. Whatever symbolic authority such cultural phenomena credited to their users or practitioners inevitably accompanied them outside their context of origin, and this created a demand in every aspiring political centre for such tokens of cultural advancement.

We can think of the city as an element of the bidding space on two levels: first, the larger cultural area, in the boundaries of which textual traffic occurs, where every city (or aristocratic court, for that matter) can make a bid for being the centre of symbolic authority. And second, each city is also a bidding space within itself, with positions open for cultural leaders of the defined territory. The two levels are linked: a bid for the outside presupposes an endorsed bid on the inside. Characterizing the organization of city life, Ascheri writes that its major characteristic is the tendency to form groups, which, although occasionally self-defeating and indicative of the weakness of constitutional mechanisms, is also a sign of vitality and movement (Ascheri 2006:96–7), because where there is nothing to argue about, arguments will not ensue. Party politics was one way of drawing borders, but there were others; a city was usually divided into a number of wards with different defensive duties, called *contrade*, and when they gradually lost their military function, they became teams in various sports – some of which, such as the horse races (the Palio) in Siena, survive till this day – maintaining strong local patriotism in each *contrada*.

The thirteenth century was a good time for cultural bidding in such spaces. The authority of the Church was in decline, and its hold on written verbal culture broken completely. But the time of magnates, such as the Medici family, still lay ahead. The symbolic authority thus rested, for the time being, on a commonly negotiated ground. Under the circumstances, it was easy for a group of like-minded people to claim it for themselves, because they could only be undermined by a similarly strong collective bid, not any separate single bidders. The collective nature of the bid also claimed for its proponents the capacity to create a broader field, a subcultural space that could accept others if they wished to enter, and this made the bid much more sustainable. If a kind of practice was to be successful in an interurban competition, it had to belong to an open group, because otherwise each other aspiring centre would perhaps have felt more temptation to assemble its own performers on a field of its own.

The poetic context

Several significant poetic bids were made during the thirteenth century. The first, called the Sicilian style, came from Frederick II's court in Palermo. In the middle of the century, the position of this school was challenged by Guittone d'Arezzo (d. 1294) and his followers. A different and less successful approach to poetry was taken by some poets from the North, who tried to reconcile the lexicon of high poetry with a more deferential attitude to the Church. Related to this bid is the work of Iacopone da Todi, whose inspired Christian verse in Italian and Latin has nevertheless remained a more or less solitary achievement. A school of poets also emerged in Siena, whose verse was characterized by irony and colloquial realism. And, finally, there was the manner of writing retrospectively labelled the 'new sweet style' (*dolce stil nuovo*), of Florence (which also spread to other cities), inaugurated by Guido Guinizelli, brought to perfection by Guido Cavalcanti and Dante Alighieri, and practised by many other poets.

The didactic poets need not seriously concern us here, because, from the point of view of cultural dynamics, their position was rather conservative and they did not attract a large enough following. Among those who did not become dominant, the group that probably deserves most attention for the present purposes is that of Guittone d'Arezzo and the poets influenced by him, because his case exemplifies in many ways the nature of the cultural bid, precisely because of its relatively short-lived success compared to its ambitions. Some of Guittone's texts have led scholars to believe that he was very consciously aspiring to become the new head of the lyrical poetry movement. A *canzone* addressed by him to Mazzeo di Ricco of the Sicilian school, *Amor tanto altamente*, follows the strophic structure of a famous piece by Giacomo da Lentini (*Madonna dir vo voglio*), the head of the Sicilian poets, but markedly opposes itself to its content – unlike Lentini, Guittone explicitly denies any wish for any reward for his devotion to the lady (Lannutti 2009:37). This is not a thoroughgoing ideological line, however. In another *canzone* (*Chiero con dirittura*) of approximately the same period Guittone becomes downright rude when addressing the object of his affections:

> There is no room in you for courtesy or wisdom; you are a creature of such haughty sort that you won't let these things affect you . . .

But, provided that the beloved changes her attitude to the speaker, she has still hope:

> If you think about it well, great courtesy cannot be absent from you, if only the pain would cease for me, your lover . . . I would lie in greater joy than any man, o haughty lady, only if without annoyance your sweet countenance, whenever I look at it, would rejoice in looking back.

130

Should we think of these as expressions of contradictory, but all too human, emotions? Or perhaps samples of different strategies for undermining the current discourse on amorous sentiments – first from one angle, and then from another? Guittone must have been truly annoyed when his efforts finally came to nothing and the torch was passed from the Sicilian school to the 'new sweet style' poets, and, in the latter part of the thirteenth century, he adopted a completely antagonistic attitude to love poetry, engaging in a strong critique of the 'new sweet style'. His sonnet *S'eo tale fosse*, in spite of containing a few notes of self-criticism (because of his own past love poems) consists in a vicious attack on one of the best-known sonnets of Guido Guinizelli, *Io voglio del ver la mia donna laudare*. Some time later (1285–90), Guittone composes a crown of sonnets called 'Of Carnal Love' (*De Carnale Amore*), in which he denounces worldly love in favour of a mystical love for God. This, in turn, is ridiculed by Guido Cavalcanti as a sample of empty reasoning with no understanding of the matter in question at its base. The sophisticated scholastic and logical terms Cavalcanti uses leave some room for interpretation regarding precisely how his critique should be read (and it may have been intentional to construct the argument so that Guittone would have had trouble deciphering it), but its general message is very clear: Cavalcanti claims that Guittone is not competent to argue against love, since his discourse lacks appropriate knowledge, something that the 'new sweet style' possesses – namely, the sophisticated metaphysics of love, expressed in Cavalcanti's *canzone Donna me prega* and other works by himself and other authors.

It therefore seems that from both sides the polemic was a part of an ongoing competition between their bids, and also aimed at the attraction of talent to their respective sides. Indeed, some poets, such as Monte Andrea, usually aligned with Guittone because they were in correspondence, actually demonstrate quite a lot in common with the 'new sweet style' in their poetic attitude and language use – so much, even, that one anthologist has grouped Andrea with Guinizelli as one of the early 'new sweet style' poets (Berisso 2006). Given the necessity for a stronger field in order to ensure the position of one's school, such polemic is quite understandable, as is the need to turn it into an ideological controversy over the nature of the subject of poetic expression.

The absence of a clear position in the early work of Guittone might have been one of the reasons why his bid was not broadly endorsed, and his all too aggressive ways were perhaps another. But the fate of the last substantial bid of the time, the humoristic school that flourished in Siena, with Cecco Angiolieri (1260?–1313?), Giacomo (d. before 1290) and Meo de' Tolomei (1260 – after 1310) as well as some others, was shaped by different kinds of factors. In fact, this school came into being as an endorsement of a bid that originated in Florence, with Rustico di Filippo (1230/40–1291/1300), but was not significantly supported by anyone in his native town. By our present standards, this poetry is very lively and much more modern than most other contemporary writing, and because of its down-to-earth humour and occasionally biting satire it must also have appealed to at least a part of its audience. Cecco wrote three sonnets dedicated to Dante, which not only indicate that they must have known each other, but also make the bid for their poetic practice to be situated on the same level. It seems Dante must have recognized that bid and responded to Cecco's mocking criticism of his sublime metaphysics, because, although his answer is lost, we have Cecco's final answer in that exchange:

> Dante Alighieri, if I am a good fool, then your spear is definitely also touching my back (i.e. you are next in line); if I have dinner with someone, then you'll appear for supper, if I bite the fat, then you suck the lard ... if I have become Roman, then you are Lombardian. So that, thanks to God, neither of us can reprimand the other of much: that would be unfortunate and senseless.

As the text reveals, both men were in exile by the time of its writing, so it has to date from after 1302. Cecco was past forty at the time, so this is no adolescent brawling. But even if he was five years older than Dante, he never became as serious or mature. While Dante did his military duty with dignity, Cecco was disciplined several times for absence without official leave, and, although born into the family of a wealthy banker, after his death his heirs had to relinquish their inheritance, because it consisted mostly of debts (Cavalli 2006:5–6). Another poet of the same school, Meo de' Tolomei, if the identification of him as the Meuccio of Dante's Rime LXIII is correct (Gorni 2008:94–95), was also a son of a powerful family and quite noted in literary circles, but he, too, had to withdraw from public office because of financial problems. These qualities define them as carriers of a subcultural practice, but also prevent them from taking the position of the carriers of high culture. The bid they made was simply a counterbid to the Florentine effort to dominate the cultural scene, meant to undermine it, but never presenting a serious alternative to it.

The other reason why this bid was not accepted may have been its countercultural nature. Cecco's verse builds on the 'low' tradition of the wandering minstrels rather than the 'high' tradition of elevated love poetry: similarly to Archipoeta, who in his 'Confession' lists one by one the sins he could not live without (Raby 1959:263), Cecco starts his sonnet *Tre cose solamente* with the statement:

There are only three things that have importance for me, of which I cannot really have enough: they are the woman, the tavern and the dice – these make my heart feel happy.

When Cecco writes of love – sometimes powerfully and with an intensely beautiful language that is in no way inferior to that of Cavalcanti or Dante – he occasionally 'lapses' into something resemblant of the 'new sweet style', which he then immediately starts to parody – for instance, in the sonnet *Io son sì altamente innamorato*, which begins with the assertion that the speaker, so elevated in love, would not consent to change places with any emperor in the world, he continues to assure that the ability to serve such a woman would make anyone say he was born under a lucky star, and ends with the anticipation of having his way with her any day now. There are other poems, of course, of which we may presume the ladies in question to be the intended audience, and which therefore conform more to the standards of love poetry, but in general the mood is clear:

I am in love, but not so much that I could not easily do without it, for which I praise myself and hold in value that I have not been given to Amor completely.

This attitude is similar to much city culture in medieval Europe, a tradition of opposition to the ideals of the 'high' culture of palaces and courts, which could, with a level of collective cultural self-consciousness, become a bid for the mental independence of the city (as with Villon, for instance), but in the atmosphere of the Italian late thirteenth century this was not productive, since the position of high culture had just been drawn out from under Church domination by a heterogeneous coalition of cultural groups, and a consolidation of high non-clerical culture was in the interest of both the aristocracy and the city. In one of his *canzones* (*Poscia ch'Amor del tutto m'ha lasciato*), Dante has criticized this type of worldview precisely on these grounds:

And then there are those who, in order to seem funny, want to be appreciated immediately by those whom they deceive, making fun of things that the blind intellect does not see. . . . Never do they fall in love with gentle ladies, . . . but, just like thieves gone stealing, they only seek to satisfy their vile desires.

133

A coincidence, perhaps, to characterize this kind of wit as 'blind' (*cieco*), which sounds very like 'Cecco'? It is clear that Dante's criticism is meant to draw a line of qualitative difference between those like himself and those who aspire to attention through the comical. The time was simply inauspicious for making use of the possibilities of expressing true and genuine feelings through the comical, although this is precisely what Cecco and his colleagues achieved in the best samples of their work.

As we shall see, the 'new sweet style' also combined different orders of symbolic resources so that, even as a kind of continuation of aristocratic poetry, the school was not its imitation, and reconfigured its elements in its own very specific way. But a proof of capacity to perform with quality in this tradition is also something that assured all parties concerned that the level of city culture was something not to be easily dismissed. These, I assume, were the main reasons why the bid of the 'new sweet style' prevailed over all others that were made in the thirteenth century: it was relatively open to performers who wished to join (access was merit-based), it took the models of the non-clerical high culture and adjusted them to the needs of a non-hierarchical society, but did that without an aggressive opposition to anyone, acknowledging its debts to its predecessors, and, as a result, emerged not as a counterculture, but as a form of expression that lent itself with remarkable ease to the task of status-building. As a cultural bid, the 'new sweet style' was a true success story.

The carriers of the practice

Of all the cultural spaces of the European Middle Ages, the self-conscious city was probably the most open to heterogeneous social and cultural flows. Its identity had not been handed down to its dwellers in entirety, but could, in part, be negotiated, and, though it was strong, it did not define a person with the same kind of finality that such attributes as one's birth in a noble family or membership in a monastic order carried with them in those sites of 'high' cultural production where these were the prerequisites for participation. It was also a heterogeneous social space in that descendants of aristocracy, as well as families of humbler origin but with a longer tradition of self-consciousness, were in constant interaction with newly urbanized and self-made people. Obviously, the cities developed hierarchies of their own, but these were, at the time, still much more merit-based. And education was one kind of merit conducive to social advancement,

134

quickly also becoming a necessary part of competence that people with high social status started to assume of each other, and a sign of dignity. The rise in status of literacy-related practices brought along what has been called 'the revolution of writing'. There exist around 5,000 original manuscripts from pre-1121 France and 2,000 from pre-Norman Britain, but come the thirteenth century, the number of manuscripts quickly starts to rise (Bertrand 2009:75). Even if a part of this growth can be attributed to a change in attitude, now more attentive to archives and preservation than before (Bertrand 2009:77), then that, too, signifies a transition. Literacy ceases to be a skill restricted to professionals. As a result of all this, 'there was reborn in Italy after an eclipse of nearly 800 years a relatively new figure in the panorama of Western medieval written culture: the literate person free to write apart from any precise social function or constricting juridical obligations' (Petrucci 1995:178). But the liberation of writing as an activity coincided with the liberation of literary self-expression from a similar professionalism. Although there had been troubadours such as the rulers Guilhem de Peitieu or Alfonso II of Aragón, a greater number of poets had traditionally been professional entertainers. And these were valuable: Indro Montanelli reports that, at the end of the twelfth century, Italian aristocrats were still likely to pay for imported entertainers their weight in gold (Montanelli and Gervaso 2004:130). However, in the Sicilian court of Frederick II, there were already no poets who would have been 'professional' in that sense (Montanelli and Gervaso 2004:292). And similarly, though we remember them for other reasons, the 'free literates' of the cities, unless they chose to depend on what their fathers earned, considered something else their primary domain of self-realization. Even Dante is said to have considered himself first and foremost a politician, for whom, in his mature years, writing was only 'a substitute for a life of practice that had been denied him' (Gorni 2008:177). Guido Guinizelli was a lawyer, Guido Cavalcanti and Dino Frescobaldi were sons of wealthy bankers (just like Cecco Angiolieri in Siena), Gianni Lapo and Cino da Pistoia notaries (Cino was also a legal scholar, author of several theoretical treatises). This was by no means a small community: Monique Bourin-Derruau reports that, in the small provincial town of Pezenas in Languedoc, with approximately 300 households, there were 10 notaries (1990:38), and we can assume that, in the bustling city of Florence, the number of people involved in the legal profession or other activities similarly appropriate to free literates must have been much greater. At the end of the thirteenth century, symbolic authority on poetry no longer lay with traditional nobility, yet none of the 'new sweet style' poets came from humble origins. Among representatives of other styles, provenance from outside that social group aptly called 'the informal aristocracy of money and war' (Ascheri 2006:96) is also exceptional, counting only a few poets like Cenne de la Chitarra, an entertainer in the traditional style.

This permits us to distinguish between actual aristocracy and an aristocratic outlook on the world. It seems that, in general, the issues of proper descent mattered less to those who had nothing to worry about themselves, while others were more concerned with status precisely because of the ambiguous nature of their own. Thus, Frederick II writes to his son Conrad, as early as 1238, that the nobility of blood without individual virtue in an aristocrat is not only insignificant, but even criminal, because, in principle, more can be asked of a noble; and one of Frederick's judges, Riccardo da Venosa, puts it in even more categorical terms, saying that if someone endowed with ingenuity is born in mud or manure, his nobility is nevertheless authentic (Fumagalli Beonio Brocchieri 2009:114). Of course, there must have been others, greater in number, who did not share this spirit of magnanimity, in part because they felt threatened by the processes it had set in motion. In Florence, that same spirit was carried even further in the reforms of Giano della Bella, author of the Ordinances of Justice, which were passed by the Florentine *signoria* in 1293 and forbade membership of governing bodies to anyone who did not work, thus depriving the traditional nobility – though only for a time – of much of their influence (Gorni 2008:65).

Dante, however, did not approve of such politics. As a representative of the middle ground between traditional aristocracy and the 'new people', he was much more status-conscious – after all, his great-great-grandfather Cacciaguida had been knighted and died a crusader, even if the family had lapsed into the business of moneylending in subsequent generations. The Cavalcanti family was also only aristocratic in comparison to those with an even shorter history. Nevertheless, Guido Cavalcanti is portrayed by his biographers as a 'gentle, cultivated ... disdainful aristocrat' (Bondanella and Bondanella 1996:119). And Dante, although he exclaims in the middle of his discussion of his family tree with Cacciaguida, its progenitor, that 'scarce is the nobility of our blood' (Paradiso XVI 1), still complains that 'new people' and quick profits have produced pride and lack of restraint in the city of Florence when the soul of Iacopo Rusticucci asks him whether valour and courtesy still reign in their home town as they used to ('Inferno' XVI 73–4). Similarly, a taken-for-granted hierarchy of people and their practices is felt throughout his discussion of various Italian dialects (*De vulgari eloquentia*). The 'free literates', most of them socially positioned between traditional nobility and the 'new people', were more likely to aspire to the position gradually vacated by the former than to associate with the latter. This is why a codal system that cast them as a spiritual aristocracy was, in their own eyes, the cognitively most adequate representation of themselves, conjoining the status of nobility with a level of cultural advancement.

The openness of the group is nonetheless illusory: it can proclaim access to it to be merit-based, but, in fact, the ways to acquire that merit – including the proper education – were accessible only to men of sufficiently high social standing in their respective communities. During the latter half of the thirteenth century, there apparently still existed a distinction between the education considered proper for a son of an aristocratic family and one of merchants. However, Dante's family was wealthy enough to provide him with not a bourgeois, but an aristocratic upbringing (Petrocchi 2008:7). The very fact that such a crossover was possible shows that the dividing line was slowly fading away.

The science of love as privileged knowledge

It is to a large extent precisely this education – sufficient familiarity with the base-texts of the textuality on which the practice relies – that defines one as a potential participant, whether active or passive. The carriers of this cultural system were open to a variety of cultural flows simultaneously, and navigated them with different levels of competence. Cavalcanti's masterpiece, the *canzone Donna me prega*, asserts that the sophisticated philosophical reasoning it contains (and which continues to trouble interpreters to this day) is addressed to a lady as an answer to her enquiry on the nature of love, which means that, at least in theory, that lady should have understood that reasoning. (Although we do not find women among the members of the poetic circle, they could in theory belong to its intended group of recipients.) Indeed, Guido's *canzone* received immediate attention and became soon enough the subject of commentary, also in Latin (Gorni 2008:86). Almost as high a level of philosophical competence is expected from the readers of Dante's *Vita nova*, which occasionally touches on similar matters – that is, the intended audience of these texts was supposed to have read beyond the quadrivium, even if they did not have proper university education. Similarly, the fictional

137

figure of Francesca da Rimini, depicted by Dante, demonstrates laudable familiarity with Boethius (Dronke 1984:372). At the same time, the audience of the 'new sweet style' was obviously supposed to be familiar with vernacular verse – both lyrics (at least Italian and Provençal) and romance literature (including French), which was indeed broadly read at the time – and the general Christian lore, as well as a sizeable part of the literature and mythology of the ancient world. In a tentative reconstruction of Dante's personal library, 'which was certainly not very rich', Petrocchi lists a dozen authors, classic and Christian, a volume on history and one on geography (or one that combined both), a small selection of Provençal, French and Italian poets, possibly the *Razos de trobar* ('Guidelines for poetic composition') of Raimons Vidal and the *Summa de vitiis et virtutibus* ('A compendium of vices and virtues') of Guido Faba – adding that, if Dante ever consulted a bigger library, like that of the Capitolare in Verona, it was 'certainly not to discover classics buried in dust or to rummage around in long-forgotten manuscripts, but only to verify the references and expressions of *auctores* whom he already knew' (2008:107). That said, a well-educated poet might easily have been among the most educated people of the time, combining in themselves the knowledges of the court, the Church and the university, the principal keepers of which were never so well informed of each other's domains. Elements assembled from separate concentrated subcultural encyclopaedias are forged into a new and more open thesaurus, which is able to claim some authority from all of them for its own, and simultaneously to provide new relevance for their respective styles of reasoning.

However, rational knowledge was by far not the only – and not even the main – characteristic that limited access to the community of 'new sweet style' participants. It only provides the base for the code with which an author may adequately express his sensitive interiority. Dante's first sonnet, *A ciascun alma presa e gentil cuore*, starts with the delineation of who is intended as its reader ('every captive soul and gentle heart'), and in *Donna me prega* (lines 5–7) Cavalcanti states in no ambiguous terms that:

> *Therefore, at the moment I am appealing to a knowledgeable reader, because I do not even hope that someone of base heart could attain to this kind of reasoning.*

Later in the poem (lines 48–9), we are told that '*also, you will see that it [i.e. love] is met most frequently in people of noble quality*'. The addressees of the text have not only to understand it with their minds, but also to relate it to their personal experiences, which, as a rule, is only possible if they have a sufficiently refined psyche. A proper understanding of the signification claim requires that both the linguistic and experiential concepts it brings together should be meaningful for the recipient.

We are thus dealing not with a literary coterie, but with an aristocratic spiritual brotherhood, united by a 'primordial' sensitivity that raises its members above those incapable of feelings of the same quality. It is not an enviable lot, as we shall see, which makes it even more noble. As Bruno Pinchard aptly notes, love had become a matter of politics, 'because it is the only kind of heroism that imposes itself on the feodality that insensibly enters the age of mercantilism' (1996:47). So poets take over from knights. In fact, even thinking of their texts as poetry that is somehow valuable for its own sake indicates a lack of understanding. Even in the *Divine Comedy*, in the famous spot where Dante is discussing poetry with Bonagiunta Orbicciani and is asked whether he is indeed the poet and author of *Donne ch'avete intelletto d'amore* (*Vita Nova* XIX), he answers: 'I am one such who, when Love inspires me, observes, and in the same way as I have been told within, signifies' ('Purgatorio' XXIV 52–4). That is, poetry is essentially a derivate, an encoding of love, not an independent practice. Poets view themselves only as servants of Amor and their designated ladies, by which move they also exclude these ladies from the circle of those endowed with a voice.

Love, on the other hand, is something on which opinions may differ. Cavalcanti's theory, for example, is at odds with Dante's roughly contemporaneous views, but this is not really a problem: just as in the discourse of philosophy, from where the terms of the discussion were being borrowed, these theoretical statements were open to argument and tolerant of each other. In fact, reasoning about the essence of love was a noble pursuit for its own sake, not necessarily a goal-oriented activity. Anyone capable of it on a sufficiently high level was admitted to the community, and thereby elevated in cultural status. In a text (*Guido i'vorrei*) claimed by some to be 'the most famous sonnet of Italian literature' (Pasquini 2006:23), Dante describes a kind of utopia quite out of this world:

> Guido, I'd wish that you and Lapo and myself would be taken by a spell and put in a ship, which would sail the sea with any wind as you and I please. . . . And lady Vanna and lady Lagia and the one under number thirty would be put there with us by the good wizard, and there we would always be discussing love, and all of them would be satisfied just as, I believe, would we.

Only in Dante's world is it imaginable that three grown-up couples could be magically moved away from the public eye and choose to discuss endlessly the essence of love instead of engaging in other related activities. Yet it is a fact that one main characteristic of the love poetry of the 'new sweet style' is precisely the thoroughly asexual nature of the love that it expresses. Although the origins of this attitude go back to the poetry of the troubadours,[1] there is a marked contrast. A troubadour would not decline a carnal reward for his devotion, and those who had occasion not to, did not: it is frequent for poets to boast that they would not trade the love of their lady for the position of any king or emperor in the world – a position vindicated even by a real king, Alfonso II of Aragón (Gadea 1990:87) – but, in *Lanquan lo dous temps s'esclaire* (lines 17–21), Bernart Marti makes this statement while lying naked in his lover's bed (Bec 1979:105), and Arnautz de Maruelh, in *Belh m'es quan lo vens m'alena* (lines 27–8), after having poured lavish praise on his lady, considers it only fair that first she gives him a kiss, and continues according to services rendered (Bec 1979:210). For a poet of the 'new sweet style', favours granted by the object of devotion are not the goal of his practice. Not dying immediately is in most cases enough. The lady is both the source of and the only possible remedy against his anguish, which creates an impossible situation:

> *I come to see you, hoping to get well, and when I raise my eyes to look at you, in my heart such a tremor arises that it makes my soul leave my arteries.* (*Vita Nova* XVI)

The novelty of this attitude is well documented in an alleged poetic exchange between young Dante and Chiaro Davanzati, a prolific Florentine author of the previous generation, on the topic of whether or not a poet should seek his lady's favours. When Dante declares his preference for 'loving without asking anything', for remaining 'desiring in desire', in order to be able to express his feelings continuously in poetry, similarly to the nightingale, whose song is pleasing only until he has fulfilled his desires, Chiaro shrugs: if a lady says 'yes' without being asked, then why not? – but if Dante's intent is not to achieve anything with her, then he is welcome to it, though he, Chiaro, had initially believed his love to be like that of others, aimed at the fulfilment of desires after one has proved oneself worthy of

---

[1] In fact, the troubadours owe this aspect of their poetics to the semi-mystical Arabic love poetry, typically practised by unhappy lovers in the desert, offering a lifetime of devotion to ladies they are never able to attain.

them. Chiaro concludes by advising Dante that, of course, there are ladies who have promised themselves to God and are averse to 'carnal men' for that reason, but to any other woman this does not apply.

To recapitulate: the 'new sweet style' of poetry was a cultural practice that emerged among the 'free literates', who appeared as a socially and culturally heterogeneous group of men in the middle ground between traditional nobility, with whom they aspired to catch up in status, and the 'new people', from whom they wanted to distinguish themselves, although their nobility 'by blood' was not sufficient to be able to do that according to the old rules. To that end, they conceived of themselves as the aristocrats of the mind, noble hearts, able to realize themselves in feelings of higher quality – a development of the ideals of courtly love, but combined with the elements of other cultural flows that had formed their cultural outlook, in particular, philosophy. This resulted in a particular body of knowledge – a 'science' – which combined the base-texts of the different cultural groups that they shared with a philosophical theory on the one hand, and a capacity to encode one's own practical experience on the other. In poetry, different subcultural and encyclopaedic knowledges were jointly turned into a thesauric whole. True, according to its own claim, poetry was only a derivate of that knowledge, something by which the level of inner advancement was made public. In order to qualify, the poet had to be in constant torment, because true love could not be mutual by definition (and, consequentially, did not necessarily interfere with the poet's actual private life). While the texts proclaimed the expression of their authors' true love as their goal, their function was rather to cast these authors as the true nobility of urban society. Aristocracy of descent had been replaced by aristocracy of practice. By the same token, a bid for a high status for that practice was launched simultaneously.

Vulgare, the medium

Modern readers of Dante's De vulgari eloquentia ('Of eloquence in the vernacular'; DVE) might well be puzzled over the strangely inaccurate opposition to written Latin of 'the vernacular', as if the latter were just one language of which French, Provençal and Italian are considered to be merely varieties, just as Tuscan or Sicilian are varieties of Italian (DVE I viii 5). But this view, indeed, is more appropriate for the linguistic reality of the time than making a clear distinction between the languages would have been. A few generations before,

Italians such as Sordel or Bonifacio Calvo had blended seamlessly into the Provençal-writing troubadour community, and even at the end of the thirteenth century, Dante da Maiano wrote some of his poems in Provençal, while Brunetto Latini wrote most of his works in French (these modern terms will be used here for the clumsier, though more adequate, *langue d'oc* and *langue d'oïl*). The proximity and distance of the variations of the Romance vernaculars is highlighted especially well in a poem called *Descort plurilingue* by the Provençal troubadour Raembautz de Vaqueiras (second half of the twelfth century), which consists of six stanzas: the first five are all in different languages (Provençal, Italian, French, Gascon and Gallego), while the last one is longer, containing ten lines instead of the usual eight, and is written in all five languages: two lines each (Bec 1979:254–6). The same Raembautz has also written a bilingual *tenzone* together with a lady from Genoa, who is unable to understand his Provençal (Holmes 2000:14). This tells us simultaneously that the number of languages/dialects, on behalf of which bids for being appropriate for literary expression could – at least in theory – have been made, was quite large, and that someone astute enough would be able to use more than one of these – which, in turn, bolstered the status of the languages that were used most frequently.

Before looking at how and why it is the language of the 'new sweet style' that *De vulgari eloquentia* proposes for the candidacy of an all-Italian literary vernacular, we should have a brief look at the other half of the opposition. The book is written in Latin, which is only natural, given that it has to judge all the possible options from a neutral ground, and, after all, Latin was the language of learning.[2] But it nevertheless seems mistaken to think that Dante is arguing for the *vulgare* against Latin, as his view is usually interpreted (Fumagalli 2001:2–3; Shapiro 1990:134–5): his dichotomy is posited in quite different terms, between *vulgare* as the kind of 'speech that we accept without any kind of rules, as if from the feeding breast', and *gramatica*, a second language that has to be studied (*DVE* I i 2–3)[3]

---

[2] According to Gorni, during the first years of his exile, Dante made a conscious effort – a bid – to establish himself as an authority in the intellectual circles (2008:191); Petrocchi supposes that his positive evaluation of the Bolognese dialect as the most beautiful municipal variation of the Italian vernacular (*DVE* I xi 6) must have been meant for the university scholars living in Bologna, who constituted a large part of the primary intended audience for the treatise (2008:109).

[3] Angelo Mazzocco would have us believe this opposition contains a generally endorsed value judgement, insisting that 'Dante's notion of Latin as an artificial, secondary language, has been accepted, with few exceptions, by all the students of the *De Vulgari Eloquentia*' (1993:213), but this seems completely unwarranted. First of all, the text

– although, in Dante's world, this second language was indeed Latin for all relevant purposes. *Gramatica*, as we are told, is 'nothing else than a certain unchangeable identity of a language across different times and places' (*DVE* I ix 11). The opposition is thus, in a certain sense, proto-Saussurean: *gramatica* is *langue*, the unchangeable, fixed system of language, as opposed to *vulgare*, which is to be met only in the shape of speech, *parole*, learned and used naturally, without paying attention to rules.[4] This view also mitigates the alleged contradiction between Dante's positions in *De vulgari eloquentia* and in *Convivio* ('The Banquet'), where he states that Latin is superior to the vernacular in nobility, virtue and beauty, because it is stable, while the vernacular changes in time (I v 7–9). After all, one of Dante's goals in *De vulgari eloquentia* is precisely to establish the conditions for the *vulgare* to have its own *gramatica*, to make the two poles of the dichotomy converge.[5]

Indeed, the conclusion that Dante reaches after a careful examination of fourteen different Italian dialects is that the *vulgare* he is looking for is none of these (*DVE* I xvi 1), but a hypothetical entity which 'belongs to every city in Italy and yet to no one' (*DVE* I xvi 6). This is indeed an original claim – even if grammatical theory had been written and a living-space for the vernacular had been claimed before, *De vulgari eloquentia* is truly, as Marianne Shapiro writes, 'the first prescriptive text to advocate to the modern world the creation of a standard language' (1990:134). But it is even more than that: it is a text that claims political language-building capacity for lyrical poetry, that of the 'new sweet style'. The success of this bid makes Italy stand out among other European nations, whose standard languages, as a rule, were based on the dialects of the capitals, where they had become standardized in official documents and regulations that were subsequently dispersed over the territories under their rule and adopted as models for local official discourses.

In fact, Dante's bid relies on the logic that the poets of the 'new

---

immediately points out that similar second languages exist in other cultures, such as Greek, which means that Dante is not talking about Latin in particular, but a non-spoken literary language in general; and second, that Italians have been positively noted to be better at grammar than the speakers of Provençal or French (*DVE* I x 2).

[4] Dante's comment on the Sardinian dialect is enlightening in this context: he accuses the Sardinians of 'imitating *gramatica* just like monkeys imitate people' (*DVE* I xi 7) – which surely was not the case in reality, even if the Sardinian dialect had (and still has) preserved many archaic words and forms, resemblant of Latin (Jones 1997:314).

[5] True, he never ceases to make the distinction that Latin poets are *regulati* ('regulated'), while the practice of the poets writing in the vernacular is judged according to their success in 'harmonizing' their words.

sweet style' were the new aristocracy. In his description of the history of language as such, he has already introduced us to the notion that linguistic variance is derived from differences in people's practice, because the languages that emerged after the Tower of Babel was destroyed were distributed according to the different professions of the builders (*DVE* I vii 7). It is therefore natural – and, as we are shown, also logically correct (*DVE* II i 6) – that different actions are in correlation with different kinds of speech; after all, language and human customs are contingent, acquired, not given, and therefore also amenable to change (*DVE* I ix 7–10). From here, there is only one step to conjoining the most noble of practices and the most valuable kind of language. Throughout the book, all the positive examples of linguistic usage have been taken from poetry, so when this happens, we are not really surprised. After all, Dante writes, 'what bigger power is there than the one that changes human hearts so that non-willing becomes willing and willing non-willing' (*DVE* I xvii 4), and then modestly adds that 'it does not really require proof that the servants [of the most noble version of the vernacular, i.e. poets] are more famous than kings, marquis, counts and magnates' (*DVE* I xvii 5).

De vulgari eloquentia thus takes the poetic bid of the 'new sweet style' one step further and recasts it, in retrospect, as a bid for reorganizing the Italian language into a noble, standardized vernacular – and places the poets as its practitioners at the centre of the symbolic power system this move creates.

Institutions and textuality

When we now move from the discussion of the medium of the 'new sweet style' poetry to the institutions of its distribution and preservation, the first issue to be discussed is the relation of poetry to music, on the one hand, and writing, on the other. Even a cursory look at the poetic texts indicates that they bear strong traces of orality: if reasonably close syllable-forming vowels follow each other in a verse, one at the end of one word, the other at the beginning of another, they are usually treated as one syllable, and depriving enclitics of their syllable-forming vowels is never a problem. It is thus plausible to assume that, slowly, in the process of its valorization, vernacular poetry was crossing over from mainly oral to mainly written form, being divorced from music in the process. Let me note that, by designating earlier poetry as 'mainly oral', I do not imply that it had been a part of an oral culture in the sense that Walter Ong (1988) and Jack

144

Goody (1987) have opposed to cultures with writing; something that is 'mainly oral' can be actualized, as a text, always or almost always in oral form, but preserved in written form. For example, we know that *jongleurs* used small notebooks, 'codices of small format and careless appearance, roughly written and lacking any ornamentation, that were intended to furnish the text of the poems to the performers who declaimed them and thus reserved for the use of a restricted category of professionals' (Petrucci 1995:177) – the texts preserved in such notebooks are a prime example of 'mainly oral' in the present sense. Therefore, the contradiction described by Holmes (2000:13), between the assertion that Dante was the author of the first Italian book and that there existed little books or performance collections before the time, is not real: the *Vita Nova* may well be the first Italian book destined as such for circulation and meant to be read as a book, not to be carried around by its owner as a memory aid. But a book such as the one of Monte Andrea, which he refuses to send to Terino da Castelfiorentino, because it contains poems by others than himself (Holmes 2000:82), is already a step in the direction of 'mainly written': we may well imagine that Andrea, a banker, did not write down his poems, and those of others, in a book just in order to be able to recite them when a suitable occasion arose, but rather for his own reading – even if he didn't share it with colleagues, for his own reasons.

Dante has also treated, at length, the relation of poetic forms to song and dance. Poetry, in fact, is nothing other than 'fiction composed according to rhetoric and music' (*DVE* II iv 2). But distinct forms have different relations to music and writing, which is relevant to their hierarchy. The *canzone*, he says, is superior to the *ballata* as a poetic genre because it is complete in itself, while the *ballata* requires dance accompaniment if it is to be performed in full (*DVE* II iii 5) – and to other poetic genres because it also comprises the art of music in itself (*DVE* II iii 8), which others, such as the sonnet, consequently do not.

In practice, matters may have been a little bit more complicated than that. Regardless of the high status Dante has accorded to the poetic form of *canzone*, the numerically bigger part of the poetic production of the 'new sweet style' consists of sonnets, which must mainly have circulated in writing. A large number of poems are written as letters to other poets, and this practice had an important role in the community. From Dante's own example (and that of Dante da Maiano), we know that one way for a poet to be accepted (or not) in the community was via a kind of initiation rite that entailed correspondence.

The first chapters of *Vita Nova* describe in great detail the mystical vision that befell Dante after his decisive encounter with Beatrice, ending with the poem he composed about it, which he sent to all 'faithful servants of Love', asking them to judge his vision. The poem received replies from Guido Cavalcanti, Dante da Maiano and Terino da Castelfiorentino, and, thanks to Guido's positive evaluation of his text (the response sonnet starts with 'In my opinion, you have seen all the glory'), and when Guido learnt who the author of the initial text was, the two became friends (*Vita Nova* III). In our terms, Dante had made a bid, which was endorsed by Guido, who in this case carried the symbolic authority, and therefore his approval of a younger colleague was sufficient. Dante da Maiano's response to the poem was quite different and offered medical advice against hallucinations. However, at a certain point before or after that, Dante da Maiano tried to do the same, sending out a sonnet describing his own dream, which received a more or less polite answer from his namesake, but was still left unendorsed – which is why Dante da Maiano is not to be counted among the members of the 'new sweet style' community.

An even more interesting example is another exchange between Dante Alighieri and Dante da Maiano, in which the latter appears anonymously. It may have been that, after Alighieri had gained fame in the poetic circles and Maiano had not achieved the same result, the latter endeavoured to start a conversation with Alighieri that would have gained him symbolic merit afterwards. Alighieri had, indeed, made his own successful bid anonymously and disclosed his identity only after Cavalcanti had praised him. This time, Maiano writes to Alighieri as if he were a humble beginner, which he definitely was not. Though Alighieri wonders about his identity, Maiano does not name himself even in his second poem, the reply to Alighieri's reply. The bigger part of Alighieri's second poem speaks really well of his correspondent and suggests repeatedly that he should identify himself. The topic of the discussion was what the biggest pain is that love can cause, and in his third poem Maiano asks Alighieri to prove his arguments with references to authorities. After this poem, Alighieri broke off the conversation. We don't know why – maybe he just did not think much of these advances from an anonymous stranger. In any case, this exchange shows that such practice was customary, and must have produced much more text than has been preserved. It also seems likely that poems that were 'sent out' as bids were freely circulated, and not kept as private matters. This would explain how Terino da Castelfiorentino, a much older man and not a very well-known poet, a cloth merchant by profession (Branca et al. 1956:22), came to respond to Dante's first poem – it seems difficult to imagine that Dante would himself have included Terino among the famous authors of his time.

The gradual change in the modes of distribution – which became the same as hitherto had only been used for preservation – opened up certain possibilities for poets, and again the authors of the 'new sweet style' were the ones to make most use of them, substantially enhancing their bid. It is easy to see how, in an atmosphere open to ambitions of aristocracy, texts that were orally performed but seemed semantically more dense, perhaps even cryptic, to their hearers at first, may have been those that were most eagerly sought for re-reading or even copied to others' notebooks, and thus objects of preferential circulation, as opposed to those that exhausted their charm upon first hearing. In this sense, the claim to 'science' of the 'new sweet style' was certainly an advantage.

One interesting question that remains to be treated here is the degree of life-defining capacity the poetic style had – how meaning-ful the philosophy of the 'new sweet style' had really become for its practitioners. In hindsight, literary history presents us with the figures of Cavalcanti and Dante as champions of almost suprahu-man love, but we may well doubt whether their poetic practice was, in fact, so strongly constitutive of their personalities. For example, an exchange, generally considered authentic, survives between Dante and Forese Donati, one of the leading Black Guelphs, that bears little resemblance to Dante's usual lyrics. We should note that Dante is the initiator of this exchange, in which he does not refrain from a fairly unambiguous allusion to the size of Forese's genitals and the resulting dissatisfaction of his wife. One would think that Cavalcanti, the consummate aristocrat of the mind, would not stoop to such rhyming. But he, too, wrote a sonnet *Guata, Manetto, quella scrignutuzza* ('Look, Manetto, at this hunchback'), which breaks with all rules of the 'new sweet style', ridiculing an old and ugly woman – according to Patrizia Bettella, a misogynistic text, a male textual revenge upon women, and particularly the cold and distant lady of his 'new sweet style' aesthetic (2005:34–5). But, since the lady is Guido's own construction, this accusation seems a little far-fetched. A more interesting reading, put forward by Gorni (2008:89–90), suggests that Cavalcanti may even have written this sonnet as a parody of Dante's *Tanto gentile e tanto onesta pare* ('So gentle and so honest she is like') (*Vita Nova* XXVI), mocking Dante's obsessive devotion to Beatrice, and this may even have been the reason why the relations between the two poets turned sour.

147

In any case, it seems clear that neither Dante nor Cavalcanti, nor, we may suppose, any other poet of the 'new sweet style', was completely defined by the aesthetic and the corresponding codes in their poetic practice. As Gorni writes, Dante was completely able to write 'with light cynicism and complete parodic competence', in any literary style of the day (2008:37), and it seems plausible that everybody else was capable of similar codeswitching. This, of course, is not to say that they were not sincere or serious in their main poetic practice, or that the devotional knowledge they claim to adhere to was simply the most efficient tactical ruse for achieving the position of symbolic authority. On the contrary – the diversity of their abilities, proven in practice, only underscores the importance of the choice they made by committing themselves to the 'new sweet style' aesthetic, which not only produced some of the finest European poetry of all times, but also guaranteed their city, Florence, the status of the major cultural centre in Italy, and paved the way for the Italian literary language to emerge.

Summary

As a group of result-texts, the poetry of the 'new sweet style' relies on two main groups of base-texts. On the one hand, it draws from the existing tradition of Italian poetry and the lyric of the troubadours, its predecessor, and, on the other, from philosophical texts, mainly Aristotle and his Thomist and Averroist commentators. The textual world of the 'free literates' also normally contains a sizeable portion of ancient Latin literature, both poetry and prose (some of which they knew from their studies, while familiarity with other texts – such as some works of Ovid, not a part of the school curriculum – could also be presupposed of an educated person), as well as French literature, including the *Roman de la Rose* and chivalresque novels. Those who were engaged in the legal profession were obviously conversant with legal texts, and the occasional appearance of medical terminology suggests a certain familiarity also with the science of medicine. But these latter areas were known, if at all, on the encyclopaedic level, while the lyric tradition and the newest philosophical discourses, tightly intertwined, were the basis of their thesauric knowledge. While contemporary poetry may have seemed to be subcultural knowledge to the keepers of ecclesiastic and ancient knowledges, these latter ones may in turn have seemed to some extent archival from the point of view of the urban audience. In the light of this new knowledge, the

148

poets of the school were able to re-code a lot of pre-existing poetic material, assigning new values to expressions formerly in poetic use. This practice strongly supported Dante's work in legislating the standards for high-quality poetry in the second part of *DVE*, even if his treatise, left unfinished, did not enter circulation at the time.

However, for those involved in the practice, this poetry was not an end in itself, but a manifestation of another practice, a selfless love for an idealized lady. The torments this love necessarily caused for any of its practitioners were compensated by a feeling of elevation that a member of the group must have felt, since the carriers of the practice, usually bankers and notaries in reality, considered themselves the true inheritors of the aristocratic mind. Not everyone was admitted to this aristocratic circle: a bid – for instance, a publicly circulated poem describing the state of mind of the applicant – had to be made and endorsed, so that the poet's peers could evaluate his level of understanding and the degree of poetic accomplishment. Although a significant amount of the base-texts for this practice were in Latin (notably the philosophical treatises from which much of its conceptual vocabulary was derived), the active medium used for self-expression was always the vernacular (though authors did use Latin for other purposes). The vernacular, however, was not just the local municipal dialect of Florence, but something of a more general character, including in itself poetic influences from other cities and deviating in the direction shown by high practice rather than street-talk whenever appropriate. By incorporating and adopting the repertoire of previously existing verse-forms, the 'new sweet style' also made use of the general tendency of the times – namely, the gradual movement of vernacular poetry from the mainly sung to the mainly written form, which permitted the authors to favour more sophisticated and sometimes obscure expressions that solicited commentaries from others, just as philosophical or theological writing had done before. The school did not crystallize into a spatially located institution – instead, by virtue of its reliance on written text, it existed as a spread-out virtual network that, when the need came, was able to unite exiles living in various cities. In that, too, the 'new sweet style' was a forerunner of future cultural practice.

If we were to assess why such a successful bid as the 'new sweet style' did not remain in the position of symbolic authority, then we would have to point to both historical contingencies and deeper structural reasons. Cavalcanti's early death and the exile of Dante must have contributed to its wavering position in the beginning of the fourteenth century, as well as the rather small group of its members, but, even more, I suppose, the changes in society and culture at large made the cognitive adequacy of the 'knowledge' appear lacking. Petrarch's worldview has inherited a large part of the devotional character of Dante's worldview, but rejects its re-codification of the poetic language as insufficient. As a result, it is Petrarch and not the 'new sweet style' poets who lays the fundament of new European poetry – something, however, that he could hardly have done without the legacy of such predecessors.

— 6 —

CASE STUDY II:
ART AND POLITICS
IN EASTERN EUROPE IN THE 1990S

When we look at the theoretical reflections on the transition from ideologically regulated cultural systems to democratic and market-dominated social configurations in Eastern Europe, we find that many authors point out an inner tension between the observer and the observed. Boris Groys, for example, has stated that Western cultural studies discourses are incapable of adequately evaluating the process because of their own structural shortcomings (2008:149–51), while Piotr Piotrowski considers the relative absence of such reflections to be a part of an imperialist project that attempts to integrate East European art into the 'normal' narrative of Western art, glossing over its differences from the mainstream (2009:11–14). At present, when a large part of Eastern Europe has been integrated into the political and economic structures of the West, we have to ask whether indeed there exists, or has existed, an Eastern Europe that could be meaningfully analysed as a whole, or whether each of the countries in the region should be treated separately (Raud 2012:206–8). But, nonetheless, both the problems that each of these cultural communities had to solve and the opportunities presented to them have only, recently, been remarkably similar. In all these countries, the traditional system of circulation of art was reorganized with the breakdown of the ideologically controlled official art institutions and the emergence of new, independent galleries and exhibition spaces. The change in art politics was almost everywhere accompanied by an intense debate on the limits of artistic expression, opposing radical forms of contemporary art to national conservatism, both of which had been suppressed by the former system. Unlikely alliances emerged, and the bidding space was fragmented along aesthetic as well as political lines as a result. The situation was further complicated by the intense

151

economic competition, as Western art collectors and buyers, as well as curators, appeared on the scene with promises of fame and/or material prosperity. As a result, the period witnessed two simultaneous transformation processes – the ideological/aesthetic change that took place in the textuality of art, and a decentralizing change in its practices – that mutually complemented each other and resulted in a radical reorganization of the artistic field. Both these processes were naturally linked to the broader changes in the social, cultural and economic environment, but it should be noted that these links were not unambiguous: support for social change did not always entail support for the changes in the field of art, and vice versa.

All of this coincided with a wave of change also in Western art, where, precisely in the late 1980s, a paradigm change had occurred as a result of new technologies becoming readily available and offering artists 'radically new capabilities now of creating work that has no referent in a non-digital world; indeed, that has no referent in the three-dimensional world as we know it' (Rush 2005:181). That said, it is nonetheless obvious that digital art in the West did not by itself displace the meta-rules that governed the process of artistic change, while for East European artists the new forms of art were something hitherto unconnected with any artistic practice, including most subversive and dissident art.

For a relatively brief period – that is, the late 1980s and most of the 1990s – the meta-rules governing the art world of Eastern European countries were all suspended and a great number of bids for recreating it on new terms were launched simultaneously. Since that time, the artistic development of these countries has quite expectedly adopted the practices, and been integrated into the textualities, of Western contemporary art in general. During that period, however, the profound changes in the social and cultural situation made artists as well as their audiences all over the area constantly question not only the legitimacy of the institutions and the adequacy of artistic languages, but also the very nature of artistic practices of the past, present and future. The carriers of artistic practices – both producers and recipients – were thoroughly transformed in the process, as were the cultural roles of the practice. All of this merits more attention, not just as an episode of recent art history, but also as a prime example of cultural paradigm change.

The institutions

It is appropriate to begin with the institutions controlling the circulation of art in society, since it is there that the change was made possible. Most authors who write about the topic bring out the dichotomy between the ideological control of the Communist Party and the alternative scene in which independent intellectuals moved, *samizdat* publications circulated, and art events were organized as well. However, the picture was much more complicated than that. First of all, the control mechanisms of the party were more sophisticated than a simple balance of rewards and punishments. Of course, in order to organize an exhibition in a public space one had to apply for permission, and the more prestigious the space, the more thorough the instances of control. A personal exhibition in an official exhibition hall usually meant that a few works were bought by the state, which ensured the artist's livelihood. Several previous appearances in official group exhibitions were a prerequisite for getting there. But most public exhibition halls were booked, and group exhibitions were organized, through appropriate organizations (for instance, the Artists' Union) and allocated by committees and boards, consisting mostly of artists and art professionals.

Thus, formally, a large part of the control over their activities was exercised by the artists themselves. Understandably, these had to be artists who were trusted by those in power to make the expected judgements, so they had to be dependent on the benevolence of the ideologues – possibly advanced beyond the standing their abilities would otherwise grant them, or complicit in dirty arrangements, or otherwise well connected and therefore interested in the well-being of the system. However, especially towards its end, the system was not completely indifferent to its own legitimacy. If possible, it would have preferred to have been taken seriously by artists who were admired by the wider public. Thus, the official organizations for creative intellectuals needed to have at least some symbolic authority as well, and anti-liberal actions did not produce any of that. Finally, not all of the regime's art officials were motivated in their work by ideological zeal. On the contrary – quite a few of them were well educated and not necessarily supporters of the political system, which they considered to be just an inevitable evil.

In addition to the ideological and symbolic capitals that the artists and art officials needed, and, of course, money, there was a fourth kind of capital in circulation, which may sometimes have been of the most decisive importance. For lack of a better term, I will call it 'relational'.

Each successful Eastern-bloc citizen had to be involved in a large and sophisticated net of relations, acquaintances, schoolmates, neighbours, etc., who were in a position to deliver to each other everything needed in life, from signatures on applications or theatre tickets to scarce consumer goods or introductions to competent dentists. One could also acquire relational capital by marital ties and sexual relations. It differs from 'social capital', defined by Robert Putnam as 'features of social organization, such as trust, norms, and networks, that can improve the efficiency of society by facilitating coordinated actions' (1994: 167) in that relational capital substitutes and bypasses publicly endorsed procedures and institutions and produces corruption, or at least what would count as corruption in a democratic society.

Art officials were obviously able to capitalize on their position, being able to prefer one artist over another in the coordination of events, prize juries, or mediating exposure to the press, including visiting Western journalists. Artists whom they treated favourably had to respond in kind. An artist returning from abroad was expected to bring a present to the art official who had facilitated the trip. But symbolic respect was also expected from them, and given. We should note that the two categories of artists that have been historically foregrounded – the loyal servants of the state, and the dissidents – actually formed a small minority,[1] while the majority of artists were not politically engaged – that is, neither ideologically committed to the system nor openly opposed to it. The picture was thus not black and white, but rather a gradient of positions, and some artists may have glided in either direction on it during the span of their career.[2] What some of these artists produced was well in line with the bleak times – 'sober modernism', as Ješa Denegri has called it: art that was unpolitical in content, unprovocative in form, and therefore considered suitable by the system (Šuvaković 2003:93). But by the very act of removing themselves from the political divide, many artists viewed themselves as politically not complicit with the system. Others, called semi-nonconformists by Alfonsas Andriuškevičius (2001:28), considered themselves to be at the forefront of the cultural struggle and constantly tested the limits of what was allowed, yet most of the time remaining in the safe area.

---

[1] Skaidra Trilupaityte has also pointed out that, in many cases, the reputation of leading artists has been based on 'retrospective assignation of the artistic legacy of morally "superior" qualities of dissent' (2007:262).

[2] For example, Paul Sjeklocha and Igor Mead discuss the work of Ilya Glazunov among the 'unofficial' artists (1967:144–5). Glazunov later became a People's Artist of the USSR, a title that could only be bestowed for services rendered to the system.

Thus, while it was impossible to convert ideological capital into symbolic – these two were counterproductive of each other – it was feasible to exchange some of either into relational capital, and then convert it into the other. It was in the nature of relational capital to be fluid and multiple; everybody needed relations of more than one kind, because otherwise the capital would be unproductive. Relational capital could also not be directly acquired for money – because that was not a very effective medium of exchange – or for any other form of material wealth. The oft-quoted Russian proverb 'You may not have a hundred roubles, but you should have a hundred friends' sums up the essence of relational capital very adequately.

The channels for converting ideological or symbolic capital into money were also limited in type and number. In addition to the state purchases from exhibitions and occasional commissions (which were limited to artists who had sufficient relational capital, and whose ideological balance was not negative), there were official art salons, where recognized artists could bring their work for sale. But here, symbolic capital was already the kind that counted: hardly anybody would purchase any art simply because it was ideologically correct. The direct sales deals between artists and buyers, however, were more dependent on relational capital. Whoever brought a buyer to an artist was owed by the artist, but this was in most cases not a service to be bought. The authorities did not encourage such activities, but neither did they actively prosecute the artists or their friends for it. A medium-sized painting by a recognized artist would have cost somewhere around 3–5 average monthly salaries, so moderately successful painters producing 7–10 paintings a year could live quite comfortably, although they would also have to sell some of their work occasionally through official salons to avoid questions about their livelihood. It is difficult to generalize over the whole cultural area, but in quite a few places it was typical for a middle-class family to own a few paintings or engravings and to exhibit them on their living-room walls, or to have a small sculpture on a shelf. Explicitly political pictures (both for and against the ruling ideology) were obviously not suitable for that role.

This network of institutions, stretched between the two poles of party control and active dissent, joined together by a flexible balance of ideological, symbolic, financial and relational capitals, and linked at various points to conversion mechanisms of one capital into another, was thrown into a complete chaos when the political and economic basis of the totalitarian states faltered, the mechanisms of ideological control became irrelevant and the relations between individual positions in the art world were radically reshuffled.[3] Especially when travel to the West became possible, but means for it were not sufficient, art became an important medium of exchange, because a lot of it was exportable. Also, more and more businesspeople and collectors from the West began to move around in the local art markets and upset them with their purchasing power.

The official salons with controlled prices were, of course, unable to continue as usual under the circumstances, especially when private galleries started to appear. Most of these were short-lived affairs with unrealistic business plans, started by people who had little or no understanding of the art trade and few had the intuitive talent of Gerd Harry Lybke, whose Eigen+Art soon developed into a major player, successfully representing its artists at major art events in the UK (Gleadell 2003:43) and America (Hasegawa 2002). Most of the gallerists, however, had imagined that now that the buying and selling of art works was no longer controlled by the ideological institutions, a bustling art market would emerge and bring huge profits – what they did not realize was that more things had become available for those who had money. The general spirit of the age was, moreover, that all cultural activities now had to bend to the laws of economy, just like any other form of production.

But the economy was just one side of the coin. Another – and for the actual practice of arts, a much more important – change was the replacement of art officials with curators. In many countries, this phenomenon is associated with the establishment of Contemporary Art Centres by the Soros (later Open Society) Foundation inaugurated by the Hungarian-born billionaire philanthropist George Soros. The involvement of Soros in East European social transition was a factor of paramount importance for the development of civil society, and projects financed by him reached into virtually every sphere of life in most East European countries, and were usually welcomed as support for the values these societies had now committed to, but had difficulties in implementing. The role of Soros in the transformation of the art world, however, was a source of some controversy.

Between 1992 and 1999, Soros funded the establishment of twenty centres in seventeen countries, 'with a mission to support the development and international exposure of contemporary art' (SCCA 1998),

---

[3] It is revealing in this context to observe how a pro-*perestroika* Soviet education official has evaluated the situation: first, he notes that other '-isms', such as consumerism, now have a legitimate position beside Leninism, and then concludes that, under the circumstances, the government must now face the task of creating a new, post-communist mentality for the people (Nikandrov 1995:48).

which initially had to abide by a very detailed and much-criticized book of rules in their operation (Czegledy and Szekeres 2009:254). Evidently, Soros and his collaborators in the headquarters of his foundation network were afraid that, should the local management be allowed more rope, the local cultural circumstances would start to affect its actions, and it would deviate from the prescribed course. And the managers of these centres had indeed been presented with a difficult task. The centres had considerable means at their disposal, but these were not used for the support of the artistic practices and artists that were considered central in the local art world. On the contrary – the standards of what constituted 'art' in the first place were radically revised, with the threshold of acceptability placed on a new level (or lowered, in the opinion of many older artists). A lot of support was given to artists engaged in forms of art hitherto considered 'alternative' and not really 'serious', such as digital and video art, or installations. Moreover, support was available on a competitive basis, and established artists had to consent to being treated on a par with relative beginners, sometimes losing out to them. And, what was most important, the paradigm of decision-making did not consider art to be the free and unregulated self-expression of the creative genius that had been the assumption behind all varieties of opposition to the totalitarian regime, but often wanted to bend it to the curatorial will.

The art curators of Eastern Europe did not form a homogeneous group. Some, such as the leading Russian curator Viktor Misiano, one of the founders of the Manifesta Biennial, had been art professionals employed by official organizations even before the collapse of the old regime. Others, such as the Polish curator and art theorist Aneta Szylak, had been active on the independent, or underground, art scene. Yet others were simply too young to have previously been active anywhere. But, compared to the regular artist, all the curators were more fluent in the theoretical idioms that were now used to articulate symbolic authority – in a certain way, these idioms had replaced the ideological vocabulary of the past, and they lent themselves similarly to the task of describing works of art in the necessary regimes of signification, making claims for them to be the expressions of certain collective experiences or shared ideas. Allan Siegel has characterized the new situation as 'the beginning of a mostly constructive interdependence of artists, on the one hand, and curatorial practice, on the other', adding that 'it would be a mistake to view this mature interdependence as simply a by-product of increased access to and mobility within the Western art world (although these are certainly factors); rather, it represents a series of reformulations, discoveries, and new critical perspectives' (2010). An immoral interdependence between the communist art official and the artist, based on relational capital, was transformed into a more businesslike interdependence between the curator and the artist, based on privileged knowledge: the writings of the curators were instrumental in enhancing the status of the artist, and, naturally, curators could not achieve their standing without the artists providing them with works to write about. Sometimes this relation was based on a sincere mutual understanding, but sometimes not necessarily. For example, Tanja Ostojić, a Serbian performance artist, has strongly problematized this relationship in her 2001 performance 'I'll be your angel', which consisted in following the once-radical curator Harald Szeemann around for days and smiling sheepishly at him – and being excluded from his projects as a result (Milevska 2005).

Indeed, since the curatorial languages were at least initially new and foreign to most of the artists, they were not always comfortable with them. When Igor Zabel was asked to comment on his work as a curator for Manifesta 3 in Ljubljana, he pointed out that there were hidden fears out there in the Slovenian art world, 'especially regarding the relationship of a relatively small culture . . . to the global art system' and that attempts had been made to 'analyze contemporary art as a system of institutions, capital and power' (Cassel et al. 2000:21) – in other words, even at that time curatorial practice of contemporary art still provoked resistance from the artists, which could not be ignored.

The carriers

By and large we can identify two main groups and three positions among the artists of post-liberation Eastern Europe: the groups of those who had and those who had not yet established any kind of relationship to the communist regime – I will call them 'old' and 'new' respectively, even if some of the representatives of both groups were of the same age – and the positions of globalism, tribalism and mercantilism. The artists of the older generation who had clearly identified themselves with the regime were marginalized in most places, sometimes carrying on in the tradition of 'sober realism', sometimes retiring completely.

The difference between 'globalists' and 'tribalists' follows here the distinction made by Achille Bonito Oliva between 'diaspora' and 'tribalism'. Diaspora, in Oliva's view, is a condition of nomadism that always implies 'a complexity of multiple references ... designed against the spectacular simplification of images', is able to 'absorb ... the spurious diversity of differentiated languages', and tenaciously keeps the artist 'away from the temptation of an easy tribal call' (2008:45). Oliva is here primarily referring to the conditions of artists who have chosen, or been forced, to live and work outside of their own cultural context, but the distinction is also equally valid for those who have stayed in their traditional environment. Thus, Sándor Pinczehelyi, who never left his provincial home town of Pécs in Hungary, or Erik Bulatov, who stayed in Moscow, nonetheless worked very much as diasporic artists.

Tribalism, in Oliva's view, is the negative opposite of the diasporic condition – the 'frequently reactionary and regressive response [to globalism], the rebirth of nationalisms and integralisms, and a new value attributed to stability' (2008:43). In this sense, tribalism implies the reduction of the multiplicity of artistic codes to one, overarching regime of signification, which is usually that of a national tradition. This is very much the effect that nationalisms have produced in many East European countries. However, tribalist rhetoric was in many cases also the only one readily available and generally understandable that could be deployed against the advance of consumerism and capitalist ideological constructs.

The 'mercantilist' position is here understood as market opportunism – the production of art that was, either really or supposedly, of interest to wealthy buyers, either Westerners or the local new rich. While the globalists and the tribalists can in most contexts be identified by the kind of artistic language they use or the way they treat their subject matter, there is no single mercantilist style, and mercantilists can adopt the techniques typical of either of the other positions, or even pose as their representatives, if they feel that this leads to material wealth. In fact, the tendency of mercantilists to gravitate towards one of the other positions[4] may have proved decisive in their acquisition of critical mass for self-legitimation. After the polarization of East European societies and the appearance of noteworthy local buyers, as well as the emergence and stabilization of domestic art markets, mercantilist styles have also crystallized into a separate category, represented by such artists as Nikas Safronov and Sergei

---

[4] For example, Boris Groys notes that many artists with 'globalist' aspirations turned to 'tribalist' artistic language when they understood that this was more appealing for Western collectors, because 'only the Soviet artist who could come to see his or her own land and its history with the eyes of an international tourist would be able to make something that could, potentially, be exported' (Groys 2003:60).

Zagraevsky in Russia, who produce kitsch ridiculed by critics but are nonetheless highly appreciated by a new rich clientele. The position they have adopted is comparable to that of the ideological artist under the Soviet system. But this only happened gradually, when the entire cultural situation changed and became paradigmatically closer to the Western art market system.

The 'old' globalists included those nonconformists and a fraction of the semi-nonconformists who had been promoting new and officially shunned, 'Western' styles of artistic practice already during the old regime. Depending on the country, they may have been completely banned from the official scene or enjoyed a certain status due to their symbolic capital. The 'old' tribalists of many countries had been in opposition previously too, and also counted the victory over the old regime as theirs. The category of 'old' mercantilists is less clearly identifiable and consists of minor artists of the older generation who had earned their keep with decorative works. The 'new' globalists, however, were those artists of the younger generation who endorsed the new standards for art and opposed themselves to the art of the past and any new production of the 'old' group at the same time. There were also 'new' tribalists, artists who picked up the national or folk art traditions and carried them on. And the 'new' mercantilists came in various guises, including imitation of globalism and tribalism, but also as producers of souvenir art and designers of commercials, which, as a 'new' profession, was not frowned upon as selling-out. In fact, it is difficult to draw a clear border between the three positions, because there was a certain overlap between them all. For example, a mercantilist bid for a non-mercantilist position had fair chances of success, if the bidder was talented enough or bold enough. So Gediminas Urbonas, a leading Lithuanian media artist, has declared in an interview that, had the old regime continued, he would have had no problems in producing sculptures of Lenin or other financially rewarding forms of art, and that he opted for new styles because he felt a change in the market (Urbonas and Urbonas 2010:42–3).

The existence or absence of contacts with the old regime was not the only thing that separated the groups of 'old' and 'new' artists. The 'old' artists of all varieties had usually had a high level of professional education in the art academies of the Eastern bloc, which prepared them very thoroughly in the technical aspects of their chosen kind of art, and also trained them well in drawing, composition and other aspects of traditional artistic work. They had not travelled very much, or possibly in groups of 'cultural workers' under the tight supervision of some art official. They usually did not speak foreign languages very well, nor were they able to read in them. They were not necessarily reluctant to discuss their own work, but neither were they very good at it. However, they were usually active socializers. In some cities, there had been closed clubs reserved for artists and intellectuals only – for example, restaurants that operated in the buildings of Artists' Unions. Quite a few among them, especially men, had regular drinking and less regular sleeping habits, and messy family lives. This lifestyle, as Boris Groys writes, was something that had been secretly envied by 'normal' citizens even under the old regime (2003:55). But the status of these artists had now risen, and accordingly also their respectability, while the adoption of neckties and other signs of 'usual' respectability was not expected of them: their artist-like appearance was taken as a manifestation of their inner freedom, through which they were even somehow more directly connected to the 'free world' of the West than were average citizens.

Quite a few of the 'new' artists took over and developed the same kind of lifestyle – for instance, by adding drugs (or at least a liberal attitude towards them) to alcohol in their transgressions. It is possible that, for some of them, it was precisely this lifestyle that made the position of the artist attractive in the first place. We should remember that it was around this time that 'lifestyle' entered public discourse as a marketing technique, as a result of the change in Western society that Zygmunt Bauman has characterized as a switch from self-realization through work to self-realization through consumption (1988:71–5). But, in most other respects, the 'new' artists differed radically from the 'old' ones. First and foremost, they had quickly picked up the knowledge that was needed for being successful under the changed circumstances. They were usually fluent in English or German, and took an active interest in the development of Western art. They were better at writing project applications and planning budgets. They also often managed to establish links to the new businesses and to solicit them as sponsors. They took every opportunity to travel, and to observe the behaviour and habits of Western colleagues. They quickly became aware of the need for self-presentation of both their artistic practice and artistic personality. Some of them mastered the curatorial idioms quite well themselves; others developed a relationship with the emerging curators and depended on them for the explanation of their works. But their professional skills were different in kind. 'Even after the great political and cultural changes of 1989', Charles Esche writes, 'when the Berlin Wall fell and Communism collapsed in Eastern Europe, contemporary art has continued to build

161

on its Western traditions. Arguably, skills in craft manufacture were then replaced by learned sociability and the comprehension of certain codes of behavior, though this switch was never made explicit in most academic curricula' (2009:103). In most art academies of the Eastern bloc, certain changes indeed took place, the emphasis moving away from the skills required to produce traditional art to practices fostering independence and originality – thus, many of the 'new' artists were incapable of realistic drawing, for example. But quite a lot of them compensated for this lack with technological skills that were beyond the capabilities of the 'old' artists, who remained much more comfortable with doing things directly with their hands rather than image-manipulation software. For the transformed standards of art, however, this was often not good enough.

Since, at least initially, the academies were not able to provide the aspiring artists with such skills, they lost a lot of their symbolic prestige, and it was also possible to become a recognized and successful artist without any formal professional training. One reason for this is that the art academies had been extremely selective of their student candidates in the past, and very difficult to enrol in, requiring a display of elementary traditional artistic skills from the candidates. Such a policy had significantly enhanced the symbolic capital of the artistic profession (which was inconceivable without the appropriate credentials), but now it started to backfire, because those very skills the academies depended upon were no longer perceived as strictly necessary for entering the field. Since the ideological control was lifted from the distribution of exhibition spaces, but the decision-making mechanisms remained largely the same (committees consisting of artists and art professionals), the revolutionized institutions were threatened with a loss of credibility: if they continued to recognize only artists who were typologically similar to 'old' artists, they could have undermined their own status. There was, of course, no real threat that the academies would be rendered obsolete or the official public exhibition spaces would have remained empty, but in an era in which traditional institutions were crumbling, even a small loss of symbolic balance was perceived as an existential threat, which inspired the new decision-makers to support reforms, and, in the sphere of art, tribalists were remarkably less successful in making reforming bids. The situation, of course, varied from country to country: in Prague, the Academy of Fine Arts was boldly and forcefully reformed under the leadership of Milan Knížák, formerly a leading figure in the Czech and international underground, while, for instance, in Budapest, the leadership of the academy might have remained content with the status quo, but was forced to revise the curricula and invite new professors by the discontent of the students.

Textuality, codes and languages

There were three separate layers of base-texts influencing the work of the artists during this period of transition: Western art (which included in most countries also their own pre-World War II heritage), the local folk tradition, and, last but not least, the communist aesthetic that had its roots in the Russian proletarian avant-garde of the 1920s, but had later crystallized into 'socialist realism' by domesticating classical Western styles and combining them with strong ideological symbolism. All of these could be identified with, or opposed – a certain kind of ironic overidentification being a variant of the latter.

Boris Groys has asserted that all the local traditions of postsocialist nations have been invented: 'the only real heritage of today's post-Communist subject – its real place of origin – is the complete destruction of every kind of heritage, a radical, absolute break with the historical past and with any kind of distinct cultural identity' (Groys 2008:155). But Groys writes from the position of a former educated Muscovite, and what he says may indeed be an adequate characterization of the metropolitan Soviet subject. For most of the cultures and societies under communist regimes, however, this is an oversimplification, and even in Russia the break with the past was not necessarily as total as Groys writes. The ethno-folkloric had been domesticated by the regime, albeit in an emasculated form, which excluded all 'vulgar' and religious elements. The alliance of ethnic kitsch and the communist system, as it has been classically described by Milan Kundera in his novel *The Joke* (1982), offered a surrogate identity to the people, something that corresponded to the first half of the definition – attributed to Stalin – of Soviet culture: 'national in form, socialist in content'. Flat assertions of ethnic cultural multiplicity, called 'governmental ethnic folklorism' by Dina Roginsky (2007:56–7), were constantly on display, but without implying any substantial difference between different backgrounds: for example, the shows by Igor Moiseev's celebrated dance troupe usually included adapted or invented folk dances of various types of national minorities, performed by Russian dancers, presenting to the audience 'a happy, contented family of nations, proud of their political order and mass culture' (Šmidchens 1999:57–8). However, the legitimacy of folklore as the authentic art of the people also provided a loophole for

163

practices of what we could call resistant folklorism, which included youth movements for collecting and protecting old objects, learning folkloric practices directly from their carriers and resurrecting them in cultural expression that clearly separated the ethnic from the official political discourses, thus helping to restore national identity and link it to the tradition interrupted by the intervention of communist ideology (Taylor 2008). Mostly defensive or celebratory, such practices belonged to relaxed counterculture, but they could, of course, help to confirm and maintain tribalist preferences, or even their participants' potentially nationalist predilections.

One particular segment of this tradition was the heritage of religious art, suppressed under the regime and rehabilitated after its fall. Religion itself had made a spectacular comeback in most areas of Eastern Europe – in some places due to its role in the liberation movement, elsewhere because of the confusion that quick social change had brought along. Even in the most secular societies there was a wave of religious self-identification, and many politicians used religious phraseology to bolster their agendas (Blagojevic 2008; Clarke and Reid 2007; Washburn 2008). This naturally created a market for art with religious connotations, and institutions to handle its dissemination. For example, since the early 1990s, the annual Forfest festival of spiritual art and music has been organized, with state support, in Kroměříž (the Czech Republic), and contemporary art has been featured prominently in the Archiepiscopal Museum of Sacral Art, called the Museum of Contemporary Spiritual Art by Elkins (2004:126), in Lublin. Possibly the strongest group to identify with the religious legacy was Neo-Byzantinism in Romania, which used the visual styles of Orthodox iconography, but was nonetheless perceived to be a carrier of artistic innovation:

> The movement was often seen as an existential alternative to the totalitarian regime and the series of exhibitions of the neo-byzantine group was interpreted at that time as a form of taking, silently, a political attitude. Even though for an outsider's point of view this trend can seem rather obsolete, neo-traditionalist and excessively oriented towards the past, the younger generation regarded it as 'avant-garde' or revolutionary. (Mocanescu 2002:14)

However, in most parts of Eastern Europe, religious symbolism did not evolve into a major cluster of base-texts. Martin Jay writes, of the 'old' nonconformist artists, that although 'at times they did revisit and reappropriate older cultural values and symbols, some nationalist, others religious, they did so without any naive belief in

164

the desirability of their resurrection' (2003:xvii), and for the most part it can be said that this attitude persisted, even when religious imagery started to carry a certain mercantilist appeal. It is possibly the churches themselves that, in their excessive desire to dominate over all forms of religious discourse, discouraged independent artistic expression of religious feelings. Particularly in Poland, the Catholic Church has alienated free-thinking individuals, including artists, who have found its spiritual dictate oppressive (Piotrowski 2009:397). Women artists have especially radically rejected the domination of the Church, which wants to subjugate them to traditional gender roles. Some of them have confronted such attitudes with forceful imagery, blending Catholic symbolism with explicit representations of the female body (Bohme 1998). In more recent years, the hostility between the Church and the art world has even led to direct confrontations, as, for example, during the events related to the 'Caution Religion' exhibition in Moscow (2004), whose participants were accused of provoking religious hatred, so that the leadership of the Moscow Union of Artists even proposed that contemporary artists be prohibited from using religious symbolism in their works (Akinsha 2005:87–9).

Another segment of the national tradition that needs to be pointed out separately is the historical one. The fall of the old regime brought with it, if only for a time, the liberation of memory – the ideological narrative of the past that had foregrounded anything conducive to the supposed triumph of communism was disbanded and a multiplicity took its place. Soon enough, a national history was constructed out of its elements, but, for the time being, stories of both pride and suffering entered circulation in various forms. This includes not only more recent events, such as the uprisings of Hungary in 1956 and Czechoslovakia in 1968 or the mass deportations of civilians from the Baltics in 1941 and 1949, but also older history, which had been reshaped in communist history books to downplay the local tradition and make Russia appear in a more favourable light. Even in East Germany, the official view of Nazi concentration camps had depicted them as sites for the killing of communists, while the Holocaust and the suffering of the Jews had been downgraded, and this had also been reflected in artistic representation (Mesch 2008:35). All these issues, energetically debated in public, were also reflected in artistic representation, including the work of artists who had no tribalist agendas. For example, one of the most prominent works of the Lithuanian surrealist painter Šarūnas Sauka is the diptych (1987) on the battle of Grünwald, a defeat inflicted on the German crusaders by the joint forces of Lithuania and Poland in 1410, in which the leading role had been assigned to a division of Russian warriors by Soviet historiography, but was reclaimed by the Lithuanians after liberation. This painting used the codes of the avant-garde, but articulated a narrative that belonged to the traditionalist domain. Occasionally, the all-too-contemporary artistic expression of such works even constituted an obstacle to their reception – thus, it is reported that the exhibition 'Where is your brother Abel?' (1995), which commemorated the fiftieth anniversary of the end of World War II with works by some of the most outstanding Polish contemporary artists, such as Mirosław Bałka, had a rather lukewarm reception, ostensibly because there were only a few directly representational works able to engage the audience (Weikersthal 2006:472–3).

After some time, however, a polarization took place that cut through generations and separated the 'globalists' from the 'tribalists'. The question of identity was no longer innocent: what had been a positive self-definition in earlier years, could now be perceived as an aggressive self-assertion, while the initial positive identity had detached itself from the national and become more cosmopolitan (and simultaneously individual). A symbolic example of this change is Romanian artist Dan Perjovschi's tattoo: in 1993, he had the word 'Romania' tattooed on his arm, but, ten years later, in 2003, he had the tattoo removed, with the comment that now Romania 'spread itself so as it is no longer visible' (Fowkes and Fowkes 2010). There were others, however, who did not share such cosmopolitanism. This had to do with the social reaction to rapid cultural change, which was perceived by many to be too quick and dangerous for the survival of indigenous traditions: a typologically expectable phase in the process of socio-cultural reorganization. Artists who endorsed such attitudes associated themselves with clearly tribalist projects, which Miško Šuvaković has labelled Nationalist Realism – that is,

> art that employs traditional means of expression and representation such as figurative painting, landscape painting, monumental sculpture, and the architecture of national styles in order to restore styles from the past ... and to reactivate them as strategies of anti-Communist, antimodernist, and anti-Western art. (2003:94–5)

But the same base-texts could also be treated with a twist, or with overidentification, as, for example, in the case of Luchezar Boyadjiev from Bulgaria, whose series 'The Fortification of Faith' (1991) depicts Jesus in traditional Orthodox iconographic style, but together with an identical twin (Piotrowski 2009:410–11). The style of these paint-

166

ings is such that, to an outsider, the difference between his work and a sincerely produced icon is not immediately visible: Boyadjiev has not broken the first-level rules of devotional painting, but he has introduced an incompatible meta-rule from postmodernist practice, which allows him to manipulate the images to express his attitude towards what they stand for.

It seems that artists could allow themselves many more liberties with the second main layer of artistic base-texts, that is, contemporaneous Western art, which was introduced, studied and imitated. But these liberties were superficial: if, here, the first-level rules could easily be broken – or were even meant to be broken – the second-level rules were upheld much more strictly, and failing to observe them could disqualify an artist's bid. There are historical overviews of the art of the period that disavow Western-type postmodernism as uninteresting and unoriginal; others see in it mainly a rebuke to tribalist bids (Šuvaković 2003:95). We might add that such postmodernism may also have seemed a promising strategy for those mercantilists who wanted to appeal to turncoat art officials.[5] But there is no denying that the influence of Western postmodernism has also inspired some very fine work, which should in no way be overshadowed by the overtly political. This is probably because the tension between the base-texts and result-texts, created by the very different social and economic circumstances of the East European artists, made meaningful signification much more complicated. After all, Linda Hutcheon's observation that Western postmodern artists had to combine 'critique and complicity' in their world (1989:138–40) was so much more true of their East European counterparts, in whose world the conflict between the many incompatible codes was much more intense and multi-dimensional. An empty bottle of Coca-Cola integrated into an installation of a Western artist was a trivial object from daily life hinting at the banality of consumerism, but in Eastern Europe it was additionally a symbol of the new becoming, a sign of freedom, an object of political desire – a metonymic representation of the now-available consumer goods coveted not only by the masses, but also by the artists themselves. At the same time, the artist was not only well aware of the meta-rules that ordered her to be cool and ironical about her attitude towards the Coca-Cola bottle in order to remain an artist, but also quite conscious of the social situation that would

---

[5] In an interview with John Bowlt, his former student, the Russian art historian Dmitri Sarabyanov has remarked that 'the Ministry of Culture is still alive and well and observes what we're doing, even though it now favors the very extreme artists, whose more moderate colleagues are not very happy about this' (Bowlt and Sarabyanov 2002:86).

unmask such an attitude, if it were openly presented, as ridiculous and hypocritical. The result of all these tensions was work such as Mart Viljus's installation *TM* (1996), a mixed-up reality of products on the shelves of a supermarket that offer us 'Pedigree Pal' cornflakes, 'Ariel' lemonade, 'Snickers' canned fish, 'Coke' for cleaning the toilet and so on.

Before the polarization of the art field, the artists thus oscillated between the two extremes of self-as-past and self-as-imitation and had to define for themselves a location on the imaginary gradient that connected them. The dark side of globalism sometimes presented itself to them with unexpected brutality: Ene-Liis Semper, a renowned Estonian video and performance artist, once told me that, during a conversation about a forthcoming exhibition, the curator showed her a catalogue of a Western art event, pointed to a work and asked her if she could do 'this' for him. She declined, but the incident shows clearly how the character of originality, in the postmodern context, has been transformed from the unique authorship of an innovative work or idea to the role of the 'authorized importer', the first person to have reproduced a practice in the local situation. This also opens up the practice of postmodern art to the mercantilist.

The third and undoubtedly the most distinctive class of base-texts for the East European art of the period is the ideologically charged 'socialist' aesthetic. Bernhard Giesen has emphasized how the subversion of commonly accepted symbolic codes was a characteristic feature of the new paradigm of art that emerged in the West from the 1960s (Giesen 2006a:317), but in the case of Eastern Europe, the semiotic of subversion carried additional overtones. Evgeni Dobrenko has analysed the nature of visual representation in late communist societies and come to the conclusion that 'Socialist Realism's basic function was not propaganda, however, but rather to *produce reality by aestheticizing it*; it was the ultimate radical aesthetic practice . . . Soviet society was precisely and above all a society of consumption: *ideological* consumption. *Socialist Realism was a machine for transforming Soviet reality into socialism*' (2004:700, italics in the original). The 'socialist realism' in question reached far beyond artistic practice: it included also the codal systems used in the media, education, even the official discourses used in workplaces for reporting and planning. Needless to say, it had no cognitive adequacy whatsoever. As long as it operated in the capacity of a utopian discourse, pretending to talk about the future, it could have some seductive power; as soon as it claimed to speak about the present reality, it failed, because it was simply unable to signify believably. Péter György has called this codal regime 'sincere cynicism': nobody was expected to believe in the discourse, but everyone was expected to behave according to the rules of the game (2003:179). But this was not only the attitude of the enlightened few. It is difficult to agree with the view of some theorists, such as Epstein, that the visual propaganda system performed without fail, 'triggering in every citizen a feeling of his or her ineradicable "Sovietness"' (1999:313). Although this was what the system itself may have claimed, its power of producing active self-identification was very limited, except perhaps for among the older generation. It seems much more plausible that the majority of the inhabitants of the Eastern bloc were able to navigate through their semiospheres so that most 'socialist realist' signification remained, for them, unseen – 'to unsee' is, in this sentence, a transitive verb used in the sense China Miéville has given to it in his novel *The City & the City* (2009): unconsciously, but deliberately, erasing from one's perception things that are not supposed to be there. In Soviet Russia, this was more difficult because of the ubiquitous slogans and bombastic monuments, but in most other Eastern-bloc countries the 'socialist realist' mode of signification was less conspicuous and limited to ritualistic sites and occasions.

Thus, when nonconformist art started to exploit communist symbols, this was not comparable, for example, to the use of Christian symbols by Catholic artists in countries where the majority are devout believers. Except for a brief moment of fascination with *perestroika* imagery in the initial stages of the reforms of Gorbachev, the symbols had never become the code for active self-identification even for those whose opinion of the communist order was positive.

The paradoxical nature of the communist text consisted in its capacity to reassume its claimed original significance, regardless of the aims and context of its postmodern artistic use. Symbols that had signified nothing but an ideological void during the time when they were used as the privileged code of power now acquired an array of different and contradictory meanings,[6] from bids to be retroactively included in the ranks of the nonconformist oppositionaries to (both honest and mercantilist) demonstrations of one's globalist position. From the ironic treatment of the socialist aesthetic in the work of Komar and Melamid to the reduction of the symbols to their bare

---

[6] Possibly the best demonstration of the emptily ideological nature of totalitarian visual culture is the incident provoked by the Slovenian artists of the New Collectivism group, who won the first prize in the 1987 poster competition for a youth festival to celebrate J. B. Tito's birthday, which was later revealed to be a reworking of Richard Klein's painting *The Third Reich* from 1936 (Erjavec 2003:168–9).

thingness in the early work of Sándor Pinczehelyi, or the overidentifi-cation with the mixture of totalitarian symbols by members of Neue Slowenische Kunst, all the artistic approaches to these signs gave them a life they had never had before, which is highly ironic.

All in all, we can say that each of the three base-textual clusters accessible to the artists of the time came with a set of limitations and meta-rules for its use. What makes this art scene remarkable and highly diagnostic of the social reality in which it emerged is precisely its ability to blend these heterogeneous streams of meaning into one thesauric code of artistic expression.

Summary

When we look at the beginning and the end of the transition process of the art field in East European countries, we see two completely dissimilar and mutually incompatible systems, although both of them have a place for artists of different aesthetic preferences. Moreover, both systems are able to accommodate a certain kind of artist who caters to the taste of the artistically inclined middle class. Museums and exhibition halls are situated in the same buildings, and sometimes even the same people are involved in the decision-making. But this is where the similarities end.

Under the old regime, the artists had a complicated relationship with the systems of power, embodied by art officials (some of whom had a similarly complicated relationship to higher instances of power as well), in which the major role was played by their relational capital, the level of connectedness to sources of various kinds of benefits. This was the only resource that could be converted both into symbolic capital and into material wealth. Such relational capital could sometimes be derived from ideological capital – that is, the benevolence of the regime – but during the last decades of the communist systems, the latter was already declining in influence. At the other end of the field (but not completely distinct from it, as some authors would suggest) was the nonconformist, dissident art world, which had internal rules of its own, but was nonetheless connected to the official art world through networks channelling relational capital – and many artists in an intermediate position. In this overall scheme, particular combinations of artistic languages and text dissemination strategies evolved, with rules for the distribution of symbolic merit and material benefits as their corollaries.

After the fall of the old regime, these combinations were reconfigured. In particular, layers of textuality were uncovered that now entered the signification practice as dominant. The reevaluation of the pre-communist past as well as the suppressed ethnic element of the national traditions, the appropriation of Western imagery (following the introduction of Western products into the sphere of everyday life) and the reaction against the communist aesthetic were all, in their different ways, conducive to the formation of new types of artist. There were those who embraced the incoming ideas and styles wholeheartedly, and others who perceived them as threatening to their newly liberated cultural identity. And there were also those who perceived in the practice of art a rewarding business, gravitating towards either of these alternatives as they saw fit, thus contributing to their critical mass and possible success in the local art world. It is remarkable that the older and the younger generation, different though they were as carriers of the practice, nonetheless formed alliances based on their worldviews rather than age. But this, if anything, allows us to conclude that, in the final reckoning, it was the tension between various artistic principles that shaped the evolution of the field, and not primarily the dictate of power, money or group solidarity.

— 7 —

CONCLUDING REMARKS

The autonomous nature of the cultural process implies that it is never inevitable that successful innovative bids should have precisely the form that they have historically taken. There are no universal laws to which the individual, articulating her own experience in her particular environment, would necessarily bend. Nonetheless we can observe certain common traits in the ways new cultural phenomena emerge and replace older ones that are losing their cognitive adequacy: there are circumstances, which, when they coincide, can invigorate the cultural process and make it possible to redefine the standards and codes on which the creation of meanings is based.

When we look for them, comparing the two cases presented in the two previous chapters, we notice, first of all, that paradigm change can occur when the legitimacy of the symbolic authority is called into question. The political climate of Italy in the thirteenth century and the fall of the totalitarian regimes of Eastern Europe both created a situation where there was no centre of political power strong enough to impose its own symbolic preferences on the entire bidding space. Balanced arrangements of subcultures were fragile and unstable. In Italy, the model of the high Middle Ages that positioned religious, aristocratic and urban cultures against each other started to fall apart in independent city-states that resisted aristocratic and religious dominance alike. The concentration of different knowledges in separate institutional sites had reached a point where none of these was able to claim symbolic authority for the society at large. The faltering of totalitarian power in Eastern Europe similarly upset the *modus vivendi* that had developed between the government-controlled, as well as underground, art institutions on the one hand, and artists with various worldviews on the other. A bipolar gradient defined by

172

state ideology and resistance to it was replaced by a multiplicity of agendas and narratives. As a result, in both contexts there appeared a situation that made possible the emergence of many simultaneous bids. These were sorely needed also because little of what was on offer in either environment was perceived to be a cognitively adequate representation of their life-worlds by their intended recipients.

Another factor contributing to the change was a development on the material side of the respective practices. The spread of literacy in late medieval Europe and the emergence of a group of free literate professionals produced a new specific group of potential carriers of poetic practice, who were able to draw on a larger repertoire of base-texts and also to expect their intended audiences to read and reread their texts at their own pace. In Eastern Europe, the introduction of digital techniques into artistic production invalidated the system of skills that had previously been the prerequisite of becoming an artist and had granted symbolic authority to art academies as the institutions where such skills were transmitted. Although this did not immediately affect the content of artistic expression, in both cases the shift created the conditions for broadening the scope of signification and challenging the existing standards of what counted as 'serious poetry' or 'art'.

This latter endeavour was grounded in a new kind of cultural knowledge that synthesized various layers of base-texts that had not had much contact before. The Italian 'new sweet style' integrated Aristotle-based (in itself, innovative) metaphysics with certain poetic modes inherited from Provençal poetry and French courtly allegorical narratives to produce a science of Love, a this-worldly equivalent of religious devotion, something accessible only to sensitive, cultivated minds. Eastern European artists used Western avant-garde and post-modern codes in order to tackle their historical, folk and religious traditions as well as the communist aesthetic, which were all re-signified in the process in different ways. In both cases, the successful appropriation of the knowledge by a group of like-minded people contributed to the success of their bids. Although, in principle, both groups were open to all independent members of the society (a category which, in Italy, did not include women), in practice the access to them was limited: in Italy, by the availability of means and leisure necessary for acquiring a sufficient education; in Eastern Europe, by a certain disposition to learn foreign languages and an inclination to learn from the Western art scene. In both cases, we also have several competing bids. The school of Guittone in Italy, without a consistent ideology and easily defeated in its philosophical ambitions as well as the Siennese school of minstrel-inspired light and satirical poetry both lost out to the 'new sweet style', because the bid of the latter, appealing to an 'aristocracy of the mind', united not by birth but by sensitivity and learning, was cognitively the most adequate from the point of view of the 'free literate' social group that had come to dominate the cultural and political scene in Italian cities. The 'new globalists' managed to tilt the balance in their favour on most Eastern European art scenes, although the narratives of national liberation provided the 'new tribalists' also with a fair chance. The newly emerged figure of the curator certainly had a role to play here: the vision of the art market shared by most 'new tribalists' (and 'old globalists' as well) saw them as unnecessary replacements for the art officials of the totalitarian system, while the 'new globalists', with rare exceptions, quickly realized the potential of a symbiosis with them. The role of the West, at the time largely perceived to represent the maximum of realistically attainable prosperity and social justice, was also not negligible. On the one hand, Western trends were followed; on the other, the taste of Western collectors and buyers directed the hand of many artists, occasionally also encouraging them to opt for less Western style choices. What united the carrier groups of successful bids was thus their ability to synthesize productive thesauric knowledge from the available cultural encyclopaedias and to address their intended audiences with cognitively adequate significations, enabling them to make sense of their own experiences in the changing environment.

However, the success of both these bids was short-lived, and not only because of historical contingencies. In Italy, the 'new sweet style' bid was superseded by the more successful one of Petrarch, whose style came to dominate West European poetry for centuries: inheriting the devotional character of the preceding generation, he nonetheless distanced himself from the privileged and aristocratically styled 'knowledge' as well as rejected the re-codification of the poetic language as lacking in a personal approach. In Eastern Europe, the most characteristic trend of the new art – the postmodern reworking of the socialist aesthetic – exhausted its cognitive adequacy after the object of its irony receded from the life-world of its recipients and became something exotic (encyclopaedic) even for the new generation of Eastern European carriers of 'new globalist' values. Both these phenomena thus had a decisive role in making cultural paradigm changes possible, but did not themselves define the codal structures of the new textuality. The 'new sweet style' poets successfully challenged the symbolic authority of the aristocracy, yet they maintained a bidding space in which some kind of aristocracy was necessary. The

Eastern European re-codifiers of the communist aesthetic introduced postmodern irony as a codal strategy to overcome the burden of their past, yet they anchored their own work in that very same heritage. Both thus performed a move that transformed the previous bidding space, but made themselves potentially superfluous at the same time.

A few final words

Let me end this book on a self-reflexive note. What it has done, in its own terms, is to launch a bid to increase the cognitive adequacy of our view of our cultural environment, which also includes, besides its present state, representations of its own history as well as what we know about other cultures. I have argued that culture can be defined in a specific way as shared practices and texts that make up a loosely integrated network. I have also presented the reader with fairly detailed models for the analysis of both textuality and cultural practice. I hope the examples and case studies have shown that the proposed models of analysis can indeed be fruitfully applied to empirical and historical material.

In an ideal world, the fate of this bid would depend solely on its capacity to deliver on what it promises, but in the one we inhabit there are a number of factors involved, some of them the choices of the author, others objective realities beyond subjective control, and some others also matters of chance. If such a bid turns out to be too timid, it will enjoy its stint of circulation and then fade into archival knowledge, but if too bold, it may overplay its hand and require too much trust from its recipients – and thus fail in its task. However, with any luck, it may also be found to be both coherent and practically useful, which will increase its life span and productivity. Which of these will happen is never predictable, except in the case of very mainstream research. Academia as a bidding space and the transformation of its symbolic power system during late modernity indeed merit a more thorough analysis of their own that will, however, have to remain beyond the scope of this book. Suffice it to say that theories of culture are themselves also cultural phenomena and can be subjected to the same procedures that have been used here for other practices. Any theory of culture inevitably appears in a particular textuality, which always has a certain limited range, a heterogeneous set of base-texts it builds upon and an environment of other theoretical result-texts it challenges into dialogue, a certain take on encyclopaedic knowledge and thesauric conceptual tools, standards of reasoning and terminological codes for argument. And such a theory is not a string of statements about how things are in an abstract, timeless space, but very much a practice with certain goals, carried out by a describable type of people, according to a definable set of rules, and transmitted in one type of institution, disseminated in others. Cultural theorists are privileged among their colleagues in being able to think about their own work in the same terms as they think about everything else that makes sense, and with the same sharpness. As it happens, how we think about why we think in the way we do is quite as interesting as the reasons why we think about how we think in that very way.

REFERENCES

Abu-Lughod, Lila. 1991. 'Writing against Culture'. In *Recapturing Anthropology: Working in the Present*, edited by R. G. Fox. School of American Research Advanced Seminar Series. Santa Fe, N.Mex.: School of American Research Press.

Agamben, Giorgio. 1999. *Potentialities: Collected Essays in Philosophy*. Stanford, Calif.: Stanford University Press.

Aitken, P. P. 1974. 'Judgments of Pleasingness and Interestingness as Functions of Visual Complexity'. *Journal of Experimental Psychology* 103(2).

Akinsha, Konstantin. 2005. 'Reporting on Tabula Rasa'. In *Continental Breakfast – The Expanded Map*, edited by G. Carbi. Trieste: Trieste Contemporanea.

Alexander, Jeffrey. 2006. *The Civil Sphere*. Oxford and New York: Oxford University Press.

Alexander, Jeffrey C. 2011a. 'Clifford Geertz and the Strong Program: The Human Sciences and Cultural Sociology'. In *Interpreting Clifford Geertz: Cultural Investigation in the Social Sciences, Cultural Sociology*, edited by J. C. Alexander, P. Smith, M. Norton and P. Brooks. New York: Palgrave Macmillan.

Alexander, Jeffrey C. 2011b. *Performance and Power*. Cambridge: Polity.

Alexander, Jeffrey C. 2013. *The Dark Side of Modernity*. Cambridge: Polity.

Alexander, Jeffrey C., and Philip Smith. 2001. 'The Strong Program in Cultural Theory'. In *Handbook of Sociological Theory*, edited by J. H. Turner. Handbooks of Sociology and Social Research. New York: Kluwer Academic / Plenum Publishers.

Andriuškevičius, Alfonsas. 2001. 'The Phenomenon of Nonconformist Art'. In *Art of the Baltics: the Struggle for Freedom of Artistic Expression under the Soviets, 1945–1991*, edited by A. Rosenfeld and N. T. Dodge. New Brunswick: Rutgers University Press.

Appadurai, Arjun. 1996. *Modernity at Large: Cultural Dimensions of Globalization*. Minneapolis: University of Minnesota Press.

Ascheri, Mario. 2006. *Le Città-Stato*. Bologna: Il Mulino.

Barrett, Justin L., and Frank C. Keil. 1996. 'Conceptualizing a Nonnatural Entity: Anthropomorphism in God Concepts'. *Cognitive Psychology* 31(3).

Barthes, Roland. 1970. *S/Z*. Paris: Seuil.

177

Barthes, Roland. 1977. *Image, Music, Text*. London: Fontana Press.

Barthes, Roland. 1990. *The Fashion System*. Berkeley: University of California Press.

Baudrillard, Jean. 1990. *Seduction*. Basingstoke: Macmillan Education.

Bauman, Zygmunt. 1987. *Legislators and Interpreters: On Modernity, Post-Modernity, and Intellectuals*. Ithaca, NY: Cornell University Press.

Bauman, Zygmunt. 1988. *Freedom*. Milton Keynes: Open University Press.

Bauman, Zygmunt. 1992. *Intimations of Postmodernity*. London and New York: Routledge.

Bauman, Zygmunt. 1999. *Culture as Praxis*. London: Sage Publications.

Bauman, Zygmunt. 2007a. *Consuming Life*. Cambridge: Polity.

Bauman, Zygmunt. 2007b. *Liquid Times: Living in an Age of Uncertainty*. Cambridge: Polity.

Bauman, Zygmunt. 2011. *Culture in a Liquid Modern World*. Cambridge: Polity.

Bec, Pierre, ed. 1979. *Anthologie Des Troubadours*. Paris: Union générale d'éditions.

Beeston, A. F. L., ed. 1983. *Arabic Literature to the End of the Umayyad Period*. Cambridge: Cambridge University Press.

Berisso, Marco. 2006. *Poesie dello stilnovo*. Milan: Rizzoli.

Bertrand, Paul. 2009. 'À propos de la révolution de l'écrit (Xe–XIIIe siècle). Considérations inactuelles'. *Médiévales* 56(Spring).

Bérubé, Michael. 2009. 'What's the Matter With Cultural Studies?' September 14, *The Chronicle of Higher Education – The Chronicle Review*.

Bettella, Patrizia. 2005. *The Ugly Woman: Transgressive Aesthetic Models in Italian Poetry from the Middle Ages to the Baroque*. Toronto: University of Toronto Press.

Blackmore, Susan J. 1999. *The Meme Machine*. Oxford and New York: Oxford University Press.

Blagojevic, Mirko. 2008. 'Desecularization of Contemporary Serbian Society'. *Religion in Eastern Europe* 28(1).

Bloch, Maurice. 2005. *Essays on Cultural Transmission*. Oxford: Berg.

Bohme, Hartmut. 1998. 'A Journey into the Body and Beyond: The Art of Alicja Zebrowska'. *Magazin Sztuki* 16(3–4).

Bondanella, Peter, and Julia Conaway Bondanella. 1996. *Cassell Dictionary of Italian Literature*. London and New York: Continuum.

Booth, William J. *Communities of Memory*. Ithaca: Cornell University Press.

Bourdieu, Pierre. 1977. *Outline of a Theory of Practice*. Cambridge: Cambridge University Press.

Bourdieu, Pierre. 1988. 'The Historical Genesis of a Pure Aesthetic'. *Journal of Aesthetics & Art Criticism* 46(3).

Bourdieu, Pierre. 1991. *Language and Symbolic Power*. Cambridge: Polity.

Bourdieu, Pierre. 1993. *The Field of Cultural Production: Essays on Art and Literature*. Cambridge: Polity Press.

Bourdieu, Pierre. 2007. *Distinction: A Social Critique of the Judgement of Taste*. Cambridge, Mass.: Harvard University Press.

Bourin-Derruau, Monique. 1990. *Temps d'équilibres, temps de ruptures: XIIIe siècle*. Paris: Seuil.

Bower, Gordon H., and Stephen G. Gilligan. 1979. 'Remembering Information Related to One's Self'. *Journal of Research in Personality* 13(4).

Bowlt, John E., and Dmitri Sarabyanov. 2002. 'Keepers of the Flame: An Exchange on Art and Western Cultural Influences in the USSR after World War II'. *Journal of Cold War Studies* 4(1).

Boyer, Pascal. 2009a. 'Cognitive Predispositions and Cultural Transmission'. In *Memory in Mind and Culture*, edited by J. V. Wertsch and P. Boyer. Cambridge: Cambridge University Press.

Boyer, Pascal. 2009b. 'What Are Memories For? Functions of Recall in Cognition and Culture'. In *Memory in Mind and Culture*, edited by J. V. Wertsch and P. Boyer. Cambridge: Cambridge University Press.

Boyer, Pascal, and James V. Wertsch. 2009. *Memory in Mind and Culture*. Cambridge: Cambridge University Press.

Branca, Vittore, Francesco Maggini, Bruno Nardi and Michele Barbi, eds. 1956. *Opere di Dante*. Florence: Le Monnier.

Bruns, Gerald L. 1982. *Inventions: Writing, Textuality, and Understanding in Literary History*. New Haven, Conn.: Yale University Press.

Burckhardt, Jacob. 1936. *Kultur und Kunst der Renaissance in Italien*. Berlin: Deutsche Buchgemeinschaft.

Burgin, Victor. 1986. *The End of Art Theory: Criticism and Postmodernity*. London: Macmillan.

Burns, Catherine. 2005. *Sexual Violence and the Law in Japan*. London and New York: Routledge.

Butler, Judith. 1999. *Gender Trouble: Feminism and the Subversion of Identity*. London and New York: Routledge.

Cassel, Valerie, France Morin, Apinan Poshyananda, Mari Carmen Ramirez, Caroline Turner and Igor Zabel. 2000. 'Beyond Boundaries: Rethinking Contemporary Art Exhibitions'. *Art Journal* 59(1).

Cavalli, Gigi. 2006. 'Nota'. In Cecco Angiolieri, *Rime*. Milan: Rizzoli.

Certeau, Michel de. 1993. *La culture au pluriel*. Paris: Seuil.

Chandler, David P. 1983. *A History of Cambodia*. Boulder, Colo.: Westview Press.

Chang, Kang-i Sun. 1986. *Six Dynasties Poetry*. Princeton, NJ: Princeton University Press.

Churchland, Paul M. 2007. *Neurophilosophy at Work*. Cambridge: Cambridge University Press.

Churchland, Paul M., and Patricia Smith Churchland. 1998. *On the Contrary: Critical Essays, 1987–1997*. Cambridge, Mass.: MIT Press.

Clark, Andy. 1997. *Being There: Putting Brain, Body, and World Together Again*. Cambridge, Mass.: MIT Press.

Clarke, Jonathan, and Duncan Reid. 2007. 'Orthodoxy and the New Russia'. *Religion in Eastern Europe* 27(2).

Cohen, Philip. 1997. *Texts and Textuality: Textual Instability, Theory and Interpretation*. New York: Garland.

Cosgrove, Denis E., and Stephen Daniels, eds. 1988. *The Iconography of Landscape: Essays on the Symbolic Representation, Design, and Use of Past Environments*. Cambridge: Cambridge University Press.

Cotterell, Arthur. 1990. *China: A Cultural History*. New York: Mentor.

Czegledy, Nina, and Andrea Szekeres. 2009. 'Agents for Change: The Contemporary Art Centres of the Soros Foundation and C3'. *Third Text* 23(3).

D'Andrade, Roy G. 1995. *The Development of Cognitive Anthropology*. Cambridge: Cambridge University Press.

Debray, Régis. 2000. *Transmitting Culture*. New York: Columbia University Press.

Dennett, Daniel Clement. 1992. *Consciousness Explained*. London: Allen Lane.

Derrida, Jacques. 1982. *Positions*. Chicago: University of Chicago Press.

Dobrenko, Evgeni. 2004. 'Socialism as Will and Representation, or What Legacy Are We Rejecting?' *Kritika: Explorations in Russian and Eurasian History* 5(4).

Dols, Michael Walters, and Diana E. Immisch. 1992. *Majnūn*. Oxford: Clarendon Press.

Dronke, Peter. 1984. *The Medieval Poet and His World*. Rome: Ed. di Storia e Letteratura.

Dufrenne, Mikel. 1966. *The Notion of the A Priori*. Evanston, Ill.: Northwestern University Press.

Duveen, Gerard. 2007. 'Culture and Social Representations'. In *The Cambridge Handbook of Sociocultural Psychology*, edited by J. Valsiner and A. Rosa. Cambridge: Cambridge University Press.

Eaglestone, Robert. 2013. 'Contemporary Fiction in the Academy: Towards a Manifesto'. *Textual Practice* 27(7).

Eaton, Marcia Muelder. 1983. *Art and Nonart: Reflections on an Orange Crate and a Moose Call*. Rutherford, NJ: Fairleigh Dickinson University Press.

Eco, Umberto. 1976. *A Theory of Semiotics*. Bloomington: Indiana University Press.

Eco, Umberto. 1979. *The Role of the Reader: Explorations in the Semiotics of Texts*. Bloomington: Indiana University Press.

Eco, Umberto. 1984. *Semiotics and the Philosophy of Language*. Bloomington: Indiana University Press.

Eco, Umberto. 2000. *Kant and the Platypus: Essays on Language and Cognition*. London: Vintage.

Elkins, James. 2004. *On the Strange Place of Religion in Contemporary Art*. London and New York: Routledge.

Epstein, Mikhail. 1999. 'Emptiness as a Technique: Word and Image in Ilya Kabakov'. In *Russian Postmodernism: New Perspectives on Post-Soviet Culture*. Oxford and New York: Berghahn Books.

Erjavec, Aleš. 2003. 'Neue Slowenische Kunst – New Slovenian Art: Slovenia, Yugoslavia, Self-Management, and the 1980s'. In *Postmodernism and the Postsocialist Condition: Politicized Art under Late Socialism*, edited by A. Erjavec. Berkeley: University of California Press.

Esche, Charles. 2009. 'Include Me Out'. In *Art School: (Propositions for the 21st Century)*, edited by S. H. Madoff. Cambridge, Mass.: MIT Press.

Fairclough, Norman. 2003. *Analysing Discourse: Textual Analysis for Social Research*. London and New York: Routledge.

Fasolt, Constantin. 2004. *The Limits of History*. Chicago: University of Chicago Press.

Feenberg, Andrew. 1995. *Alternative Modernity: The Technical Turn in Philosophy and Social Theory*. Berkeley: University of California Press.

Feldman, Jerome A. 2006. *From Molecule to Metaphor: A Neural Theory of Language*. Cambridge, Mass.: MIT Press.

Felski, Rita. 2003. 'Modernist Studies and Cultural Studies: Reflections on Method'. *Modernism/Modernity* 10(3).

Ferguson, Tamara J., Brendan G. Rule and Dona Carlson. 1983. 'Memory for Personally Relevant Information'. *Journal of Personality and Social Psychology* 44(2).

Fillmore, C. J., and Keith Brown. 2006. 'Frame Semantics'. In *Encyclopedia of Language & Linguistics*. Oxford: Elsevier.

Fish, Stanley Eugene. 1980. *Is There a Text in This Class?* Cambridge, Mass.: Harvard University Press.

Fontanille, Jacques. 2006. *The Semiotics of Discourse*. New York: Peter Lang.

Foucault, Michel. 2002a. *Archaeology of Knowledge*. London and New York: Routledge.

Foucault, Michel. 2002b. *Order of Things: An Archaeology of the Human Sciences*. London and New York: Routledge.

Fowkes, Maja, and Reuben Fowkes. 2010. 'Contemporary East European Art in the Era of Globalization: From Identity Politics to Cosmopolitan Solidarity'. *ArtMargins* (September).

Fox, Richard G. 1985. *Lions of the Punjab: Culture in the Making*. Berkeley: University of California Press.

Fox, Richard Gabriel, and Barbara J. King. 2002. *Anthropology Beyond Culture*. Oxford: Berg.

Frege, Gottlob. 1960. *Translations from the Philosophical Writings of Gottlob Frege*. Oxford: Blackwell.

Friedland, Roger, and John Mohr. 2004. 'The Cultural Turn in American Sociology'. In *Matters of Culture: Cultural Sociology in Practice*. Cambridge Cultural Social Studies. Cambridge: Cambridge University Press.

Friedman, Jonathan. 1994. *Cultural Identity and Global Process*. London: Sage Publications.

Frobenius, Leo. 1921. *Paideuma: Umrisse Einer Kultur- und Seelenlehre*. Munich: Beck.

Fumagalli Beonio Brocchieri, Mariateresa. 2009. *Federico II: Ragione E Fortuna*. Rome: Laterza.

Fumagalli, Maria Cristina. 2001. *The Flight of the Vernacular*. Amsterdam and New York: Rodopi.

Gadea, Ferran, ed. 1990. *En So Vell i Antic: Antologia de Trobadors Catalans*. Barcelona: Edicions de la Magrana.

Gaonkar, Dilip Parameshwar. 2001. *Alternative Modernities*. Durham, NC: Duke University Press.

Gascoigne, John. 2002. *Cambridge in the Age of the Enlightenment*. Cambridge: Cambridge University Press.

Geertz, Clifford. 1993. *The Interpretation of Cultures: Selected Essays*. London: Fontana Press.

Giesen, Bernhard. 2006a. 'Performance Art'. In *Social Performance: Symbolic Action, Cultural Pragmatics, and Ritual*, edited by Jeffrey C. Alexander, Bernhard Giesen and Jason L. Mast. Cambridge: Cambridge University Press.

Giesen, Bernhard. 2006b. 'Performing the Sacred: a Durkheimian Perspective on the Performative Turn in the Social Sciences'. In *Social Performance: Symbolic Action, Cultural Pragmatics, and Ritual*, edited by Jeffrey C. Alexander, Bernhard Giesen and Jason L. Mast. Cambridge: Cambridge University Press.

Girardin, René Louis. 1979. *De la composition des paysages; (suivi de) Promenade ou itinéraire des jardins d'Ermenonville*. Paris: Éditions du Champ urbain.

Gleadell, Colin. 2003. 'The Frieze Effect'. *Art Monthly* (272).

Goodman, Nelson. 1968. *Languages of Art: an Approach to a Theory of Symbols*. Indianapolis: Bobbs-Merrill.

Goody, Jack. 1987. *The Interface between the Written and the Oral*. Cambridge: Cambridge University Press.

Gorni, Guglielmo. 2008. *Dante: Storia di un visionario*. Rome: Laterza.

Grayling, A. C. 1997. *An Introduction to Philosophical Logic*. Oxford: Blackwell.

Greimas, A. J. 1983. *Structural Semantics: An Attempt at a Method*. Lincoln: Nebraska University Press.

Griswold, Wendy. 2008. *Cultures and Societies in a Changing World*. Los Angeles: Pine Forge Press.

Groupe Mu. 1982. *Rhétorique générale*. Paris: Seuil.

Groys, Boris. 2003. 'The Other Gaze: Russian Unofficial Art's View of the Soviet World'. In *Postmodernism and the Postsocialist Condition: Politicized Art Under Late Socialism*, edited by A. Erjavec. Berkeley: University of California Press.

Groys, Boris. 2008. *Art Power*. Cambridge, Mass.: MIT Press.

György, Peter. 2003. 'Hungarian Marginal Art in the Late Period of State Socialism'. In *Postmodernism and the Postsocialist Condition: Politicized Art under Late Socialism*, edited by A. Erjavec. Berkeley: University of California Press.

Hampson, Sarah E. 1988. *The Construction of Personality: An Introduction*. 2nd edn. London and New York: Routledge.

Hampson, Sarah E., and Andrew M. Colman, eds. 1995. *Individual Differences and Personality*. London and New York: Longman.

Hannerz, Ulf. 1992. *Cultural Complexity: Studies in the Social Organization of Meaning*. New York: Columbia University Press.

Harrison, Charles, Paul Wood and Jason Gaiger. 1998. *Art in Theory, 1815–1900*. Hoboken, NJ: Wiley-Blackwell.

Hartley, John. 2008. 'The Future is an Open Future: Cultural Studies at the End of the "Long Twentieth Century" and the Beginning of the "Chinese Century"'. *Cultural Science* 1(1).

Harvey, Brian Peter. 2000. *An Introduction to Buddhist Ethics*. Cambridge: Cambridge University Press.

Harvey, David. 1996. *Justice, Nature, and the Geography of Difference*. Oxford: Blackwell.

Hasegawa, Yuko. 2002. 'Selections for the Tenth New York Digital Salon'. *Leonardo* 35(5).

Hetherington, Kevin. 2001. 'Moderns as Ancients: Time, Space and the Discourse of Improvement'. In *TimeSpace: Geographies of Temporality*, edited by J. May and N. J. Thrift. Critical Geographies. London and New York: Routledge.

Hjelmslev, Louis. 1959. *Essais linguistiques*. Copenhagen: Nordisk sprog- og kulturforlag.

Hobsbawm, E. J., and T. O. Ranger. 1983. *The Invention of Tradition*. Cambridge: Cambridge University Press.

Holmes, Olivia. 2000. *Assembling the Lyric Self*. Minneapolis: University of Minnesota Press.

Holzman, Donald. 1978. 'Confucius and Ancient Chinese Literary Criticism'. In *Chinese Approaches to Literature from Confucius to Liang Ch'i-Chao*, edited by A. Rickett. Princeton, NJ: Princeton University Press.

Hopper, Paul. 2007. *Understanding Cultural Globalization*. Cambridge: Polity.

Hutcheon, Linda. 1989. *The Politics of Postmodernism*. London and New York: Routledge.

Jakobson, Roman. 1985. *Verbal Art, Verbal Sign, Verbal Time*. Minneapolis: University of Minnesota Press.

Jay, Martin. 2003. 'Foreword'. In *Postmodernism and the Postsocialist Condition: Politicized Art under Late Socialism*, edited by A. Erjavec. Berkeley: University of California Press.

Jenkins, Adelbert H. 2008. 'Psychological Agency: A Necessarily Human Concept'. In *Psychological Agency: Theory, Practice and Culture*, edited by R. Frie. Cambridge, Mass.: MIT Press.

Jones, Michael. 1997. 'Sardinian'. In *The Romance Languages*, edited by M. Harris and N. Vincent. London and New York: Routledge.

Kant, Immanuel. 1781. *Critik der Reinen Vernunft*. Riga [Latvia]: J. F. Hartknoch.

Kelley, W. M., C. N. Macrae, C. L. Wyland, S. Caglar, S. Inati and T. F. Heatherton. 2002. 'Finding the Self? An Event-Related fMRI Study'. *Journal of Cognitive Neuroscience* 14(5).

Kennedy, Hugh. 1986. *The Early Abbasid Caliphate*. London: Croom Helm.

Kitagawa, Joseph Mitsuo. 1966. *Religion in Japanese History*. New York: Columbia University Press.

Knauft, Bruce M. 2002. *Critically Modern: Alternatives, Alterities, Anthropologies*. Bloomington: Indiana University Press.

Kristeva, Julia. 1982. 'Psychoanalysis and the Polis'. *Critical Inquiry* 9(1).

Kroeber, A. L., and Clyde Kluckhohn. 1952. *Culture: A Critical Review of Concepts and Definitions*. Cambridge, Mass.: Peabody Museum of American Archaeology and Ethnology, Harvard University.

Kuhn, Thomas S. 1962. *The Structure of Scientific Revolutions*. Chicago: University of Chicago Press.

Kundera, Milan. 1982. *The Joke*. New York: Harper & Row.

Kuper, Adam. 1999. *Culture: The Anthropologists' Account*. Cambridge, Mass.: Harvard University Press.

Kymlicka, Will. 1995. *Multicultural Citizenship: A Liberal Theory of Minority Rights*. Oxford: Clarendon Press.

LaCapra, Dominick. 1989. *Soundings in Critical Theory*. Ithaca, NY: Cornell University Press.

LaFleur, William R. 1992. *Liquid Life: Abortion and Buddhism in Japan*. Princeton, NJ: Princeton University Press.

Laland, Kevin N. 2011. *Sense and Nonsense: Evolutionary Perspectives on Human Behaviour*. Oxford and New York: Oxford University Press.

Lannutti, Maria Sofia. 2009. *La letteratura italiana del duecento: storia, testi, interpretazioni*. Rome: Carocci.

Latour, Bruno. 1993. *We Have Never Been Modern*. Cambridge, Mass.: Harvard University Press.

Lawson, E. Thomas, and Robert N. McCauley. 1990. *Rethinking Religion: Connecting Cognition and Culture*. Cambridge: Cambridge University Press.

Le Goff, Jacques. 2005. *The Birth of Europe*. Malden and Oxford: Blackwell.

Le Goff, Jacques. 2008. *La Civilisation de l'Occident Médiéval*. Paris: Flammarion.

Lévi-Strauss, Claude. 1962. *La Pensée sauvage*. Paris: Plon.

Lévi-Strauss, Claude. 1983. *The Raw and the Cooked*. Chicago: University of Chicago Press.

Lotman, Yuri. 1970. *Struktura Khudozhestvennogo Teksta*. Moscow: Iskusstvo.

Lotman, Yuri. 1992. *Izbrannye Stat'i vol. I*. Tallinn: Aleksandra.

Lotman, Yuri. 1993. *Izbrannye Stat'i vol. III*. Tallinn: Aleksandra.

Lotman, Yuri. 2010a. *Culture and Explosion*. The Hague: De Gruyter Mouton.

Lotman, Yuri. 2010b. *Nepredskazuemye Mekhanizmy Kul'tury*. Tallinn: Tallinn University Press.

Lowenthal, David. 2002. *The Past Is a Foreign Country*. Cambridge: Cambridge University Press.

Lukes, Steven. 2005. *Power: A Radical View*. Basingstoke and New York: Palgrave Macmillan.

Lynch, Aaron. 1996. *Thought Contagion: How Belief Spreads through Society*. New York: BasicBooks.

Malinowski, Bronisław. 1960. *A Scientific Theory of Culture and Other Essays*. Oxford and New York: Oxford University Press.

Mandler, George. 1985. *Cognitive Psychology*. Mahwah, NJ, and London: Lawrence Erlbaum Associates.

Mannheim, Karl. 1985. *Ideologie und Utopie*. Frankfurt: Vittorio Klostermann.

Mannikka, Eleanor. 1996. *Angkor Wat: Time, Space, and Kingship*. Honolulu: University of Hawaii Press.

Marrone, Gaetana, Paolo Puppa and Luca Somigli, eds. 2006. *Encyclopedia of Italian Literary Studies*. Boca Raton, Fla.: CRC Press.

Marzolph, Ulrich, Richard van Leeuwen and Hassan Wassouf. 2004. *The Arabian Nights Encyclopedia*. Santa Barbara, Calif.: ABC-CLIO.

Mattia, Joanna di. 2003. '"What's the Harm in Believing?": Mr Big, Mr Perfect, and the Romantic Quest for Sex and the City's Mr Right'. In *Reading Sex and the City*, edited by K. Akass and J. McCabe. London: Tauris.

Mazzocco, Angelo. 1993. *Linguistic Theories in Dante and the Humanists*. Leiden, New York and Cologne: Brill.

McCullough, Helen Craig. 1985. *Brocade by Night*. Stanford, Calif.: Stanford University Press.

McGann, Jerome J. 2001. *Radiant Textuality: Literature after the World Wide Web*. New York: Palgrave.

McRobbie, Angela. 2000. *Feminism and Youth Culture*. Basingstoke: Macmillan.

Mesch, Claudia. 2008. *Modern Art at the Berlin Wall: Demarcating Culture in the Cold War Germanys*. London: Tauris.

Miéville, China. 2009. *The City & the City*. New York: Del Rey Ballantine Books.

Milevska, Suzana. 2005. 'Objects and Bodies: Objectification and Over-Identification in Tanja Ostojić's Art Projects'. *Feminist Review* (81).

Miller, Uri. 1997. 'Thesaurus Construction: Problems and Their Roots'. *Information Processing & Management* 33.

Mocanescu, Alice. 2002. 'National Art as Legitimate Art: "National" Between Tradition and Ideology in Ceausescu's Romania'. In *The Contours of Legitimacy in Central Europe*. Oxford: European Studies Centre, St Anthony's College.

Modood, Tariq. 2013. *Multiculturalism*. Cambridge: Polity.

Montanelli, Indro, and Roberto Gervaso. 2004. *L'Italia dei comuni. Il Medio Evo dal 1000 al 1250*. Milan: Rizzoli.

Moretti, Franco. 2000. 'The Slaugherhouse of Literature'. *Modern Language Quarterly* 61(1).

Nikandrov, Nikolai D. 1995. 'Russian Education after Perestroika: The Search for New Values'. *International Review of Education* 41(1/2).

Ogden, C. K., and I. A. Richards. 1923. *The Meaning of Meaning: A Study of the Influence of Language upon Thought and of the Science of Symbolism.* London: K. Paul, Trench, Trubner.

Oliva, Achille Bonito. 2008. 'The Globalisation of Art'. In *Belonging and Globalisation: Critical Essays in Contemporary Art & Culture,* edited by K. Boullata. London: Saqi Books.

Ong, Walter J. 1988. *Orality and Literacy.* London and New York: Routledge.

Ortner, Sherry B. 1990. 'Patterns of History: Cultural Schemas in the Foundings of Sherpa Religious Institutions'. In *Culture Through Time: Anthropological Approaches,* edited by E. Ohnuki-Tierney. Stanford, Calif.: Stanford University Press.

Panofsky, Erwin. 1991. *Perspective as Symbolic Form.* New York: Zone Books.

Pasquini, Emilio. 2006. *Vita di Dante.* Milan: Rizzoli.

Patterson, Orlando. 2004. 'Culture and Continuity: Causal Structures in Socio-Cultural Persistence'. In *Matters of Culture: Cultural Sociology in Practice,* edited by R. Friedland and J. Mohr. Cambridge Cultural Social Studies. Cambridge: Cambridge University Press.

Peirce, Charles S. 1931. *Collected Papers of Charles Sanders Peirce.* Cambridge, Mass.: Harvard University Press.

Penny, Benjamin. 2008. 'Introduction'. In *Daodejing.* Oxford: Oxford University Press.

Pessoa, Fernando. 2002. *The Book of Disquiet,* translated by Margaret Jull Costa. London: Serpent's Tail.

Petrocchi, Giorgio. 2008. *Vita di Dante.* Rome: Laterza.

Petrucci, Armando. 1995. *Writers and Readers in Medieval Italy: Studies in the History of Written Culture.* New Haven, Conn., and London: Yale University Press.

Pinchard, Bruno. 1996. *Le Bûcher de Béatrice.* Paris: Aubier.

Piotrowski, Piotr. 2009. *In the Shadow of Yalta: Art and the Avant-Garde in Eastern Europe, 1945–1989.* London: Reaktion Books.

Pollock, Sheldon. 2009. 'Future Philology? The Fate of a Soft Science in a Hard World'. *Critical Inquiry* 35(4).

Putnam, Hilary. 1988. *Representation and Reality.* Cambridge, Mass.: MIT Press.

Putnam, Robert. 1994. *Making Democracy Work: Civic Traditions in Modern Italy.* Princeton, NJ: Princeton University Press.

Raby, Frederic James Edward. 1959. *The Oxford Book of Medieval Latin Verse.* Oxford: Clarendon Press.

Raud, Rein. 1994. *The Role of Poetry in Classical Japanese Literature: A Code and Discursivity Analysis.* Tallinn: Eesti Humanitaarinstituut.

Raud, Rein. 2007. *Japan and Asian Modernities.* London and New York: Kegan Paul.

Raud, Rein. 2012. 'The Gloomiest of Destinies? Intellectuals and Power in East-Central Europe'. In *Yet Another Europe after 1984: Rethinking Milan Kundera and the Idea of Central Europe,* edited by L. Donskis. Value Inquiry Book Series. Amsterdam: Rodopi.

Reyna, Stephen P. 2002. *Connections: Brain, Mind, and Culture in a Social Anthropology.* London and New York: Routledge.

Riffaterre, Michael. 1978. *Semiotics of Poetry*. Bloomington: Indiana University Press.

Roginsky, Dina. 2007. 'Folklore, Folklorism, and Synchronization: Preserved–Created Folklore in Israel'. *Journal of Folklore Research* 44(1).

Rosaldo, Renato. 1993. *Culture & Truth: The Remaking of Social Analysis: With a New Introduction*. Boston: Beacon Press.

Rosch, Eleanor. 2008. 'Principles of Categorization'. In *SAGE Benchmarks in Psychology*, edited by K. Lamberts. London: Sage.

Rosenwein, Barbara H. 2006. *Emotional Communities in the Early Middle Ages*. Ithaca, NY: Cornell University Press.

Rumelhart, David E., James L. McClelland and G. E. Hinton. 1986. 'A General Framework for Parallel Distributed Processing'. In *Parallel Distributed Processing: Explorations in the Microstructure of Cognition*, vol. II. Cambridge, Mass.: MIT Press.

Rush, Michael. 2005. *New Media in Art*. London: Thames & Hudson.

Russell, Bertrand. 1940. *An Inquiry into Meaning & Truth*. New York: W.W. Norton.

Saussure, Ferdinand de. 1966. *Course in General Linguistics*. Toronto: McGraw-Hill.

SCCA. 1998. 'Soros Centres for Contemporary Arts Network'. Budapest, Open Society Institute.

Schleiermacher, Friedrich. 1998. *Hermeneutics and Criticism*. Cambridge: Cambridge University Press.

Sebeok, Thomas A. 1994. *Signs: An Introduction to Semiotics*. Toronto: University of Toronto Press.

Sewell Jr, William H. 1999. 'The Concept(s) of Culture'. In *Beyond the Cultural Turn: New Directions in the Study of Society and Culture*, edited by V. E. Bonnell and L. A. Hunt. Studies on the History of Society and Culture. Berkeley: University of California Press.

Shapiro, Marianne, ed. 1990. *Dante Alighieri: De vulgari eloquentia*. Lincoln: University of Nebraska Press.

Siegel, Allan. 2010. 'Shifting Perspectives on Curatorship'. *ArtMargins* (December).

Siegel, James T. 1993. *Solo in the New Order: Language and Hierarchy in an Indonesian City*. Princeton, NJ: Princeton University Press.

Silvia, Paul J. 2005. 'What Is Interesting? Exploring the Appraisal Structure of Interest'. *Emotion* 5(1).

Simão, Lívia Mathias, and Jaan Valsiner. 2007. *Otherness in Question: Labyrinths of the Self*. Charlotte, NC: Information Age.

Sjeklocha, Paul, and Igor Mead. 1967. *Unofficial Art in the Soviet Union*. Berkeley: University of California Press.

Šmidchens, Guntis. 1999. 'Folklorism Revisited'. *Journal of Folklore Research* 36(1).

Sperber, Dan, and Deirdre Wilson. 1998. 'The Mapping Between the Mental and the Public Lexicon'. In *Language and Thought: Interdisciplinary Themes*, edited by P. Carruthers and J. Boucher. Cambridge: Cambridge University Press.

Spivak, Gayatri C. 1988. 'Can the Subaltern Speak?' In *Marxism and the Interpretation of Culture*. Urbana: University of Illinois Press.

Stalin, Joseph. 1972. *Marxism and Problems of Linguistics*. Peking: Foreign Languages Press.

Stock, Brian. 1987. *The Implications of Literacy*. Princeton, NJ: Princeton University Press.

Strathern, Marilyn. 1996. 'The Concept of Society is Theoretically Obsolete: For the Motion'. In *Key Debates in Anthropology*, edited by T. Ingold. London and New York: Routledge.

Strauss, Claudia, and Naomi Quinn. 1997. *A Cognitive Theory of Cultural Meaning*. Cambridge: Cambridge University Press.

Strawson, P. F. 1950. 'On Referring'. *Mind* 59.

Suddendorf, Thomas, and Michael C. Corballis. 2007. 'The Evolution of Foresight: What Is Mental Time Travel, and Is It Unique to Humans?' *Behavioral and Brain Sciences* 30(3).

Šuvaković, Miško. 2003. 'Art as a Political Machine: Fragments on the Late Socialist and Postsocialist Art of Mitteleuropa and the Balkans'. In *Postmodernism and the Postsocialist Condition: Politicized Art under Late Socialism*, edited by A. Erjavec. Berkeley: University of California Press.

Taine, Hippolyte. 1866. *Philosophie de l'art en Italie*. Paris: G. Baillière.

Taplin, Oliver. 2001. *Literature in the Greek World*. Oxford: Oxford University Press.

Taylor, Mary. 2008. 'Does Folk Dancing Make Hungarians? Táncház, Folk Dance as Mother Tongue, and Folk National Cultivation'. *Hungarian Studies* 22(1–2).

Thornborrow, Joanna, and Jennifer Coates. 2005. *The Sociolinguistics of Narrative*. Amsterdam: John Benjamins.

Toulmin, Stephen Edelston. 1992. *Cosmopolis: The Hidden Agenda of Modernity*. Chicago: University of Chicago Press.

Trilupaityte, Skaidra. 2007. 'Totalitarianism and the Problem of Soviet Art Evaluation: The Lithuanian Case'. *Studies in East European Thought* 59(4).

Trouillot, Michel-Rolph. 2003. *Global Transformations: Anthropology and the Modern World*. Basingstoke and New York: Palgrave Macmillan.

Tsukioka, Settei. 2007. *Onna Shimegawa Oeshibumi*. Kyōto: Kokusai Nihon Bunka Kenkyā Sentā.

Tylor, Edward Burnett. 1871. *Primitive Culture: Researches into the Development of Mythology, Philosophy, Religion, Art, and Custom*. London: John Murray.

Urbonas, Nomeda, and Gediminas Urbonas. 2010. 'Experiences of Artistic Freedom in Lithuania before and after the Wall: a Conversation'. In *A New Deal: Post-Soviet Realities Meet Welfare State Models*, edited by M. Tillberg. Stockholm: The Swedish Art Critics Association Press.

Valsiner, Jaan. 2001. 'Process Structure of Semiotic Mediation in Human Development'. *Human Development* 44(2/3).

Valsiner, Jaan and Alberto Rosa. 2007. *The Cambridge Handbook of Sociocultural Psychology*. Cambridge: Cambridge University Press.

Valsiner, Jaan and René van der Veer. 2000. *The Social Mind: Construction of the Idea*. Cambridge: Cambridge University Press.

Vega-Redondo, Fernando. 1994. 'Technological Change and Path-Dependence: A Co-Evolutionary Model on a Directed Graph'. *Journal of Evolutionary Economics* 4(1).

Warren, W. L. 1978. *King John*. Berkeley: University of California Press.

Washburn, Daniel Gavin. 2008. '*Toska*, Nation, and Religion in Russia: An Ethnography of Three Informants Interested in Religion'. *Religion in Eastern Europe* 28(4).

Weikersthal, Felicitas Fischer von. 2006. *'Zerstörer Des Schweigens': Formen Künstlerischer Erinnerung an die Nationalsozialistische Rassen- und Vernichtungspolitik in Osteuropa*. Cologne and Weimar: Böhlau Verlag.

Weil, Simone. 1999. *Oeuvres*. Paris: Gallimard.

Whyte, William. 2006. 'How Do Buildings Mean? Some Issues of Interpretation in the History of Architecture'. *History & Theory* 45(2).

Zittoun, Tania. 2007. 'The Role of Symbolic Resources in Human Lives'. In *The Cambridge Handbook of Sociocultural Psychology*, edited by J. Valsiner and A. Rosa. Cambridge: Cambridge University Press.

Zittrain, Jonathan. 2008. *The Future of the Internet and How to Stop It*. New Haven, Conn.: Yale University Press.

INDEX